ARRIVEDERCI NEW YORK

Arrivederci New York

A novel
by
EUGENE CHRISTY

Adelaide Books
New York / Lisbon
2020

ARRIVEDERCI NEW YORK
A novel
By Eugene Christy

Copyright © by Eugene Christy
Cover design © 2020 Adelaide Books

Published by Adelaide Books, New York / Lisbon adelaidebooks.org
Editor-in-Chief
Stevan V. Nikolic

All rights reserved. No part of this book may be reproduced in any manner whatsoever without written permission from the author except in the case of brief quotations embodied in critical articles and reviews.

For any information, please address Adelaide Books
at info@adelaidebooks.org or write to:
Adelaide Books
244 Fifth Ave. Suite D27
New York, NY, 10001

ISBN: 978-1-951896-22-5
Printed in the United States of America

This story is dedicated to my grandchildren,

Eoghan, Grace and Oscar

Volume I
Of The Twentieth Century Quintet

The past is never dead. It's not even past.

– William Faulkner

Contents

Chapter 1   *A Game Of Chance*   **13**

Chapter 2   *193 Mott Street Apt 2B*   **26**

Chapter 3   *A Mountain Looms*   **40**

Chapter 4   *Like A Needle And Thread*   **60**

Chapter 5   *Domenico, The Iceman*   **77**

Chapter 6   *L'anima Di Una Scarpa*   **104**

Chapter 7   *Wrong Turn On Rivington Street*   **126**

Chapter 8   *A House Made Out Of Chocolate*   **138**

Chapter 9   *The Thread In The Spool*   **150**

Chapter 10   *The Tangled Cloth*   **170**

Chapter 11   *Maestro Of The Plaza*   **196**

Chapter 12   *The Uprising Of The Women*   **222**

Chapter 13   *The Fire Above*   **250**

Chapter 14   *Arrivederci, New York*   **275**

Acknowledgements   **281**

Chapter 1 Acknowledgement   **287**

About the Author   **289**

Chapter 1

A Game Of Chance

The boy who started down the mountain, on foot and alone, from the town of Alta Villa, in the province of Campania, in the year 1899, was at that time ten years old. His name was Antonio LaStoria, and he was running away, taking with him nothing but his name, although in his right hand, he clutched a handkerchief, knotted around his palm, with his passage-money gripped against his tightened fist. His mother had thrust on him a few coins and a last, mournful kiss. His only other possession was the *mandolino* strapped to his back.

The life he was leaving he would remember inscribed on his skin, which seemed to have a memory of its own, imprinted with the back of his father's hand. There, he felt his mother still crushing him to her body, and then thrusting him away. On his cheeks he felt tears carving rivulets into his face, the way the rivers of time and place chiseled ravines into the mountains. Inside, he felt a stone, and the stone was his heart, weighing him down, as if he were already an old man, as ancient as the stones themselves, which were everywhere in Alta

Villa, all around, on the ground, in the fields, under the grass, in the very walls of the houses; in the teeth of the mountains, on all sides, stones, all the way to the jagged, cloudy horizons.

It all started because his father had betrayed him. Instead of caresses, he had received blows. Scolding, threats and curses, which never seemed to end.

As young as he was, Antonio knew this was not right.

All he could think of to do was to run away from this *miseria*, to flee headlong downhill, on the rocky unpaved cart-path that went winding round and round down the mountain-side, a thousand feet down, to the sun-sparkled city of Avellino in the valley below. Night after night, in his narrow house he had dreamed of the road to the sea, past Vesuvius, puffing in the distance, to Napoli, and a ship on the open ocean, which would carry him back to America.

He missed New York. He missed speaking English, a man's language, with marching feet.

His father, who was called Enrico LaStoria, had taken him there only the year before. Thinking to open his own tailor-shop in Manhattan, the father took the son with him. Like a door-stop in hot weather, it might be useful to have the boy. He could do the fetching and carrying, run errands, sweep up, a thousand things. Meanwhile, he, the father, would do his duty and pass on to his son the useful trade of tailoring–just as his father before him had, and his father before that.

But would the boy do his duty, would he obey? After all, he had left his wife, the boy's mother, behind. She would have cost him. She was one who knew how to spend. No, no, Enrico LaStoria needed to be free, free to cater to the paying customers, not to his wife. Enrico LaStoria would develop his clientele, through the exercise of his courtesy, fawning, yet full of guile, obsequious to his betters, resentful and dismissive only behind their backs; and of course, his suit-coats, vests and trousers, would be impeccably crafted, measured to fit nobly, to grace the better-off person who would purchase and wear them.

However, the father hated the place, this New York, and the people, too, these *Americani,* from the streetcar conductor to the policeman, with their unmannered, rude behavior, and their grotesque, barbarian tongue. The noise, clutter and distraction of the teeming city street, the gutter-ugliness of a life where no one knew their place and all rushed to and fro in mindless chasing after— what? The almighty buck, that's what. The very thing Enrico LaStoria lacked.

It offended him. His own people, the Avellinese, were being poisoned by the attitudes and habits of this place.

Yet his own *paesani* combined to offend his nostrils even more, with the system they had, in this benighted New York, that controlled and drove down the independent tailor.

They called it the sweating system. After all, if you were the *padrone,* why pay rent for space to work the cloth? Let the stitchers pay for their own space! They had to live somewhere, didn't they? In the hard New York winter, they would have to sleep indoors at night, no? So, parcel out the work in dribs and drabs to the docile, malleable ones, on the basis of an independent contracting arrangement— and everybody's happy! Let the fathers and the mothers worry about pushing the production out of their 7-year-olds and their adolescents. Sell them the raw cloth, let them turn it into market-rate rags, and buy it back from them wholesale. You could even make them buy their own sewing machines, and carry them home on their backs.

And who do you suppose sold them the sewing machines?

Enrico LaStoria fled back to his wife in the old country. Who could compete with the sweating system? He fled, dragging his protesting son, Antonio, by the hand, taking him, against his will, from the only people who treated him decently—his friends in the street, the other eight-year-olds and nine-year-olds who played in the gutter and were happy not knowing any better.

For a year, young Antonio brooded, biding his time, plotting his revenge, all the while suffering abuse and beatings from his father. His poor mother could not protect him from the paternal wrath. She was afraid of that man. Already she had been abandoned once before. She cowered. What good was it, then, to dream of finding refuge in her lap?

That year took an eternity to crawl by. Antonio was tormented by the thought that he was losing his English with no one to practice on.

In the end he determined that the only way to get out was to be as hard and implacable as the very stones of Alta Villa.

On the day he ran away, finally, Antonio started downhill at a run, but soon he was forced to go easier, until he had slowed himself to a walk, with a heaving chest, and his heart beating, and in the end he found himself plodding along dusty country roads, accepting rides from farmers' passing wagons, eating grapes and peaches and apples, which he picked himself, watching over his shoulder, even as he dried the tears from his soul, scolding himself for being an ignoramus and an infant, only to find the growling of Vesuvius growing more voluminous and menacing, until finally he began to feel pursued, like Aeneas fleeing a burning Troy, in the print that used to hang in the front room in Alta Villa, that cheap reproduction, which went into hiding every time you flung open the front door, the house was so narrow.

Ah, but he must banish such weak thoughts, and face forward to the wind, and let the open air dry the tears on his cheeks, no matter how much he still felt the sting of his mother's kiss and the caress of his father's slap. In this way, fury and folly, both, pursued him.

He fell asleep on a pedestal under the stone bowl of a fountain, in the middle of a village *piazza*. A fountain where women filled their *brocche d'acqua*, even as he slept in the dust at their feet. He was so tired and hungry he did not have the strength to waken, even when, from outside somewhere, he heard a voice.

"*Allora*," said a woman. "What have we here? "

He opened one eye, and spied a woman standing in a doorway a few steps away. Her arms were folded on her chest as she leaned against the doorjamb. She was dressed all in black, like a nun, but without white wings, and with rouged cheeks and red lips. He eyed her suspiciously.

"Como ti chiama? Eh, ragazzo? "

Blinded by the sun, he held one hand over his eyes. "Antonio," he said, resenting being awakened from his dream, in which he was already in America.

"Ah. Antonio. A good saint's name. Well, little Antonio, why don't you come here? I'll give you a drink. You must be thirsty after all your travels."

He roused himself to get up, but the neck of the mandolin was pinching his own neck. She crooked her finger at him *"Ven ca!"* When he did not come immediately, she scowled impatiently.

Reluctantly, he rose. Some attraction in her voice, some power in her crooked finger, made him. He was not menaced, but *che brutta*, pulled by a string.

Inside, it was as dark as an oven. Sleep, and the hot day, and the suddenly evaporated sunshine held him in a spell of temporary blindness. He heard water from a *brocca*, pouring into a cup. He drank, and realized he was hungry.

"What's that you got in your hand, eh?"

Her voice seemed to come from several places in the room at once. He glimpsed her pale face, with her red cheeks and lips. *"Niente."*

"Nothing? Then why you got your hand wrapped so tight?" Roughly, she grabbed it from his side. "And where are you going? Running away? What's this? You got money! Where did you get money?"

"My mother gave it to me."

"Is that so?" Antonio wanted to run, but she had him by the hand. "Maybe your mother didn't give it to you. Maybe you stole it. Want me to send someone to fetch her, eh?"

"No! I'm going to America!"

"Oh, I see. *Allora*, Antonio, you'll need a lot more than that. To live in America *è molto costoso.*" She let go of him, to make the common gesture that signified *soldi*, rubbing her thumb back and forth across the first two fingers.

Antonio took back his hand. It was an instinct. He clutched the handkerchief wrapping his hand tighter. He felt the coins hot against his sweaty palm. His eyes had adjusted to the dimness. There was a man in the room, too, a man who wore a *veste* over a rough undershirt and suspenders, and a table, and a chair where the man sat, with three walnut shells on the table in front of him, which he deftly and sibilantly slid back and forth with crisscrossing hands. He lifted one, and there was a dried pea. He covered it again, and slid his palm over to reach for a deck of cards.

"*Ciao, Antonio.*" The man's voice was kind. "*Benvenuto.* You come to the right place. *Come stai?*"

"*Nun sto molto bene,*" said Antonio.

"*Ma, perché?* What's the matter? Afraid? A big boy like you?"

"I say, call the carabinieri," said the woman.

The man ignored her. "Nothing's going to happen to you, Antonio. Relax." The man riffled the cards with his thumb. "*Le piace carte? Vo' giocar'?*"

"No!"

"Maybe you prefer the shell game?"

"Maybe he prefers we call the cops and have him dragged back home!" said the woman.

The man turned on her. "Leave the poor boy alone! Why don't you fetch him something to eat, eh? The poor kid must be famished!"

"Well, he's a runaway, isn't he? I wonder what his father might say when he gets hold of him again!"

"Go down the street to the bakery. Get him some bread to eat!"

Furiously, with a swoop of her voluminous black skirts, the woman rushed out.

"There! That's better. Now we can breathe again. Us men, we got to stick together, you know– after all, it's a man's world, isn't it?"

The man sat back and regarded Antonio, who was beginning to feel he would never get out of there.

"Listen, boy—say, what's your name again? Antonio. *Va bene.* By the way–what's that you got on your back? Do you play? You know how? Why don't you give us a tune?"

"I don't feel like it right now."

"Non importa." The man sat back and lifted his elbows in the air, placing his hands behind his head to cradle his neck with locked fingers. "Listen, Antonio, sit down. Make yourself at home." He smiled. "In a minute, you'll have a slice of bread, maybe some *pastavazoule*, you'll feel a whole lot better, you'll see. Are you really going to America—all by yourself?"

"Of course."

"And what you going to do there? Sing for your supper?"

"I'm a tailor."

"Is that so?" The man seemed to ponder something. "So—that's your passage money wrapped in your hand—and you got it from your mother—she gave it to you?"

"That's right," said Antonio, suspiciously. He thought he could divine a sort of a game in progress. He wondered *why don't I just run out the door?* Ah, but another voice said, *And how far would you get?* At that very moment, the old woman swept back into the room.

"Good," said the man. "All right, now, let's eat—let's eat first. And then we'll talk. Just you and me, Antonio. Man to man." The woman shoved a *piatto* of bread and beans under Antonio's nose and clapped down a spoon for good measure.

Morosely, with no appetite whatsoever, Antonio shoveled it in. He was beginning to lose heart. He could see that he was outmaneuvered. Whatever game they were playing—they had him coming and going, all right. He pushed away the plate.

The man wiped his mouth fussily on the back of his hand. "Have some more!" He sat back and loosened his belt. "No?"

The man in the vest was taking his time. *Un gatto con un topo.*

"Well, now," he began, while the old woman cleared off the table, "which do you prefer the most—in your heart of hearts—the money, or the mandolin?"

Antonio said nothing.

"Because, you know, that's a very nice instrument."

The man made a calculating face, nodding with his lower lip stuck out. He was thinking that this boy was not entirely stupid, that he was bold enough to run away from home, that he had *testicoli*.

"Well, the proposition I'm going to offer you is–your money, or your mandolin. After all, I don't know how much money you got there. The instrument might be worth a lot more. And, of course, we're not thieves, you know. Nobody can accuse us of that! We play fair and square. A game of chance is what I propose, that's all. I will wager three times whatever you got in your hand there for your mandolin–depending on who gets the high card. Or, if you prefer, the shells and the pea! What could be fairer than that, eh?"

Antonio could do nothing but squirm in his seat.

The man was playing with the shells and the pea. Covering. Uncovering. "Come on," said the man. "Take a chance. What's the matter? Afraid? You're not afraid of anything, are you, Antonio? Leaving home all by yourself. Going all the way to America. That's taking a big chance. Anyhow, what's life without taking a chance, I say. Come on. Don't try my patience. Make up your mind. Remember-when you win, you gonna get three times as much money as that! Come on–I can see you're itching to do it."

Antonio left that village with only the mandolin on his back, and an empty handkerchief in his hand. All he could think to do was to stuff it in his pocket, to save it for later, when he would need it, because inevitably he was going to reach the moment when the enormity of his own stupidity would swamp over him, and the hot tears of shame would scald his face and send him reaching for the handkerchief.

He trudged all the way to Napoli with only his own thoughts for company, and the ever-present laughter of Vesuvius, over his shoulder, mocking him, driving him onwards. He could not turn back.

The volcano was smoking. A plume rose up lazily into the air, spreading out at the top, like a *loricato* pinetree. He kept on and on, tired, hungry, thirsty and footsore. Would he ever escape that volcano, or would it haunt him to the end of his days?

And with every step his empty palm scalded him. His hand felt naked without the handkerchief wrapping it tightly. He heard his mother's voice in his ear, as hollow as a seashell, saying, *If you put the passage money in your pocket, you'll forget it's there. This way, every minute, you'll grasp it in your fingers.*

When at last he reached the scattered edges of the sprawling slum called Napoli, one of the world's most ancient cities, he decided to make his way from the outskirts directly to the docks, without detour or diversion, no matter how difficult it was to decipher the maze of streets, squares and alleys, trusting only his own nose for the smell of *il mare*.

And the harbor was there, in the air, along with the thousand odors of the overcrowded narrow streets, where you had to watch your head for chamberpots tipped out of second-storey windows, and mind your step for the *cacca di cavallo* lying in wait in lumps on the cobblestones. Unlike his mountain home, in the town of Alta Villa, here in Napoli there was not a breath of a breeze. In the swelter of August, the steaming bowl of the Tyrrhenian Sea hung humidity in the air; the wider waters were concentrated in the Bay, which lapped up to the very walls of the promenade, topped with balustrades, that fronted, in a concave ring, the *centro città;* until, in that tropical haze, the entire city took on the stink of rotting vegetables moldering in one vast open sewer.

At last, without stopping or speaking or seeking counsel or directions, or barely breathing, Antonio attained his destination, trying not to openly hold his nose. Tangled among the spears of spars, amid tilting cranes and the hillocks of warehouses, there rode the carcasses of the hulking black iron ships.

He hung back on the fringes of the milling crowds of travelers and their mounds of baggage, to listen in, and overhear. In his desperation he did not know what to do. In despair he muttered under his breath a prayer to his patron saint, Saint Anthony, to beg him for a miracle. *Sant'Antonio*, he prayed, *if you help me now, in my hour of distress, if you rescue me from myself, I will pay you back! I will never forget!*

But in the back of his mind, if he had to, only if he absolutely had to, there was the mandolin— he might be forced to have to sell it.

The milling crowds became gradually not strangers to be feared, but faces to look into, eyes to search out. He made himself small and forlorn, but not invisible. He took a station standing on the side, out of the way, but where he might be found. And he waited, praying, his fingers, in his pockets, moving as if he were counting beads, or money. How many times, back home, after Sunday mass, in the small medieval stucco church in Alta Villa, which the people called *Saint Mary of the Mountains*, how many times had his mother taken him by the hand, to light a candle, to put a coin in the slot? How many times had he looked up to see the statue of the Christ Child cradled in the arms of the stone saint who looked down on the infant boy with love in his tender expression? How many times had he himself, in the narrow house, when his father had gone out shooting rabbits or squirrels for their supper, sought solace in unslinging his mandolin, to play something to comfort himself? Would St Anthony abandon him now? Would no music come to sing him a lullaby of reassurance? Now more than ever before in his short, tormented life he needed that strong male figure, of authority, sanctity, and musical gentleness, to reach down a helping handful of love.

Then he spotted a group of travelers knotted in a bunch like grapes, who looked to be a family. The man seemed to be anxious about the family's place in the long, winding queue waiting to board the gangplank. Around him were gathered those who depended on him: four children, all small and young and very, very quiet. The mother cradled an infant in her arms. She rocked the baby and turned her body from side to side in a swaying motion that made her long faded blue flowery dress dance. She gazed into her child's eyes, and as Antonio watched, he felt a longing rise within him, as if he had struck a chord on the strings, and heard it resonate back to him from the clammy cold walls of the narrow house in Alta Villa.

Then, suddenly, the woman with the baby in her arms turned her head, quickly, a birdlike motion, to look over her shoulder, as if for something missing. But her gaze instead fell on Antonio.

Then she looked away. Something frightened her. A thought. Adamant, she swore she would not look again. She clutched her baby closer to her breast. Antonio prayed as hard as he could—*Sant' Antonio, patron of lost children, hear my plea and help me!*

The lady in blue turned her head, in spite of herself, toward that *ragazzo* again, she couldn't help it, something made her, and in that instant, she noticed that Antonio was a fair-haired boy, with rosy cheeks, almost like *mele pallide;* and then she saw, strapped to his back, *il mandolino.*

What possible difference could that make? Yet, it did.

Shyly, the boy Antonio took one step towards her. He continued, hesitant, yet drawn. There was a momentum in the air, as if a wind from somewhere were puffing him out like a sail, forward off his feet. And once in motion, *che pace*, that string again, only this time, *con tenerezza*, like an invisible thread, weaving him to her.

And as he came nearer, his eyes downcast, out of bashfulness, suddenly his eyelids lifted, with a flutter like autumn leaves, and he looked up at her.

The honeyed sunlight of the South was coming over her shoulder, to pool in his eyes, and when he looked up at her, this lady in blue, with his eyes big, golden, just-turning-to-brown, they were eyes to break a mother's heart.

Suddenly Antonio was standing next to her, his hand slipped into hers. She glanced up at her startled husband, who gave her an alarmed look, and she warned him by furrowing her brows, while squeezing to her breast the *bambino* in her other arm.

Nearby stood the bearded official with the peaked cap and the cracked visor who had taken their tickets, now with his back turned, gnawing on a twisted stalk of stringy celery.

"He won't notice." Urgently, superstitiously, the lady in blue voiced to her husband this thought: "The Blessed Mother has sent us this lost lamb."

And so Antonio sailed for America.

Chapter 2

193 Mott Street Apt 2B

Mid-ocean, in 3rd-class steerage, below-decks on the *R. M. S. Ultonia*, Antonio was one more sack of flour thrown onto a hill of sacks. Above-decks, in daylight, in the sun, spray and slashing wind, he was a troubadour, strolling from town to town with his *mandolino*, free as a passing cloud.

This second crossing gave Antonio solitude, time at the ship-rail, by himself, gazing out over the open sky and sea, his back turned even to the family which had taken him aboard. Freedom was intoxicating. He was grateful to the lady in blue, but resentfully, because it was shaming, too, to be obligated. The year before, his father had been there at his elbow, every time he turned his head. *"Where do you think you're going? You stay here—where I can see you."* Now there was no one to say him nay, no one to forbid him, and he was damned if he were going to submit himself to authority from *her* husband. No—nobody was ever going to tell him what to do, ever again.

R.M.S. Ultonia was no luxury liner. She was nothing more than a converted freighter, relegated by the Cunard Line to the Italian immigrant trade, with room in 3rd class rated for a capacity of 675, though 1000 passengers, picked up in Trieste, Fiume and Napoli, were packed into steerage. If clouds shrouded the ship, or foul weather reduced their headway, Antonio began to feel uneasy. If the rail crowded with seasick wretches heaving their insides out, he would feel spontaneously prey to moroseness. Then he would have to fend off attacks of remorse. A hole burned in his hand where the coins his mother pressed upon him for his passage money were once so tightly wrapped. The lady in blue? Every time her husband looked at him, Antonio wanted to run away all over again.

After fourteen days, fourteen miserable days in the clanking iron darkness of steerage; fourteen artificial nights deprived of day, devoid of light, breath, or sleep, humid with overheated humanity; endless days on a slow, overburdened freighter which seemed sometimes to drag them almost backwards: out of the fog came the lady in the harbor, holding aloft her light. She stood solidly. What held her up? She seemed to float in a cloud. The rail was crowded with onlookers who wished to marvel, who wanted, desperately, after two weeks below-decks, to memorize this moment of moments. Having seen this before, and having been bitterly torn away from the city he loved, the harbor of his destiny, the thrill was no longer the same for Antonio, and he had to turn his back.

R.M.S. Ultonia docked on the far side of Manhattan, at the Hudson River piers, to disembark.

Passengers on the first deck—perhaps returning New Yorkers, Americans—had to be let off first. The old wooden immigration processing station in Ellis Island had burned down two years earlier, and the new one of brick and limestone and Beaux Arts design was still under construction. The authorities first met the steerage passengers from the *Ultonia* at dockside as they came down off the gangplank loaded with baggage, and then herded them on foot through the streets to the temporary station set up at the Barge Office, which was actually a vast warehouse on the west end of the Battery. Antonio marveled at the ignorance of his fellow immigrants—they muttered and murmured, unable to understand this procedure, feeling they were being herded like goats in a back garden. Antonio, who had been through this same scenario the year before, wanted to say, *Listen, it's like this*—but he swallowed this arrogance.

The Barge Office had been commandeered for this immigrant-duty. Unlike Ellis Island, nothing here was set up for efficient and speedy processing. Ellis Island, with its railings and pens to group families together in the order they were listed on the ship's manifest, had at least attempted to minimize discomfort and disorder. Now, in the Barge Office, people were sent here and there, with this group and that, in what seemed like happenstance, with questions, forms, delays, inspections by doctors, questionings by officials, detours, re-groupings, and then waiting, forms, and delays again, passed back and forth like dirty wash-water in a sloshing tub. Antonio was chained to the family who had saved him. He longed to be free of them. The lady in blue was perspiring. She was under the eagle eye of her husband, who blamed her for the nuisance caused by Antonio. The boy's presence made them all nervous and anxious. The officials could turn people away from entering the country by a decision called debarment. One could be debarred for flat feet or enlarged glands. For conjunctivitis or trachoma when the eye doctor peered with his light. Everybody had to produce their vaccination certificates, without which they would not have been allowed on board the *Ultonia* back in the old country. All the men, heads of families and wage-earners, had been schooled by their relatives and the Italian government officials on how to answer the question, "Do you have a job arranged in the United States?" Many did have such a job fixed up before their departure from home; but if you slipped, and answered "Yes," you were debarred. You had to answer that question with a firm "No," because the American authorities did not want immigrants coming in and stealing jobs from Americans. All this worry, plus the interminable waiting, in an overcrowded Barge Office, for two to four hours, or even longer, with no chance for food or water, and long lines for the too-few toilets, and this after a final night on board a ship full of insomniacs, who could not sleep because they knew that now they were so near to America, the America of all their hopes and aspirations, and yet, still, so far away, all this was added to the anxiety on the part of the family of the lady in blue. Were they about to get caught pretending that Antonio was one of their own? Then, *di sicuro,* all of them, mother, father and four children, would be debarred. Antonio himself, every time the husband or wife looked at him, felt excruciating guilt for being the one who was putting them through this anxious, tortuous wait.

He longed, before departing, and never seeing her again, to kiss the hand of the lady in blue, to bow his head in humility, to hold the back of that hand to his forehead a long moment, till he could feel the warmth of her being pass through his skin.

To thank her seemed so miserably inadequate. He had not the words to say to her *I will never forget you.* Nor could he repay her kindness, not in the next million years. The acts of this woman were beyond the scope of mere gratitude, they put her in the company of the angels.

Yet, because of all that was going on in the Barge Office, he was forced to act deaf, dumb and stupid, and make no demonstrations.

Thus, when finally it came time to be released, young Antonio LaStoria, ten years of age, an immigrant, without papers, from an impoverished land, ran away from the Barge Office at the west end of the Battery and headed east, as fast as he could. At first he walked, then he walked faster, then he was skipping, and then running. Soon he was racing, racing against himself, to put the foul smells of steerage behind him, to feel his feet on solid ground, to get away, yet again, from yet another episode of shame and failure, stuck in the past, the past that was chasing him, the yesterday that was dragging at his heels; racing to put that yesterday and *all the past* behind him, to erase it, with one swipe, to start again, to begin clean his new existence, *subito presto;* to cancel the lady in blue, and all that he owed her, he raced, to wipe out the stain of his own ingratitude, he raced, to flee from the shadow that chased him, the shadow that was his own shadow—*his mother.*

And then, after a time, after some blocks, he found himself racing just because he could, racing because in his loins and in his legs he felt it, because in his mind he demanded it, racing because he was free, free, gloriously free to do whatever he pleased.

And then it was suddenly raining out, and the rain forced him to halt and turn the mandolin strapped across his shoulder bowl-back out, so that rainwater would not get inside, and he did not want to halt, he wanted to race, he wanted to race because *he would outrun the rain.*

And why should it not be raining in the streets of New York, the greatest city in the world?

Everything happens in New York!
I made it! Andiamo!

Antonio was headed for a building on Mott Street, No. 193.

He flew, his only worry in the world being the precious instrument on his back, his mandolin.

Until he could get under some shelter somewhere, he had nothing to cover it with.

Then he was standing in front of it. No. 193, a big ancient clapboard double-decker, as wide as an ocean-going vessel.

Somehow it was smaller than he remembered, from a year before. In his memory, it was as big as a landlocked dreadnought.

But quickly he must get up the three steps. On the porch, out of the rain, he took a breath, his first breath. Shaking the water from his hair and eyes, his door was there, on the right, next to the alley. He rushed up one flight, three steps at a time. The long mahogany-dark hallway ran the length of the deep house, with two apartments, of three rooms each, their front doors on the left, facing windows thrown open. If you reached out an open window, you could touch the brick wall next door.

He came to the door of 2B. When that door opened, everything would begin.

You knock, of course, that's only right.

You walk in, you sit down, they offer you something.

So, loudly, brashly, with his last ounce, vigorously, he knocked.

The door opened, and there was his uncle, Zi' Eugenio, his father's brother, looking down at him, blinking.

Behind the startled uncle, the cousins came crowding around, gaping. An unexpected knock on the door at suppertime usually spelled trouble, the police, the *padrone*, the truant officer.

This time they were so astonished their mouths opened in unison, while nothing came out.

"Where did you come from!" said Zi' Eugenio. He looked up and down the landing. "Where's your father?"

"I didn't bring him."

"What do you mean? *You* didn't bring him! You came by yourself? How? *Nun possibile!*"

"Papa, Papa! Let him in!" Everyone was crying at once. There was bound to be a story in this.

"If you came by yourself, you can go right back again, by yourself!"

"No, Papa, no!"

Antonio's uncle was trying to shut the door in his face, but his excited children were in the way, all babbling. The three oldest, Enrico, Maria, and Luigi already mixed up pidgin English and bastardized Neapolitan. Zi' Eugenio himself went back and forth easily between each native tongue in the house. "Hey, you *piccoli marmocchi*, who's in charge here?"

"*Mamma!*"

"Si, si, I let him in! *Perché no!*"

Zi'Marietta, Uncle Eugenio's wife, now intervened. "*Adesso, entra, ven ca, le coso povero, chiude la port'.*" She was a Donatelli, also from Alta Villa, like her husband, Antonio knew from his mother, who had schooled him in all the family relations and their intertwinings. Zi'Marietta spoke only the *dialett'* from back home spoken by everyone in the family.

Antonio was desperate. *"Zi Marietta, pe' favor, nun saccio a-che fa'. Do settimane fa', vini a Napuli, ora song acchi, aggio lavora', aggio vivere, tu nun tiene nu posto pe me? e dove? Nun saccio a-che fa'. Si tu nun me po' aiuta', me vado a durmi' nel parco, o pe le strade, o da qualche parte."*

Antonio threw his arms around her and buried his face in her pregnant midsection. He shut his eyes tight, to stop the tears. His own bravado had suddenly trembled his heart. Now that he was really here the enormity of his awful gamble was overwhelming. He was afraid to show his face.

Uncle Eugenio crossed his arms on his chest, and looked at his wife. *"Si, a salutamentissimo e mannagia la miseria!*–plenty of room for another boarder!"

Zi'Marietta hastened to reassure poor little Antonio that nobody was going to send him to sleep in the street. *"Assetate, assetate guaglio'. Tienne fame? Vo' mangia' na cosa? Hai sete? Vo' bere na cosa?"* She gave a reproving look to her husband. Everyone was talking so excitedly all at once that the dishes on the table shook.

"What the hell is going on?" said the uncle. "Can anybody tell me that!"

With his eyes tightly shut, clinging to the refuge of his aunt's protective embrace, somehow Antonio became conscious of watching eyes. "Who are those people?"

Zi' Eugenio said, "For your information, those people are my boarders, the Castellanos, who took your place last year when you and your father ran back home."

Antonio looked up with appeal in his eyes and said to Zi' Marietta, "I never wanted to leave you." The cousins, witnessing this spectacle, knew there was only one side to be on, Antonio's side. *Ah, yes, nobody knows how we children have to manage things just to be let alone to survive, to live.*

Gently, Zi' Marietta detached herself. Moments before they had all been living in some other world, a workaday world of endless toil, unending sameness, stultifying repetition, which no longer existed, and they began to breathe again, but in a brand-new world composed of sudden, swift strangeness, of incomprehensible drama and spontaneous surprise.

The cousins found an extra chair from somewhere, God knows where. If you could find anything in that place, you had good eyes. Everything was on top of and underneath everything else. The children made a place at the table for Antonio to sit down.

Now Uncle Eugenio pulled out a chair, with emphasis, and he, too, sat down.

Eugenio LaStoria rented this three-room cold-water flat, Apt. 2B, No. 193 Mott Street, for the family to live and work in. An enormous claw-footed cast-iron stove with its pot-bellied oven door occupied half the main room. On the stove, a big pot steamed, putting clouds into the air. To feed all these people—let's see, there were six LaStorias, and the four Castellanos in the other bedroom, mother, father and two children—you had to be cooking, boiling, stirring all day and all night to keep everybody going. A huge soapstone sink, crowned with the modern glory of a single giant spigot, provided running cold water—inside the house, no less. The sink had to be big enough not only to wash dishes, but to do all the laundry for ten people—and where else do you think people took a bath, after you hung up some bedsheets on a rope? In this same room.

All these things cost money, the furniture, the groceries, the bedsheets, the pots and pans. So you had to store all the materials for making your living—where? In this same room, of course. How were you going to pay for a place to sit and eat and cook and clean and wash and scrub and talk and chat and relax and enjoy life if you didn't work for a living? And where would you do that? In this same room, of course—unless you owned your own shop somewhere, or maybe you had a convenient storefront or two, just lying around.

In order to pull the table out for supper, they had pushed back up against the walls a pair of Singer sewing machines, with foot-operated trestles.

From these machines they made their living. Spools of thread and bundles of cloth and coats, pockets and sleeves and buttons, were everywhere, on top of, underneath, beside.

Plenty of room for another boarder!

Antonio looked around. Where was he going to put his mandolin, so he could eat? Uncle Eugenio had his chin in his hand and he was rubbing the skin away.

Antonio met with the trusting brown eyes of his six-year-old cousin Maria. Only six, but young enough in her innocence to fall into adoration with an older cousin, who magically came and went, appearing out of thin air. And furthermore, did she even remember him? A year is a long, long spell when you have only six of them. Antonio could see in her eyes she was thinking that her heart would burst, it was so exciting. Enrico, eight years old, was thinking, *my friend is back, my playmate!—now there will be trouble, and plenty of it!* Little Luigi, only four, did not know what to think, but watched his older brother and sister to find out what to say and do. Angela, the baby, was upset with all the commotion, but her cries for attention were going unheeded. To the cousins, anything new, sudden, unexpected, out of the routine, seemed so amazing, *it was like the Pulcinella-show breaking out!*

They were arguing about who to squeeze him into bed with, at the same time, pushing food and drink at him. And clamoring for more details of his adventures, because *di sicuro* he was a miracle in their midst, and only God and the Holy Mother and all the saints could have pulled him through, crossing the ocean like that, by himself, no less!

But Antonio noticed that Uncle Eugenio was unhappy. He looked tired to Antonio. Worn-out. Diminished. So pale, white, almost. Indoor living had drained away all his color.

Antonio's father, big-brother Enrico, was a tall man with a face like a thunderstorm. As soon as he thought of his father, even here, with an ocean between them, Antonio saw him walking away from him down the street in Alta Villa, heading to the countryside with his rabbit-gun slung over his shoulder.

But his uncle, in the flesh, at the opposite end of the supper table, was not the man Antonio remembered. *He's smaller—shrunken—thinner. So skinny and bony. His suspenders fall straight to his belt. His drooping moustache has lost its pride. He keeps his fedora on indoors. I have made a mistake,* Antonio thought. *A big mistake.*

A little refreshment got Antonio talking again, with his mouth full. Beginning at the beginning, he carefully omitted that shameful episode with the foul witch and the conniving card-sharp who robbed him of the money that his mother, God help her, somehow had collected from God knows where.

He looked around the table thinking it was impossible to believe his own exaggerations and fibbing embellishments, even as he uttered them. But the eyes of the cousins were dancing with credulity, brilliant with admiration, and when he got to the part about the lady in the blue—they were looking at each other, mouths open, hands fluttering, blessing themselves with the sign of the cross.

Antonio suddenly remembered his mandolin. But he did not feel like playing. When he looked into his heart there was no song there. The Castellanos, all four of them, had come out of their rented room to sit at the table when supper was in the offing and there was someone to gawk at and a story to unravel. And why should they not? They belonged here. They paid their room and board. Antonio did not.

This year was not last year. He was no longer nine, now he was ten. Before, he was doing as his father wished. He was a good boy.

Now, he was a runaway.

An orphan, begging for a place at the table.

Zi'Marietta was big and round, expecting another baby.

Now I show up.

The poised spoonful had lost its flavor all of a sudden.

He watched himself put the spoon down slowly in the wooden plate which, a moment ago, he was scraping clean.

"I will go, Uncle," said Antonio. Everyone in the room was speechless.

Antonio retrieved his mandolin and prepared to depart.

At the door, he turned to look at them all, stunned into silence, and he said, to his uncle, *"Mi dispiace disturbarti."*

Outside it was getting dark now, but it had stopped raining. That was fortunate. Antonio did not really want to spend the night in the park, but he had to walk, so that he could think.

He knew that if he had to stay out all night, he could find shelter, right at the back of No. 193. But first he had to walk.

He had to walk until he figured things out. He had to walk until he was tired and could go to sleep.

The thing he was afraid of was that his thoughts would keep him awake all night.

But these were his streets. They were as familiar to him as the lines crisscrossing the palm of his right hand. This night would pass and the morning would come. The mandolin on his back was not his only friend. It was early September and the nights in New York were still steamy. Almost everyone was outdoors late at night; the miserable ones were those stuck in the airless indoors. Tomorrow he would see his own friends again. Not tonight. With his friends, he needed to make a dramatic entrance.

Tonight was the night to be alone with his thoughts.

After wandering aimlessly for a couple of hours, gazing at the families all gathered outside on the stoop in the hot night, trying to escape the ovens of their apartments; looking up, to see strong men who built brick walls, and dug pipelines in the street, and worked on the docks as stevedores, lying down in utter weariness on their backs on fire-escapes to try to gain some rest for the night in the oppressive heat; hoping that darkness would hide him and his troubles from prying eyes, when he knew that he himself would collapse in the next few steps if he did not lie down, Antonio found himself, he forgot how, at the end of the narrow alley beside No. 193.

In the courtyard at the back of the building there was a shed where the garbage pails were kept, enclosed behind a door tight-shut with yarn.

This was the hideaway of the year before where he and his playmates played aggies or cards. Now, closing the door behind himself, he fell into exhausted sleep on the ground, by the barrels, dreamless sleep, the sleep of the dead.

In the morning he was awakened by someone nudging his shoulder. "Move over."

It was Uncle Eugenio, who was lowering himself to the hard ground to sit beside the yawning, stretching, shivering boy.

"How did you find me?"

"Did you think I don't know where you went when you don't want to be found?"

"This is our clubhouse. No grownups allowed."

"Eh! I used to be once upon a time a kid, too, you know."

Antonio now moved over a little more and was sitting up in the dirt, shoving over a garbage pail with his foot.

His uncle said, "What are we going to do, eh? You see how things are. I don't have money to send you home. You got any money?"

"No. I spent what I had to get here."

Even as he said this, he cringed inwardly at the lie. Thank God Uncle Eugenio couldn't read minds.

"Anyway, you don't want to go back."

"I can never go back there."

"What are you going to do then?"

"Don't worry about me, I will find work."

"You're ten years old."

"I'll think of something."

"Come home with me, Antonio. To where you belong."

"You have no room for me."

"I can't very well kick out the boarders. I need the money. But—you are my brother's boy. To tell the truth—I'm a little ashamed of myself. You catch me by surprise. Of course, your cousins would never forgive me. Then, there's my wife. You know I can't very well do without her, and she—she— then, there's the neighbors to think about, with the big mouth flapping all over the place up and down the street. You know as well as I do you're gonna end up starving for something to eat and your pals gonna bring you upstairs to their mother, and then what? Why you wanna bring shame on the family like that?" Uncle Eugenio crossed his arms, his mind made up. "Come on, let's go upstairs. You come with me and stay where you belong. Hey. Don't forget the *mandulino*. You gonna leave it here?"

Chapter 3

A Mountain Looms

Breakfast was last night's beans fried over. Shoveled onto a plate. Tear off a piece of bread to mop up with. Big hands reaching, children's hands, grabbing. Meanwhile, Uncle Eugene was not finished speaking to Antonio. "You know, lately, they been making a *bell'affare* over school for you kids."

Scuola? Antonio hadn't given it a thought.

"The lady from the settlement house been sticking her nose in everybody's business. They wanna know from me, are you brushing your teeth, are your fingernails clean?—are you feeding these kids?"

I should have known, thought Antonio.

"Eh–the rats around here are better fed than we are," said Zi' Eugenio. "Last week, the big *formaggio*, Roosevelt himself, was walking down the middle of Mulberry Street, pointing his finger. A little army following him around making note of his every word."

Allora, how's school going to get me money?

"Don't look at me like that, Antonio. It's not my idea. I don't make the rules. Or did you forget, last year, when you were here, your father had to put you in school, no? I thought you liked it. You seemed to catch on to the lingo pretty quick. You learned all the bad words, all right." Uncle Eugene paused for a moment to be amused with himself.

But his nephew was not amused. *How am I ever going to pay back my mother? For the money I threw away. On a stupid game. That was rigged against me.*

"You know he's police commissioner now, that Roosevelt. You'll be next on his list, Antonio, so you better watch your P's and Q's, like the *Americani* say."

Auntie Marietta and Signora Castellano, the two mothers, paid no heed to Uncle Eugene at all, but carried on their own conversation in rapid dialect. Castellano himself, nodding continually, seemed to back up everything Zi' Eugenio was saying, but really, Antonio could read his face. He was sure the man couldn't understand English at all.

I'm in the soup now. Just like that time with the man in the vest and the old witch.

Life at 193 in New York was on a rigid schedule. A task was twenty raglan overcoats, finished right and tight, and returned to the *padrone* in the morning, in exchange for new bundles of parts for the next task. *Taskers* is what the newspapers called them whenever they ran exposés of conditions in the slums.

But there was an old-country proverb from the rugged region around Avellino that Zi'Eugenio preferred to quote. *"After we climb one mountain, another looms into view."*

Uncle Eugene got a dollar a task, a dollar a day. It didn't matter if his crew couldn't finish twenty coats in 12 hours. If they did, so much the better, but if they didn't, they had to work

14 hours: they had to finish. One task every day. No days off till Sunday. You had to keep one day ahead of the schedule to make sure there were always enough parts in the house to produce.

If you didn't produce, the *padrone* would turn off the faucet. No more bundles, no more work. He will give it all to someone else, who's faster.

To stitch, they had to eat. To eat, they had to cook. If it took longer to cook and eat, it took longer to finish the twenty coats.

To make the day go, they made a competition out of the endless drudgery. They split into two teams so that the two teams could race each other, the Castellanos vs the LaStorias.

They raced, because they had to cook, clean, go down the hall to relieve themselves, produce finished coats, get the kids to school and back, wash and clean, take care of the baby, all at the same time, all in the one room.

First Auntie Marietta took her place behind one of the Singer machines. When the mother's legs gave out from pushing on the treadle, the father would take her place. The Castellanos, on the other machine, did the same, switching back and forth between the parents. Both mothers were pregnant, as usual, so it was up to their husbands, as the stronger sex, to go as long as they could before giving out, and letting the women go for a spell on the treadles for as long as their calf muscles could hold out before cramping up entirely.

Uncle Eugene was paying $2.50 rent on the apartment every week, so he threw a little money the way of the boarders, but it came back to him. To get the Castellanos to live in, Eugenio had to offer a split of the weekly. Castellano wanted 50-50, but Eugenio was stubborn and held out for 60-40 in his favor. He told Castellano that they weren't the first he had refused. He banked on how desperate they might be, and they were. They were the ones he'd been waiting for.

Right now, after breakfast, Zi' Marietta was lining up the kids for a good scrubbing. They sent Antonio down the hall, but it was *occupato*, so he had to go downstairs, out in the back, in the courtyard where there were two outhouses up against the fence between their yard and the brick apartment house from the next street over. Back upstairs, his aunt had found a new set of clothes for him, scratchy. One of Uncle's white cotton shirts, oversized, and a pair of knickers, too small, because they were cousin Enrico's. "I can't send you to school in those rags you're wearing that came across the ocean in the bottom of the boat," said Zi' Eugenio. A short-brimmed floppy cap on his head, and that was his school uniform.

Antonio pulled and pushed at the sleeves and shoulders, his sense of fitness offended, and the itchiness intolerable, and since he was ten now, in case they hadn't noticed, he hated being put in short pants, and, what's more, the tails of his Uncle's big shirt bunched up around his waist intolerably, so that he felt ridiculous, and was sure that he looked ridiculous, too.

While the kids were getting washed and dressed for school, Zi' Eugenio had to hustle down the street to the *padrone's* with yesterday's finished coats piled on his back, only to return, as quickly as he could, with tomorrow's bundles of parts, so voluminous that he was hidden under them, stooped over with the dead weight.

Since, in order always to keep one day ahead, he had to keep not one but two heaping hills of cloth parts in the apartment, as overcrowded as it already was, there was hardly space to turn around before you met yourself coming back. They spent all day and evening reducing one pile of parts while maneuvering around another pile, tomorrow's pile, just as big.

After we climb one mountain, another looms into view.

The trouble was that Uncle Eugene and the Castellano man, the two heads of families, found out quickly that their original deal didn't work. With five LaStorias in the house, and four Castellanos, they just couldn't feed nine people on $3.50 a week after Eugenio and Castellano each put in $1.25 for the rent. Both families were country people. Back in the old hometown, they would have had a vegetable plot in the communal gardens on the outskirts. Here in New York with four apartments in their building alone, there was no way you were going to grow tomatoes in the courtyard out back. So they had to go shopping at Ferrara's *groceria* on the corner to get imported Pastene or Nina canned *pomodori.* Lucky for them they started shipping tomatoes from Campania and Basilicata and Calabria to New York virtually as soon as the first immigrants got there from Italy. A pound of macaroni was 10 cents; a pound of coffee 15 cents; loose pea-beans 9 cents a pound, and you had to soak them in water overnight. Ground round to make meatballs on Sunday was 14 cents per lb., but 1 lb. wasn't enough for ten people, as they were only getting meat once a week, twice if they were lucky and went with chicken. Usually, it was only pork rinds, just to flavor the *pastavazoule* or *polenta* they had five or six nights a week. In the winter, the mothers could bake bread in the pot-bellied oven and heat the apartment that way, but in the summer, they would have died of heat prostration, and they had to buy bread by the loaf at Vincenzo's Bakery on the block, 5 cents a bag for a nice fat Italian bread. Same for making spaghetti from scratch at home, except that Sunday was the only day they had free enough to spend that much time, and even then, they had to start at six in the morning. For the kids, they had to have milk, 8 cents a quart. Thank Christ for mother's milk or infants would never survive. Breakfast in the morning tended to be leftover *polenta* or *risotto* or *farina* in sauce from the night before. A 2-lb. sack of the flint cornmeal imported from home to make the *polenta,* 18 cents. They were not potato-eaters, but they became potato-eaters, because a 10-lb. paper sack of Long Island spuds at Ferrara's was all of 14 cents. So they boiled them, doused them in tomato sauce, and made do. Still, they didn't have enough to eat. If it wasn't for the settlement house lady, and the food pantry at St Anthony's of Padua up on Houston Street, their parish, the children would never have seen a fresh vegetable like a red pepper or a cucumber. Butter at 26 cents a lb., eggs at 21 cents a doz., sugar at 31 cents for 5 lbs., they went without. *Allora,* drinking their coffee black was no hardship, where they came from.

Still, after all the scrimping they weren't making it. Nothing for it but for Castellano to sign himself up with the *padrone* and finish a second task per day, to bring in an additional 6 bucks a week. So now, every morning, two husbands were leaving the house, to stagger back loaded down with bundles of parts to haul up to the second floor. Every day there was not one, not two, but four vertiginous piles of sleeves, fronts and backs, pockets and collars, stacked everywhere and wherever, that you had to work around in the already-swarmed-under apartment.

After we climb one mountain, another looms into view!

But, at least now, the kids could have a cup of hot cocoa for a treat on Sunday night, if they were good all week. Hot cocoa, 25 cents a lb, a luxury, stirred into water just brought to a boil, a splash of milk on top, and they were living like royalty on $9.50 a week after the rent was paid. *Ahh, New York!*

When it was Antonio's turn, Zi'Marietta rubbed the ears off both sides of his head with a soapy, rough washcloth. She insisted he had to button up, and have his hair combed, too, and wash his face, and hold out your fingers. She had to cut his nails for him, but there was no time, there was so much to do, she was digging the dirt out from under them with her scissors, the big ones she used for the raglan. *How many ways can they dream up to torture a kid!*

Out came the sewing machines from both walls in the kitchen. The table they pushed back, and the two teams formed up. The kids had to be at school at eight o'clock, but there was still almost an hour and a half where they could push out some production.

Antonio being the oldest now, he was going to be expected to help out on Uncle's team.

Working on a team was a kind of way of paying for your room and board. Enrico and Maria, as young as they were, were the basters on the LaStoria's team. Enrico was 8 and Maria 6. Luigi and Angela were too young really to work, but, soon enough, soon enough. Uncle and Auntie appointed nephew Antonio to now be the finisher on their team, trained as he was in the needle arts by his father. That was the law, that was the system, from now and henceforward.

But as Antonio observed, in his own mind, without any prompting from himself, *this system, it didn't put any cash into your hand.* The two weekly pay packets from the *padrone* went into Uncle Eugene's pocket, by arrangement with Castellano, and from there he doled out the other family's share to the signore, but his own wife and kids were left out of the disbursements, and that included young Antonio.

For once in his life, Antonio began to see the logic of his father from the year before. If that man had gone to work for his younger brother, his pocket would never have seen any walking-around money. It was simply beneath his dignity.

Hence, he found the best job he could that would bring in weekly cash, at Levy and Sons.

Time enough to sleep when we're dead, Uncle Eugene always said. He had a storehouse of wise sayings. *You're only young once. Work never killed anyone.* "And if you want to hold your head up on Sunday, you better have a little spare change left over for the collection box at Mass." *Easy come, easy go,* he always said.

"And furthermore, we were born into this trade, and no other. To make clothes for other people to wear. The needle trade, that's the LaStoria family business. Consider yourself fortunate. A roof over your head, food on the table. Would you rather be digging the ditch for the pylons on the 2nd Avenue El, or maybe breathing the air in the sewers? Do you know what it means in this life to have a trade, eh?"

Uncle was exasperated from lugging the parts on his back through the streets, and then in the end, up the stairs to the porch, and finally upstairs to the apartment. "*Ascolta mi*—last year, you and my brother ran out on me. First, your father lands here, with you, expecting me to put him up. *Va bene,* I do it. What am I supposed to do? He's my brother. Then, come to find out, he's too good for the *padrone* to patronize him, my high and mighty brother. He's gonna go work for Levy & Son. So, he makes piece-work, and he pays me for the room. In other words, he's my brother, but he's a boarder. Well, now I got a new boarder, and Signore Castellano works on my task *and his,* with me and my family, every day, every hour, and don't give me no trouble. That's what you call teamwork. That's what you need to hold your head up in this bloodthirsty sweating system that's drinking our blood. Yes, you too, Antonio. You're not too young to see the writing on the wall. You know what's the problem with you and your father? You're *orgoglioso. Sì!-Orgoglio..* You got your *dignità* stuck up your *culu.*"

So that's the way it is.

Antonio's road in New York was becoming as tortuous and winding as the road down the mountainside from Alta Villa.

What a strange world adults dwell in! Antonio could not fathom it. People like his uncle, or the Castellano man, the husband of the lady in blue, his own father. Was it some secret only grownups knew? Would he ever grow into it himself? *No, no, no, I will never be like that when I grow up.*

"Antonio," said Uncle, sharply. "Wake up. Daydreaming again? You want the Castellanos to get ahead of us, eh? See if you can put a move on, if it's not too much to ask."

Between spending all morning in school, Antonio was thinking, *and all afternoon slaving away on a team—when do I get out of the house to make some money?*

But Zi' Eugenio's words rang stolidly in his ears. *You're ten years old.*

And stubbornly he had replied, *I'll think of something.*
But what?
After we climb one mountain, another looms into view.

Outside, with his two cousins on the way to school, Antonio turned to Enrico. "You take your sister. I'll meet you there."

"Where you going?"

"I gotta go see a man."

"You gonna get in trouble."

"If you don't say anything to your father, I'll be all right."

"You gonna get *us* in trouble," said Enrico, who now had six-year-old Maria, a first-grader, by the hand. She was looking up at Antonio with big eyes.

He explained to her. "What are they gonna teach me at school? I know how to make change! If I had any money! Now—be a good girl—you go, and tell me all about it tonight. Right now, I gotta go see a man."

Antonio watched them disappear into the bobbing heads of the street, which was boiling with people. Now he could go where he wanted, do as he pleased, see everything. He was in his element, outdoors, unfettered. The sight of New York stirred him up. You didn't know where to look first. Here, at the corner of Mott Street and Spring Street, were waves of people, big and little, well-scrubbed and dirty, men, women and children, working, shopping, or idling, sloshing back and forth like soap bubbles in a galvanized tub.

But Antonio's special pleasure was the animals. Dogs, mules, donkeys and above all, horses. All the menagerie of New York. Especially the horses and the dogs. It was one of the things he most missed, back in Alta Villa, about the great city.

In Alta Villa, animals were few because the people were few, and poor. Cow's milk was unheard of—only a goat could manage the top of the mountain where Alta Villa was perched, on the spine of the Appenines, where, on the far side of the next ridge over, the land slanted down to the Adriatic. Only the farmers down in the valley around Avellino kept dairy cattle.

But here in New York, you went to the corner store, and they had cow's milk, in bottles. Where it came from, nobody questioned. You just went to the store and put your eight cents down on the counter and they handed you the quart of milk.

As in Alta Villa, you pictured the dairy cows somewhere else—maybe not down in the valley below, but certainly, somewhere out there in the vast countryside outside New York. You would no more think to see a cow on the streets of New York than you would a grizzly bear.

Still, in the city itself, animals were plentiful and ubiquitous, especially the horses. Magnificent dray-horses that pulled the beer-wagons, plodding plow-horses who hauled the streetcars, humble ponies between the shafts of ice-wagons and coal-wagons.

To Antonio LaStoria, the boy of ten, these animals had personalities, you could see their souls in their faces, they were without guile, you could befriend them, the horses, and the dogs, too.

As he had learned on the road to Napoli—people, you had to beware of. Animals, on the other hand, you could trust–except the cats.

Those, he hated. Once when he was little, on a trip to Avellino, his mother had taken him into a shop that smelled of bread. It was so warm in the shop, so inviting, with glass cases full of pastries, he felt so welcomed by the aromas and the odors, from wood to cake to sawdust. A cat stuck its nose around the corner, hunting. Little Antonio stooped, sliding forward on his knees, and reached out to stroke and pet the cat, which snaked out a paw, raking the back of his hand. Tears jumped out of his eyes, and he wailed in fright and confusion. His mother, at the counter, pulled his head into her skirts, and went on talking with the woman of the bakery.

Ever since, Antonio had loathed cats with a sense of disgust and hatred. They would not work for you, or be your friends. They lurked about like shadows. Sliding past you up against the walls. Aloof, and independent. They would only come if you coaxed them. Otherwise, they ignored you and behaved as if they were the only breathing beings in the room. But cats were also calculating and deceitful. They would jump on your lap when they wanted something. And they were hunters, who preyed on animals smaller and weaker.

Horses, mules and dogs—the noble horse, the humble mule, the faithful dog.–those Antonio loved with fervor. They were animals full of gratitude for your concern, who could return your love a thousand-fold, animals who had innocence, and a soul without sin, without deviousness.

Today on the crowded street he was dodging people, who plagued the city with noise and argument. But the horses, patient, docile, peaceful, the horses who were everywhere, who toiled and waited, who worked for their living, accepting whatever came their way, without needing to control the world, or question life, but simply existing, each according to his own nature–these were the creatures who had called him back to New York.

Dogs, too, were attracted to him, as he was to them. When he turned the corner onto Spring Street, he noticed a dog trailing after him. He was not surprised. He was happy to have the company. Whether the dog belonged to anyone or was just a stray, it meant that he was not without a friend in this neighborhood. He need not stop for this dog—the dog would understand, they always do.

At the moment, Antonio thought he would head for Mulberry Street, to see the sights, but not for long.

The solution to everything had come to him.

It was not pride, as Zi' Eugenio said, that made him who he was, but a craving for independence, for God knows, he had more to be ashamed of than to be proud of, especially whenever Alta Villa intruded on his thoughts, or he remembered the benevolence of the lady in blue, or his mother's love, and her desperate wishes for a better life for him, her only child, her beloved son, even if it should mean losing him forever.

Whenever he thought of his mother he was crushed with guilt.

How could he have left her like that, when he was all she had? Why had he been unable to save her, to save both of them? That stone in his heart that was choking him the day he left her to run down the mountain now rose into his throat again.

I am the same, like my father, Antonio said to himself, *a selfish bastard.*

His mother had made for his sake the ultimate sacrifice—she let him go, so that he could have his freedom, and a chance at the life he wanted—never once putting herself before her only boy. She even put the money into his hand to enable him to leave her.

I will go to work where that man did, at Levy & Sons, *where they paid him wages each week. How else will I ever get the money to send for my mother, to rescue her, to get her away from him!* Now that was settled, Antonio could breathe.

I am going to get the money to save my mother, no problem, you'll see, di sicuro. I promise you, Mamma.

For a boy out of school in the morning, Mulberry Street was like the circus. Everybody was on show. There, that man with the handle-bar moustaches, stripped to the waist, he was the lion-tamer. There, that other one, with the bowler hat, he was the ringmaster. There, that fellow exercising on his fire escape, he was the acrobat. The fat lady and the juggler and the snake-charmer, they were all there, too.

And where had he seen the circus before? Certainly not in Alta Villa—in New York, of course.

There were so many things about New York which had agitated his sleep, back in the narrow house in Alta Villa: the cousins, the apartment, his friends from school, his studies, his passion for the Americans' way of talking, their English language, the horses; they agitated his sleep and pulled him out of his bed, to plot and to strive, to struggle to return. Now at last he was face to face with the chance to really learn the lingo, to perfect it, to perhaps almost be an American himself, if that could ever be.

And it was easy as long as you were immersed in the streets of New York. All the boys he knew, his friends from the neighborhood, from school, reveled in talking English. At times, it could be their secret language, the thing which enabled them to fool and manipulate and get around their parents. Not only that, but their families depended on the children to teach the grownups enough to help them get along in their daily lives, in the street, on the streetcars, in the markets, at the banks. English was not only a joy, it was a necessity.

In Mulberry Street, there were wagons and carts and pushcarts, cafes, drugstores, restaurants, barrooms, shops, dress-shops, hat-shops, barbershops, grocery shops, delivery drivers and peddlers, beer-wagons and rag-men, and horses everywhere, so that you had to watch where you were stepping. Both sidewalks were crowded, you could hardly move, and many people had to walk in the street to get around obstacles and pedestrian traffic. Wagons were parked on both sides at the curb, and there was only room for one horse-drawn vehicle at a time to go down the middle—if two had to pass, going opposite ways, it was an argument.

The women were all bare-headed, and had their long hair tucked up in buns and unruly mops with strands and wisps falling over their ears and down in their eyes, and all the men wore hats—or most of them—bowlers and fedoras and trilbys and straw hats, and hats with turn-down brims and satin hatbands, or cotton twill hatbands, or plain dark hatbands, or printed flowery hatbands, and straight plain ribbons or fancy pleated ribbons—or else soft, flat caps with short bills, the kind some people called a newsboy's cap, made of wool or tweed or plain old cheap cotton, the kind you wore for everyday or when you couldn't afford better, the kind most of the kids wore, if they were boys.

And there were boys everywhere, it seemed hundreds of boys, milling around in groups or hanging around pushcarts and fire-hydrants, strolling in packs, or hanging onto their mothers. All the women in the street looked like they were somebody's mother, although there was no shortage of girls around, if they were young enough—the ones old enough to attract the stares of men, but who weren't yet married, were all indoors.

The men doing the staring were mostly those lounging at the outdoor café tables, with a bottle of wine or beer in one hand, and a cigarette in the other. Antonio wondered where they got the money, to be sitting there, paying for drinks in the daytime. He looked up and saw a man with a white shirt with billowy sleeves puffed out fastened at his wrists, standing on a fire-escape, on the second floor over *Mazzo e Figli*. This man looked as if he had nothing to do but stand there surveying the street in his fancy button-down vest, which looked like it cost a pretty penny. *Maybe it's Mazzo himself,* Antonio thought. *Where did that dog go?*

The buildings, surrounding you, everywhere you looked, themselves looked like top hats, tottering over the crowded thoroughfare—most of them four or five stories tall, some as much as six, ganged together practically wall to wall, three feet apart, adorned with plain and ornamental fire-escapes, some, on the upper stories, hung with laundry drying, like white flags on a brick-colored sky.

Antonio was jostled out of his daydream when someone bumped against him and he was propelled into a wagon-wheel hub that stuck out into the street, but he forgot about that instantly when he heard someone call out his name.

"Hey, Naso!"

When he turned around it was Mousey, a school friend from the year before. "You're back!" cried the smaller boy, who threw himself around Antonio's neck. "Yeah," said Antonio, "but when I seen you, it's like I never left. Get off me!"

"Where did *you* come from? I thought I'd never see you again. One day you were gone, you disappeared, just like that!"

"That kid still pickin' on you, Mousey?"

"Nah. Not since you took care of him. He's still lookin' around corners. Wait'll I tell Knickers I seen you!"

"Why ain't you in school?"

"Double sessions, *strunz*."

"Oh, yeah. I heard from my cousins."

"You back in the building?"

"Where else would I be? Hey, you remember that time we snuck into the circus?"

"Like yesterday! We almost got caught, too."

"Where's that dog?"

"What dog?"

"That dog, Dingo. That's what I named him—Dingo. You see him anywhere?"

"You got a dog?"

"Nah. He's just a stray dog keeps following me around. Like you."

"You know something, you *testa di cazz*. I missed you!"

"Okay, *pazzo*. I'll see you later. I think I see that dog."

"But when am I gonna see you again? What do I tell the boys? We gonna get together? Like old times? What do I tell Knickers and Long-johns & Il Gatto? They're gonna wanna see you. They're not gonna believe it when I tell 'em you're back!"

Antonio was laughing. Mousey was still the same—he hadn't grown any bigger, that was sure. Still twitchy like a rat. "Okay, okay, Mousey—tell you what. Meet me at the clubhouse out back about five—I'll have some news for you then—right now I gotta be someplace."

"Aw, Naso, don't go! Ya just got here."

"Five o'clock. The clubhouse. Be there, you *testa di mulo*. Bring the guys!"

Levy and Son was located at the corner of Baxter and Walker. You couldn't miss it. Old man Levy had put together a four-story building complex there, to make his garments, and sell them, too. It was enormous. From where Antonio was, you had to go back to the corner of Mulberry and Broome Street—Baxter was only one street over. So, either you could go down Mulberry a couple of blocks past Hester Street and down to Canal Street, and then hook a right—Walker Street began right there—or, you could cut over from Mulberry on any cross street to Baxter itself and just go down two blocks to the corner of Walker—and there it was, *Levy and Son*—couldn't miss it.

Antonio felt happy being back in the streets. He was proud of himself because he hadn't forgotten his way around. How many nights had he lain in bed in the narrow house in Alta Villa rehearsing his knowledge of the streets and alleys and short-cuts—how many times had he revisited in his dreams the apartment, the courtyard out back, the clubhouse, the school, that time he and his gang got into the circus . . .

Not for the first time that day, Antonio found himself, unbidden, thinking of his father. How the man learned to loathe *Levy and Son*. He could not get over the fact that the factory-manager, or even the floor-lady, dared to inspect his work. It disgusted him how they gave it the once-over. *A craftsman like himself!* They didn't even know what they were looking at. Once, he dropped a stitch or two, or three or four, on purpose—they saw nothing. *And these were the people who paid piece work to the help—and saw themselves as superior? You know what they were? Scum of the earth! That's right.*

Matsa Christa.

"Why do you call them that?" Antonio wanted to know.

What's the matter with you? Don't you know a yid when you see one?

Although Enrico LaStoria disdained to learn English, he picked up words such as *kike* or *sheeny* without any problem at all, because it was essential to him. Indeed, he made a point of inquiring about them when he heard them flung around by the other Italians who worked at *Levy and Son*—and he enunciated them, with a sneer, and a secret self-satisfaction. From the moment he first stepped on the premises he held it against the owners that they were Jews.

To nine-year-old Antonio, it all seemed to him very mysterious, part of that world of the grownups that often appeared to him so opaque, and yes, ugly.

Yet because he absorbed his father's every nuance it was important to him also to know, or to try to find out.

"So—how can you tell—just by looking at them?" Antonio wanted to know.

Listen, stupid, his father said, when you get to be my age, then you'll be smart, like me.

Enrico LaStoria often spoke to his son Antonio in this manner. The boy asked too many questions. But Antonio persisted. "Can't you just tell me?"

Look at me, said his father. I'm going to explain something to you. Judas, he sold Christ for thirty pieces of silver—and Judas was a Jew, no? And then the Roman soldiers, they got a hold of Gesù and they hung him up on a cross—to suffer, and die. That's the Jews for you.

Antonio did not care if they did pay piece work at *Levy and Son*. He was not nine years old anymore. He had separated himself from his father. It was his life now. He had divorced himself from the overbearing presence, the never-ending dictatorship. All he needed was two or three dollars a week. He was just a boy. If he could buy a penny candy once in a while or a *gelato* on Sunday for himself, what more did he need? He didn't have to worry about supporting all those people at Uncle's place— just give a little something to help out. Uncle was getting a little something from here, there, and everywhere, to help out. If Antonio contributed a buck or two a week, a little more or less, then—he could keep his head up.

I am going to get the money to rescue my mother, no problem, you'll see, for sure, I promise.

Finally, he was there, at the back door of *Levy's*. Ready to start. That very day.

The man who was sweeping up at the rear dock said, "Yeah. I remember you. You used to hang around, gettin' in the way. But we don't need no bundle-boys right now. We got all we need. What? Last year was last year. Lemme tell you, kid—the only reason your father wanted you around was to translate for him. And so we had to put up with you. Jesus Christ–kids today! More trouble than they're worth. Now, get outta here. I'm busy."

Chapter 4

Like A Needle And Thread

Antonio headed back to Mott Street with his head down. When he stuck his hands in his pockets, they were empty. The curt rejection in the man's hoarse voice telling him to *"get out"* rattled, stinging in his ears.

Not for a moment had he figured into his calculations this kind of total, final defeat. Indeed, he had counted on Levy and Sons as the solution to every contretemps. Losing his passage money to the man in the vest, turning his back on the husband of the lady in blue, his frustration at finding himself under the control of Uncle Eugenio, to whom he now owed his very sustenance and shelter, all these were solved by Levy and Sons. But not now. Now he was stymied, blockaded, by the very people he thought owed him a living. Why could he not twist the world to his own command? He wanted to cry in fury, and he knew he could not let himself; he was so angry he wanted to bite the insides of his own mouth.

He had to get to the clubhouse. He needed to see his friends. He needed to feel good, *not like this, like it's the end of the world.*

When he spotted Knickers, keeping a lookout from the alley-corner next to No. 193, the other three popped their heads out over his shoulder.

"Naso!–Mousey told us he bumped into you!"

"Yeah—he thought he seen a *spettro*."

"Why the hell didn't you meet us at the clubhouse like you was supposed to?"

"Yeah, we were there waiting for you!"

"Hey, hey," said Antonio, "one at a time."

"Come on!"

"What's the idea, Naso?"

"You trying to stand us up?"

"All right, all right, *basta!* Last one to Mulberry Street's a rotten egg!"

Then in an eye-blink they were running down the street, dodging back and forth between hydrant and lamppost as if they had never been parted, but were simply picking up an unfinished race. They ran and ran, from sheer idiocy, till they were tired and stopped running, five breathless boys, and gradually slowed down, and looked at each other, and started laughing. Five former friends who suddenly had discovered the severed arm, the missing limb, that had been torn from them for the entire past year.

The sudden burst of energy, thrashing arms and legs, relieved Antonio of that plug at the base of his throat. He jumped up and down, senselessly, threw punches at the air. This was what he needed, animal release.

Having discovered themselves to have willy-nilly circled back to Mulberry Street, Antonio started a shoving match with Il Gatto, among the pushcarts. They managed to accidentally bump into old man Zammuto, who started swearing at them, while Mousey pinched a peach behind his back. Antonio grabbed it away as they ran off. "I'm starved!" he cried. "I didn't have nothing to eat all day long!"

"Hey," said Long-johns, "let's go over my house. We'll get my mother to give us something."

Long-johns' mother, Signora Ciccone, whose husband worked on the sewers, had her table set for his homecoming when they got there: said she, "What? I gotta feed the whole street now? Sit down, you good-for-nothings."

Antonio thought he had never tasted pea-beans so good in his life, and there was a couple of big pieces of sweet, tough pork rind buried in there, that just hit the spot, and gave him something to slide it down with. "I could eat a *vacca intera*," he told the Signora.

Back in the clubhouse, the cracks in the slatting let in enough twinkling from the windows of the courtyard for them to play *scopa* in the looming darkness. They scooped their deck of cards from its hiding place in a hole behind the clapboarding and passed them to Antonio to deal, just as in days of old. He said to Long-Johns, "Your mother never even knew I was gone!"

"No-she figured you got sent away to reform school."

"I wish I was—it woulda been easier."

Knickers said, "So—you gonna tell us the whole story?"

"Why should I?" Shuffling the cards made him think of *that man.*

"Nevermind, we got it all out of your cousin with the big mouth," said Il Gatto.

"Little Enrico?" Il Gatto had the untrustworthy oval eyes of a cat, which is why Antonio bestowed on him that nickname. "What did he tell you?"

"Some unbelievable story about a 'lady in blue' helping you stowaway on a ship."

"Yeah, was any of that true, or did he make it all up?" said Long-johns.

Antonio had dealt out three cards each and turned four cards face up in the middle. It would be a short round as there were five of them and only forty cards in the Napolitane deck they used. He told them, "Every word is true. I couldn't make up something like that. I wouldn't believe it myself except that it happened."

"And why didn't your father come back?" said Knickers, who earned his sobriquet from the short pants which drooped around his ankles: his mother was saving money. She had leftover material and she said he would grow into them.

"You guys ask too many questions. My old man's my own personal business. Are we playing *scopa*, or what?"

"Scopa!" cried Mousey.

"*Aspett,*" said Antonio. "Whaddya think you're doin,' *stupido*? Three and four's seven, not eight. Put that back."

"But we wanna know why you came back without him," said Mousey. "Weren't you scared?"

"Takes a lot of *nervo*, if you ask me," said Il Gatto, who was as skittish as his namesake.

"So maybe I took a chance," said Antonio. "What's wrong with that? I was always lucky. I was lucky my father brought me here in the first place. But my lucky streak's been letting me down lately. What I wanna know from you puddle-brains is where can I find me a paying job—or I'll have to be scrounging off you guys all the time."

"What about Ferrara's?"

"The grocery store?"

"Did you try Sal the barber?"

"How about Terranova's newsstand, down on the corner?"

They knocked it around awhile, but deep down they knew you needed a heaping dose of Antonio's uncanny luck, at their age, to get someone to take you on, unless you knew somebody, or you had a cousin or an uncle that could get you into the pushcarts or the restaurants or the streetcars or the nickleodeon, anything. Trouble was everybody already had a cousin of their own they had to take care of. And at ten years old, you couldn't go out on the construction sites or down to First Avenue, where Knickers said he heard they were gonna start building a train tunnel, underground.

"We'll all be old men by the time they start something like that," said Antonio. He was looking at the seven of coins in his hand, thinking, *that's worth a point right there, hold onto that one.*

"No, it's true, I swear. You ask my Pa—he'll tell you. It's been in the papers."

Always an argument with these guys, Antonio thought. "Okay, Knickers, you got that round. Who's keeping score?"

"I will," said Long-johns.

"Right, so take the stick and mark it on the slats," said Antonio. "And no cheating. We're only gonna play to eleven this time, first one to eleven. I don't have the time tonight to go to 21." He collected all the cards to start the second round, dealing out three cards each, and four cards face up in the middle, *which adds up to 19 already, so only 21 left in the deck—these rounds are gonna go quick, which is good, cause I'm bored already.* "Mousey, you can play all night if you wanna. You keep playing this game, you'll even learn how to count."

The rounds did go quickly, and the cards, *Coppe, Denari, Spade, and Bastoni,* Cups, Coins, Swords and Clubs, flashed from Antonio's fingers, and at the end of each round, whoever totaled the most points won the round; during a round, all the numbered cards, 1 through 7, and the three face cards, *Fante, Cavallo and Re,* Infantry, Knights and King, which counted as numbers 8,9, and 10, were used to *scoop* cards from the face-ups in the middle; a match took a face-up card, and that was one point; but you got a *scopa*, a scoop, if, out of the three cards in your hand, say you had a *Cavallo*, which represented the number 10, and two face-up cards were showing, a 7 and a 3, which added up to ten; your *Cavallo* took the two cards *plus* all the other ones face up, too, and you announced out loud, *Scopa!*, removing these cards from the round. The dealer, Antonio, then had to deal out 3 cards to each again, to start the next round; and the new round kept going till all the cards left in the dealer's deck were gone; Long-johns then tallied 1 point for the winner of that round on the slats, with the stick, for winning that round, the winner being determined by adding up how many points you got in that round. Every match you got and every *scopa* was worth 1 point, but the Seven of Coins was worth 1 point all by itself, so if you had it in your hand, you tried to hold onto it. Finally, and it only took half an hour, Knickers made 11 rounds, by the tally on the slats, and Antonio called the game, saying he had to get going. "Knickers, you got the luck tonight."

"Nah, nah, it was nothin.' You brought the luck back from the old country, Naso."

"And for cryin' out loud, call me Tony, willya, youz *buffone*? I don't like, *hey, Strunz!* And I hate *'Naso.'* Leave my Roman nose out of it. From now on, I'm Tony—you got it?"

That night Antonio lay there, in a tiny pallet on the floor with his cousin Enrico, so little room to himself that it was like a needle lying next to a thread in a sewing box.

He was being kept awake by his uncle's snoring and by his own disquieted thoughts chasing one another round his perspiring temples. Listening to Auntie Marietta breathing. His little cousin Maria sighing, the baby Angela sometimes whimpering. The *famiglia LaStoria* was forced to share one bedroom because Uncle Eugene needed to sublet the other one to the Castellanos. Despite the heat, they couldn't sleep out on the fire-escape outside the Castellanos' window because it was raining heavily tonight. So Antonio was trying to sleep in a bedroom the size of a walk-in closet, with two parents, an infant, himself, and three smaller cousins, seven people in one room; an inner room sharing a party wall with the cold-water flat that took up the other half of the second floor; an inner room with no windows, not a breath of air, human body-heat rising, the humidity of the hot night lying as heavily on your chest as three woolen blankets, your nose plugged with stuffiness.

Every time Antonio thought he might finally be drifting off, Auntie Marietta had to get up for the baby. How his cousins slept so easily, blissful as angels, he didn't know: *they must be without sin, or without a conscience. Not like me, worried about everything all the time, so I can't sleep at night. If only I didn't make so many mistakes. I can't wait till I'm 14. Then I can get my work permit. I wish I could just grow up, just like that. Then all my problems would be solved. Yeah—that's what you thought when you were trying to get to sleep in your bed back home. If only I could get back to New York again, all my problems would be solved. And look what happened . . .* Then he was running, running, running through the streets, dodging fire hydrants with the others, and he didn't realize that he was running in a dream where he was dreaming of running, until– . . .

The new day woke Antonio with the sensation of fresh ideas. He didn't know why, but he thought he did his best thinking when he awakened from a deep sleep. *Because your head is full of rocks, you pazzo from Alta Villa!* Take just one block of Mulberry, alone. In that one block, there's four shoe repair shops, four bakeries, and four barber shops, and they're all making a living. Little Italy is overrun with thousands of people. Maybe, if you could figure out what they wanted, or what they needed, there must be a lot of things. *If it was winter right now, maybe you could shovel snow. Everybody needs their sidewalk cleared off.*

But *primo*, first, he was going to find that garment factory where they needed bundle-boys. There were other places to ply his trade besides *Levy and Sons*.

And ply his trade he must. Whenever he tried to picture himself doing anything else but measuring, cutting, fitting, sewing, his mind rejected the image, a blot on a mirror, and set off a violent reaction in his blood, which rose up in his throat tasting like sour gruel. Antonio's destiny and the family's devotion to the garment trade, *like a needle and thread*, that's how they fit together.

And again, as soon as they were outside, out of sight of Uncle Eugenio, Antonio sent his cousins, sworn to secrecy, down the street off to school, while he went his own way. In spite of tormenting himself with worries late at night, he was ten years old; and he woke again each day bouncing with the excess of everything, energy, plans, hope, and hunger, and each day he told himself the same thing—*no more stinking old Napoli smelling like a rotten cabbage. This is New York.*

He began by knocking on every other door. That was to tempt fate and increase his luck. Today he would try one side of the street, time enough for the other, *domani*. He trusted in his luck. He counted on it. *Got any work for me?* He told himself all the time that he was a lucky boy. How lucky was it, to have made it this far, to have crossed the ocean, to have a roof over his head? Obviously his luck could not falter now. He told himself, *I'll eat later. I'll eat when I'm hungry. I'll eat off the pushcarts.*

Something will turn up.

At back door after back door, loading dock after freight elevator, the answer was the same—no work today. Come back some other time. Maybe when you grow up. The lady from the settlement house, the truant officer, too—they been poking around, trying to catch us breaking some damned law, you know?

Let's see—shoveling snow—shoveling dirt—shoveling cucca di cavallo—*gotta shovel something.* All around him in this beehive of a city he could see men working, standing in holes, digging, building, covered in dust, wiping away the grimy sweat. But he was neither big enough nor old enough for such things. For many money-paying jobs, you had to have your working papers. *Why can't I be 14 already? What can a kid of 10 really get away with, to make a buck? Collect cigar butts out of the gutters?*

Each day he told his cousins the same excuses, sending them off to school without him, swearing them to secrecy. "Run along—I'll see you at the house, later, tonight, you know?"

And he avoided the clubhouse and his friends. He would put them all off until he had something to show for his perseverance. After all, he was Antonio LaStoria, his father's son, and he had to keep up appearances.

When he had gone on solidly this way for two weeks, he still had not been to school yet.

Next morning at Uncle Eugenio's, just when he thought he would slip out the door again, same as yesterday, Antonio opened the door quietly, *so far so good.*

But somebody was there, as if waiting for him.

A big man with a big moustache, and dressed in a good-fitting suit, a store-bought suit, with a weighty ledger-book in his hand, held at his side, casually, in his left hand, in curled fingers, the way a schoolboy would carry a schoolbook.

"Thank you," said the man. "I was just about to knock."

"Oh, come in!" said Zi'Eugenio, from inside. The big man took up the whole doorway as he entered. "Do you know who this is, Antonio? He came to see you."

The visitor smiled one of those wide, put-on smiles, which melted away as he bent over to put his nose close to Antonio's. "I'm the truant officer."

"Come in, come in," said the uncle, who had gotten up in his undershirt and suspenders, baby Angela on his arm, gaping over his shoulder. Zi'Eugenio was apparently unaware that he ought to be embarrassed at his state of undress before the visitor. Indeed, he seemed very satisfied with himself, as if he had pulled off a trick at cards. "Sit down, Mr Engel—please. Have a cup of coffee."

Mr Engel pulled out a chair and placed his ledger before him on the table. Auntie Marietta got little Maria to set a cup and saucer before the guest. The other children all drifted in one by one to watch this latest show, the Castellanos' kids, too—and their parents.

With the gawkers-gallery filled, Antonio's embarrassment was complete.

He sped an angry dart with his eyes at his cousin Enrico—*you told!*

Mr Engel said to him, as he flipped pages, "I believe I have your name in here." Antonio had been out-flanked. There was no question now of slipping out the door.

"Let's see," said Mr Engel as he lifted his cup to his lips to sip. "Uh—LaStoria. Is that correct?"

Antonio raised an eyebrow and turned down his mouth, sticking out his bottom lip, as if to say, *maybe*.

"Capital L. Capital S. Hmm. Not an easy name to forget."

The bad boy wished only to melt into the floor, to disappear, and not to have anyone remember him, *ever*.

"Well, Master LaStoria," said the truant officer, "I am a busy man. I would like it if you did not give me any reason to be even busier. The law is the law. You must go to school. And that's that."

A warm flush seemed to cover Antonio from head to foot. The other children smothered giggles at his discomfort, they could not help themselves. His uncle was jiggling the baby in his arm, up and down, while he leveled a look at his nephew that said, *think you're smart, eh?* Auntie Marietta bustled about the esteemed visitor, offering mutely the sugar-bowl, and a teaspoon to stir with.

"Yes, please, and thank you." Mr Engel seemed to have natural good manners, and it seemed that he did not wish to make these people feel uncomfortable, on account of their mode of living, or lack of English, so, he enunciated, slowly and clearly, so as not to lose the opportunity of a teaching moment.

The poor man must have been in places much worse than this, in this neighborhood, Zi' Marietta was thinking, or hoping.

But it also was obvious that Engel was stealing a look here and there where he could. His otherwise placid face, with its well-fed cheeks and Prussian moustache, betrayed a judgmental side to his carefully-polished, professional manner. He had introduced the word *law* into the atmosphere, a word which cut the room into *us* and *them*, like a wall descending.

But Uncle Eugenio LaStoria needed a five-foot slab of lumber to knock some sense into Antonio and Mr Engel was just wooden enough to fit the task.

Antonio could do nothing but watch them being nice to each other. They proceeded to act as if he were not even there. Meanwhile, he brooded. Some loathsome kitten was purring and pawing around the cuff of his shirt. Or his sock was falling down on his ankle, tickling. He could not quite put his finger on it.

Presently, not so quickly as to gulp, Engel finished his coffee, and rising, to politely excuse himself, he nodded to the lady of the house, and shook hands with Zi'Eugenio, who was thanking him for taking the time. Then he was saying, "Goodbye, now, and have a pleasant day, all," and closing the door behind himself.

"Wait!" cried Antonio.

Mr Engel opened the door again. "Yes?"

"I have a question, Signore!"

"My boy—you may address me as 'Sir.' That is the correct form."

"Yes, sir. I'm sorry, sir."

"And what is the question?"

Zi'Eugenio interjected. "Antonio, Mr Engel is a busy man—."

"How old must I be—," the boy blurted out, "what does the law say?—before I am permitted to work?"

Mr Engel looked at the uncle, the wife, the other children—and he deliberately let his eye go wandering over the sewing machines stowed away against the walls. "Fourteen, Master LaStoria. And then you may apply for a work permit."

There was a rebuke to Zi'Eugenio hidden in these words. His nephew Antonio, who wanted to be called 'Tony' these days, had pricked him between the ribs with a pointed little interjection.

The city administration was full of reformers. Zealots and crusaders, products of the Progressive wave of the times, they made the objects of their solicitude, the immigrant poor, feel like they were aborigines, designated for conversion into Americans by a baptism in boiling water by missionaries.

No one felt this more keenly than Uncle Eugenio, who wished every day with all his heart that he could somehow lift his family out of the slums, if only so he could wash off his skin the stigma he saw in their eyes whenever he caught the American officials looking him up and down.

One day Antonio happened to be in Ferrara's *groceria* when the boy mopping the floor, with a wide sweep of his wet-mop, knocked over the bucket of sawdust standing in the corner onto the wet floor-boards, while there were housewives crowded into the tiny shop, filling it noisily with the customary combativeness.

Signore Ferrara slammed down his hand on the counter. From behind that cramped surface, he and his wife kept watch on every little thing. He sped around the corner—and that was a thing he never did—he might leave his wife's side, but not the cash register's.

"Porca vacca! Che cosa fa! Fare i gattini!" A river of abuse followed, and the old man threw the boy out, aiming one good kick at the fleeing miscreant, which missed, further engorging Ferrara's red face. *"Lei leccaculo! Si ri licenziato! Uscire!"* And under his breath, *"Figlio di puttana!"* With his hands on his hips, he surveyed the clean-up. *"Che stronzo! Che cosa fo addesso!"*

The perspiring old man went to fetch a brush and dust-pan, while Antonio was trying to think quickly.

He had been sent to Ferrara's by Zi'Marietta with 8 cents for a quart of milk. Now he stuck the pennies back in his pocket and said, "Signore—please!—I'll help you! Let me. Don't worry. Go back to your counter—I'll take care of it."

Antonio went around on his hands and knees between customer's legs, sweeping up, and when everything looked restored, he brought the implements of dust-up back to Ferrara, which gave him entrance to the back of the counter.

Ferrara was making change, and he said *"Va bene,"* and "Thank you," sideways to Antonio, who got up his courage, and said "Prego."

Losing his nerve at the last second, Antonio was going to wait, and try coming back tomorrow, making some excuse, but it occurred to him that somebody might beat him to it, when, just then, Ferrara said to him, "I seen you around here before. What's your name?"

"Tony. Tony's my name."

"Who you belong to?"

Antonio told him, and Ferrara said, "Yes, I know your uncle—he owe me money—like everybody—I wait—when they get it, they pay, that's all right. Anything else? Good job. Thanks to you. I'm busy, you can see."

Antonio said, "I thought that boy who worked here was your son." Ferrara said, "That *testa di cazza!* Why you ask?"

"Because you fired him."

"So?"

"So you need somebody? I'm available—for after school—every day, after twelve—till whenever you want—all day Saturday!"

"What can *you* do? Whadda you know about grocery?"

"You can teach me. I'll work for next to nothing. What were you giving the other kid? Give me the same."

So they made the deal for three dollars a week, for six days—not including Sunday. "But you gotta start right now—that is, if you're available."

"Just let me get a quart of milk for my aunt—I'll be right back."

And Antonio started stocking shelves and helping customers, bagging groceries and sweeping up. Everything you had to do so that Ferrara could sit on his ass. From long ago, the old guy was tired of telling his wife to do it, and getting looks from her.

But Antonio, after a couple of weeks, found out that Ferrara was not the easiest to please, either, or to deal with. The first week he asked for his *paga-paga* on Saturday—and Ferrara told him, the till is short–maybe Monday.

When Monday came, Antonio was shining with pleasure because he was able to go home and put into Auntie's hand three whole dollars, of real money. It gratified him, and eased his guilty sense of obligation, but also he meant it as a sign of things to come, that they could depend on him. They should use this for extras, and "Please, Zi' Marietta, call me Tony. Please? I'm ten-and-a-half now, almost eleven. "

He felt an immense new status when Auntie was combing his hair in the morning—he stood up straighter.

But then he found out at school that the boy who had the job before him was going around bragging that he had told off old man Ferrara, and quit, and what's more, the new kid was working for fifty cents a week less, *what a laugh!* So, when Antonio went to Ferrara and asked for the additional fifty cents, since it was his due, because that was the deal they had made, Ferrara, pointing out that Antonio had said he would work for next to nothing, and now all of a sudden he was bigger than his *pantaloni* size, and thought he knew more than somebody like me who's been in this business for forty years, and you're not such a good stock-boy, anyway, and furthermore, now that I think of it, I do remember your father, and he owes me money, too, so now, I take it out of your pay, how's that? "Always daydreaming, I have to call you three times before you hear."

So Antonio quit, right then and there.

Wasn't much of a job, anyway, he was thinking as he walked back home with his hands in his pockets. *Let the old man treat somebody else like dirt under his feet.*

But still he was downcast—he had made such promises to Auntie and Uncle, it seemed—now what was he going to say to them?

But Auntie and Uncle did not blame him. "Why you want to fool around with that man?" said Zi'Eugenio.

Still, Antonio felt badly, and he couldn't help pouting a little. "You don't understand," he muttered.

His uncle said, "What? What's to understand? You go to school, and after school, stay here and— and that's all!"

His aunt tried to soften her husband's tone. "It's just that this way I don't worry about where you are, Antonio—*scusi,*–Tony."

Her husband looked exasperatedly at her, and turned to his nephew to insist, "There's nothing out in the street for you—and what about the family business! You gonna forget everything your father and me ever taught you? That's how you show your gratitude? Ten years old!"

"Oh, yeah, I'm ten years old. And soon I'll be eleven, and what then?"

"*Ascolt'*—don't talk back! Did your father wear out his hand dealing with you?"

"Whadda *you* think?"

"Eh!—I thought so!" The nephew looked so woefully chagrined, at being reprimanded, and yet defiant, just the same, that Uncle Eugene threw his hands up in the air. "But, what am I gonna do with you?"

Zi'Eugenio stopped short of saying anything more, because, of course, he did not want his own children to feel he paid more attention to Antonio than he did to them. And, of course, he could not use corporal discipline with this one because he was not his father.

But it was even more complicated than that. If he should spank Enrico for something he did, or slap Maria's wrist for some infraction, and yet, never lay a hand on their cousin, the next thing you know, they'll all be crying "Not fair, not fair!" *Madonn'!*—this *dolor' nel culu* nephew Antonio simply did not understand everything the head of a household had to contend with!

Uncle Eugenio stuck his thumbs in his suspenders, and declared to Antonio, "Now you make me put my foot down. You go to school–and before school, and after school—you stay here, and work, like everybody else. No questions. No answers. No explaining. No *backtalk*." Said Uncle, with emphasis. "*And so, that's the end of that.*"

Chapter 5

Domenico, The Iceman

Saturday night was bath night at 193 Mott Street. Out came the big circular galvanized tub into the center of the floor, up went the bed-sheets on clotheslines. Everybody had to take their turn, from the biggest to the smallest. You went inside those sheets looking like a coal-shovel and you came out as shiny as a green grape, shivering and pulling blankets around yourself, rushing out of sight into the bedroom to get dried and back into some warm clothes.

Afterwards, they used to clear the table and the whole family played *scopa* or sometimes *briscola,* for a change, till everybody was stretching and yawning, and then they went to sleep happy, from the sheer joy and relief of playing cards instead of working.

It was just the same at Mousey's and Il Gatto's and at Knickers' house. You had to keep the family sane. It didn't cost anything, you had a laugh or two, and, so what? where's the harm? All the families in Little Italy were living the identical stale-bread lives, heedlessly skating on the knife-edge of existence, and nobody was any better than you were. They were the egalitarian poor.

On Sundays, Auntie Marietta rose at six to make macaroni and spaghetti by hand. Out came her big breadboard. Then came the flour, next the rolling pin. Rolling out the dough, four fingers wide, somebody had to hold up the long strip from behind her while she fed it slowly through the machine, turning the handle, and somebody else had to collect the separate strands coming out the other end, and cut them to length, and collect them and stack them to dry. You had to start early to leave time for drying. Because of the expense, they only had macaroni once a week. Sometimes they made meatballs, with egg, fennel, and breadcrumbs, or sometimes they would boil a chicken cut up in the sauce, but more often, it was *zozziicce*—sausages were cheaper.

Sunday mass at St Anthony of Padua was at eight o'clock or nine o'clock or ten or eleven, sharp. If you were late even a minute, you could find yourself out of luck. Thousands of people went there on Sundays; even though the main church held fifteen hundred, they had to send all the overflow into the basement, for two masses were held at each hour, the numbers were so great.

As they left the house and turned north on Mott Street, they were headed to Houston, and both sidewalks, on either side of the street, were thronged. And everyone was dressed in the best they had. The women had all saved their flowery hats decorated with ribbons and bows, not to wear at the fishmarket, but for this day, for Sunday, for walking to Mass. In every cold-water flat, all the children, in every family, were required to devote themselves to polishing their shoes. The mothers of many children became children themselves as they got their one good dress, their one good coat, out of the closet or the wardrobe, where during the week it was stored and ignored. This was no day to appear in the street in an apron, with your hair in tatters. In front of their mirrors, the women primped, after spanking the dust particles out of their bonnets, slapping them against their thighs. They placed the hats on their heads, and adjusted, profiled and posed. Their husbands, weary and worried and debt-ridden and plagued all the week long, were dressed by their wives, as if they too needed a mother—*straighten that collar, tuck in the cravat, button your vest, you ignorante, do you think I want to be seen with you like that!*

Once out in the street, they and their families would be examined up and down, ranked and rated from head to toe, judged solely, and for always and ever, by the degree of their magnificence, no matter how tawdry might be their daily lot— even as they themselves examined the examiners, appraising and judging. They might have been the poorest population in the entire city, yet they behaved as if they were a herd of heifers, calves and prize bulls, competing for the ribbon.

When this coagulating flood finally reached its destination at the corner of Sullivan and West Houston, it was as if the entire city of brick and cobblestone had liquefied into the bloodstream of one massive artery, only to arrive at the beating heart, the magnificent Church of St Anthony of Padua.

As befit its stature, this church seemed to crown its humble surroundings complacently, like the mitre on the head of a bishop who had somehow taken a vow of poverty.

The pennies of the poor were vested in the gold and marble vault of this beautiful building. Yet the stonework breathed with the pulse of a living organism. The prayers, supplications and superstitions of centuries were bound up and woven into its very walls, so that it seemed to beckon, a lamp on a dark ocean, shining here at the western terminus of a voyage which already had lasted seven lifetimes.

When the mass was over, finally, and Antonio made his way at last outside to the front steps, while he squinted to see, and raised his hand over his eyes, as he looked up, the sun washed his face.

Then it was home for the big Sunday dinner, a little nap afterwards, and then, the highlight of the week, *La Passeggiata*. the Sunday afternoon stroll, maybe about four o'clock, down to Mulberry Park, where the quality from uptown came to watch the show, idling their Fifth Avenue stagecoaches, parking at the four curbs ringing the Park, listening to the music from the bandstand, while they ogled the gypsy lower-classes, with their quaint European customs and native costumes.

There was a music teacher at PS 130, and unlike most of the teachers, he was Italian, or, one should say, actually, Sicilian. This was Professore Siragusa, and—put it this way, he spoke both languages, pretty good English, and Sicilian, which, to Antonio's Napolitano ears, was a third language. Nevertheless, when Antonio found out about him, he went to see him, with his mandolin in his hand.

"So, you play? Tell me—who taught you?" The Professore was a little skeptical that an underfed boy like this who needed a haircut—*well, he probably taught himself—he thinks he can play–*.

"My mother used to take me to lessons."

Signore Siragusa looked dubious, so Antonio added, "She had a cousin down in Avellino who was the music teacher in the town."

"*Veramente?*"

Antonio did not want to think about his mother. He tried to avoid it, because it caused him the pain of a guilty conscience. Yes, that was it—his conscience. But the man was waiting—patiently? Interested? No matter how much attention Antonio got, somehow he still felt nobody was really interested in him. Reluctantly, he replied, *"Sì, veramente."*

"Continua." Like the educated Sicilian he was, the professore knew how to make himself understood in good Italan when he wanted to. The teacher took a seat.

"*Allora*—we used to ride down the mountain in a farmer's cart, *ogni mercoledì*. My mother liked it—she got out of the house, she left me with her cousin, if she had anything she needed to buy in the city . . ." Antonio caught himself saying too much.

"*Strano*," said Mr Siragusa. "I thought you were one of Mother Cabrini's boys."

"A convent kid? Listen—I got a mother and a father! I'm not no orphan."

"*Va bene, va bene!* How do you make a C-major chord?"

"With a C, and E, and a G!"

"How do you make a minor chord?"

"You flat the 3rd."

"I see somebody taught you something. You have an instrument?"

"The mandolin my mother bought me." Antonio showed the teacher, who seemed not to have noticed the stringed instrument in his hand.

"Show me how you play the *tremolo*," said Signore Siragusa. He reached over and set a metronome in motion. "First, quarter notes, to the beat."

Antonio struck his D-sring, downward, hitting the A-string, then liftng his wrist, back up to the D, in time to the beat.

"Now, eighth-notes."

"Now sixteenths." The maestro listened. "*Adesso, trenta-secondi.*" Then he put the metronome up two notches. Watching, Antonio reflected that it was the very same metronome his teacher back in Avellino used. Siragusa said, "The *tremolo* is the essence of the *mandolino.*" He spoke to his students by pronouncement, by *fiat,* by declaration. "If I take you—you understand you must *learn.* Pay attention. Study. *Practice.* Above all, *practice.* Now, play something for me."

"What?"

The teacher looked dismayed. "A song, *mannaggia lo.* Something you know. Something you *like.*"

Poor Antonio was now sweating under the glare of this auditioning. Deliberately, he selected a favorite song, but with a slow tempo; he was afraid he would not pass; he would hate to be rejected by this martinet. He played *"Santa Lucia."* This would give him the chance to display his tremolo technique, which the professor had said was essential to mandolin. Strenuously, he played, but, with touch, he thought, with emotion, closing his eyes to listen.

Thus he did not see the Signore lean back, fold his arms, and sigh, as he delivered a pronouncement: *"Ah . . . molto bene. I take you."*

At Maestro Siragusa's rehearsals, which were held after school, none of the boys felt like fooling. The Professore did not permit girls in his orchestra, it was a sanctum of male privilege, and the boys all felt the prestige, the status, that conferred. When he tapped his ruler on the black music-stand at the front, they lifted their chins, stopped talking and glued their eyes to him. He told them the page to turn to. He was teaching them to become an orchestra that would play every Sunday in the pergola at Mulberry Park, and for that, you needed discipline. At the end of the school year, and even before, at Christmas, they were going to give a concert for all the parents, and they had to be note-perfect. There was no question of misbehaving in his classroom. He did not throw chalk or erasers at your head. He was very soft-spoken. You had to listen to hear him. He never raised his voice, but his eyes were demanding. When he tapped his ruler, he compressed his lips, and it was as if he looked straight into your soul—but there, he found music, and he slowly drew it out of you. His students adored him, without question, and without knowing why.

One day after practice, when he had gotten to know a little more about Antonio, the taciturn one, the circumstances of his home life, who he was living with, and the family's background and fortunes, Signore Siragusa ventured an opinion. "So—you were an only child. Very unusual."

Antonio was shouldering his mandolin, fiddling with the strap, and he ended up walking away, bothered.

It was disturbing how the Professore could insinuate into your mind, with a look, a gesture, an expression of his eyes or downturned mouth, something that stopped you cold in your tracks; something that made you ponder, doubt and question, to accuse yourself, so that you were uncomfortable, all of a sudden, in your own clothes.

Antonio supposed that the Signore would be surprised to find out some things about him. For instance, that he was somebody who was looked up to, among his own *gruppo*. But it was true. He supposed—no, he knew—it had something to do with his miraculous reappearance in their world. After an equally mysterious absence. He was there, and then he was not, and then he was there again. And none of them could lay claim to having run away from home, or made their way across the Atlantic, on their own. But Antonio had done it—and in their eyes, the deed was bigger than the boy. It cloaked him with an aura. This aura came from envy. His friends wished to be him, and they knew they could not.

Wouldn't the Professore be astounded to know that.

Antonio had not yet given up entirely on finding paying work. But the problem was, *ovviamente,* Uncle Eugenio.

How to get around that block of cement? For the moment, right after the visit from the truant officer, Engel, for the next couple of weeks, at any rate, Antonio was blockaded, frustrated, stymied. He had been out-and-out outmaneuvered by that cagey uncle of his, who had proved, in more ways than one, truly, to be his brother's brother. At night, lying there in the dark, his mind grinding away on the gnashing gears that kept him awake, convinced he would never fall asleep, the long day that began with his ears being twisted off his head by his auntie's harried washcloth, and then proceeded to all the dragging and pulling of setting up the machines after breakfast, while waiting on the two fathers, LaStoria and Castellano, to creep back up the stair loaded down with cloth-parts; only to end up spending every next available minute, down to the last dregs on the clock, till getting pushed out the door to school, with the two teams racing to produce, produce,

produce, swallowing up another hour and a half; then, four hours sitting in the classroom fighting off the yawns, and also, the other students, with their stupid games and tricks, not to mention the teacher, with her long-armed yardstick; *Madonn'!* Turns out one's life was not one's own after all!

And to think that, after school, when the bell rang and they had to go home to make way at noontime for the next shift of double-sessions, it was right straight back to the grind again at No. 193 Apt. 2B. Four walls that closed in on you like a stone prisonyard. The endless drudgery till the debate ensued about which team won and did they have time to top for supper and were the twenty coats, or forty, pardon me, were ready to return-deliver to the *padrone* in the morning on the bent backs of the *due padri*, and could finally stop now and put away the machines, pull out the table and have a bite to eat before collapsing on a pallet on the floor in sheer idiotic exhaustion?

And in the sleepless dark later the dawning realization creeping into Antonio's bewildered brain that *I can see perfectly the point my father had last year—unless you get out from under Eugenio's sweating system—you'll never make it in this town!*

Appalled, the old man who lived inside the body of the boy Antonio lay there in the dark, eyes wide open, dreading the thought—*in the end, I have turned into my own father, after all . . .*

Antonio tried figuring out who really needed windows cleaned at home—because they couldn't do it themselves, for one reason or another. Maybe they were too old or sick. Maybe they were too tired— or they had so many small kids, too young to help out. But would they pay?—and how much? He got a few jobs that way going around the neighborhood, but they were few and far between, and not steady enough. He found out that if there was an old lady living all by herself in a building, there was probably a good reason why. He did get his face around, and the name "Tony." People started to get to know him, and some people would send him here and there, or make suggestions, that ended up putting a little something in his pocket. So and so's had a death in their family, they're gonna be at their wits' end this week, poor things, run over and see if they'll want you to wash down all the steps in the building, maybe they slip you a little. La famiglia Torrino, they just had another kid, she's laid up—go see them, see what they need. He ended up doing all sorts of odd jobs—but then he found out soon enough that he was running around crazy and it didn't really pay in the long run. Either he had to wait for the money, or they cheated him, and what could he do? Or he felt awful taking money from some old cripple who was even worse off than he was.

Now this mania for making money he was pursuing in every available *stolen moment* in the day—after school, not before.

He had been forced to become just as calculating as his nemesis-uncle. *Now we'll see who will outfox who.* His acquiescence lasted only so long. When weeks had gone by, the uncle would slip; his vigilance would relax; thinking his victory complete, his guard would be down. *As long as I don't give him any excuse to drag in reinforcements from Engel—I should get by. Just go to school every day— then, after school—aha!*

Bit by bit, an inch first before a yard, then, taking a mile, Antonio was edging away. He made sure to always turn over every cent he made on his odd-jobs to Auntie; so, gradually, he was winning her over; not so difficult, as her sympathies were with him anyway; *and you can understand why, as I'm the one putting a little pin-money in her hand which she doesn't have to wheedle and cajole out of her husband.*

Uncle Eugene said, "Antonio—I never see you anymore."

"Please, please—it's Tony!–you know I'm almost 12 years old now, don't you?"

"I don't know even what you're up to, where you go?—you come and go as you please. You don't even tell your Auntie. Don't you know, she worries? "

"But I'm here every day, ain't I, working on the team?"

"Oh, si, as long as you making your own office hours! I ask my kids—where is he?–have you seen him?–it's like asking headstones in the cemetery—their lips are sealed!"

"But, Zi' Eugenio!—you're always telling them kids are to be seen and not heard!"

Uncle Eugene threw his hands up. "If your mother could see you now! And when's the last time you wrote her a letter, by the way? With all your money, you can afford the stamps."

Mousey thought he should try the newspaper want-ads—or maybe even sell newspapers himself. Maybe at one of the busy corners, or out in front of church Sunday mornings, or maybe he could get a route and deliver door to door. Tony looked into it and found out he could not make enough money—not even the three dollars a week Ferrara had been paying him. He would love to find something, anything, as steady as what Ferrara had going, a grocery open 7 days a week, to replace the odd-jobs, the day-jobs, which came and went. But where? Il Gatto told him he had found out Antonio could make a lot of money selling gum at the trolley stops, a nickel a pack—but Antonio quickly figured out it would cost him 3 cents a pack to get the supplies, and then if he didn't run around to every trolley stop within three miles, how would he get rid of them all, and if he didn't get rid of them all—*madonn'! it's not worth it!* Besides, it was one of those things—they weren't giving out that gum for free—if you wanted to make money, you had to have money to begin with.

Then one day he was in the street after school with no prospects but to head home and stitch some bundles with the rest of them, when he came across an accident. Two wagons had collided in Mulberry Street: a beer wagon and the iceman's cart. No wonder—it was so pinched and over-crowded all the time, people spilling from the sidewalks, pushcarts, delivery vans. It was a lot to take for *il cavallo*. They got nervous, started whinnying, didn't know which way to turn. The iceman's horse shied, and then he bolted. The two wagons got their wheels locked, the drivers jumped down and started stupidly arguing, like always.

By the time Antonio came along, a crowd had gathered, a fist-fight was about to break out, and nobody was paying the least bit of attention to the poor animals. The iceman's horse was twisting and writhing and trying to break out of the shafts; he was still so agitated, Tony ran over, without thinking. For a second, he didn't know what to do—but then he grabbed the bridle, and the poor frightened horse plunged his neck vehemently, and then reared back, and the boy almost broke his arm, but he held on, and reached up his other hand over the horse's left eye, and then he stroked his cheek, and he held onto the thrashing bridle, and kept stroking and petting, and put his hand over the horse's nose, and the horse was snorting and breathing hard, and Antonio started talking to him, softly, trying to sound soothing, asking, "What's your name—poor boy! Oh! Oh! Oooh! All right, all right, take it easy—what's your name, eh?" The horse started to respond a little, and maybe begin to calm down somewhat, and so far, the boy had avoided his hooves, so maybe—when he heard somebody behind him, laughing, saying, "That dumb animal, his name is Fiorello!"

Tony never found out who said that because the whole incident was so confused and quick, all over in a minute. By the time they got the wheels untangled, both drivers were all argued-out, the crowd was dissipating, because the fun was over, and Antonio himself got shoved out of the way, and separated from Fiorello.

A couple of days later, he was going home to Mott Street again, after school, when he heard somebody call out, "Hey, Naso! Come here!"

"My name is Tony!"

"Whatsa matta? Some kid told me. I was asking after you. He said you answer to *Naso* because you always sticking your big nose into every little thing. Must be *amico* of you, no?"

"My name is Tony!"

"So, come here, Tony!" It was that hot-tempered delivery driver who drove the horse called Fiorello; the man was planted, standing next to an ice wagon with the name DOMENICO painted on the side-rails.

This Domenico, if that's who he was, built like a barrel, was short, stubby-legged and dressed in a long white butcher's apron, down to his knees. His torso he covered with a leather vest, and a wet sack-cloth over his right shoulder, he tied on with a loop running under his left arm. "I been looking for you!"

Antonio approached him, and the man said, "I asked around after you. They said you was always around somewhere, so now, here you are. You like my horse, eh?"

"Is his name really Fiorello?"

"Yeah, he's my Little Flower, all right. How would you like to ride him?"

"For sure. Okay. Why not?"

"Well, I tell you what. See—I'm looking for a dummy-boy, to climb up, and sort of keep him in line. In other words—well, you know these horses, they cost me fifteen, sixteen bucks apiece—and they're always dying or something, breaking a leg, gobbling too much feed, getting sick, farting in my face all the time—so, I need you to—well, you interested?"

"You mean, a job? *Di sicuro.* Okay. Why not? But it's gotta pay. I can't afford to work for nothing. A lotta people wanna hire me, you know."

"Well, I mean, yeah, but I gotta tell you, it's hard work, and very long hours, and seven days a week—."

"What do I have to do?"

"Well, you ride on his back, and sort of lean close on his neck, talk to him, keep him calm and relaxed—but the main thing is you gotta warn away the traffic in front of him—you seen what he did the other day—"

"How much? I gotta get at least three bucks a week—that's what old man Ferrara used to pay me in his grocery shop. You can ask him."

"I already did. He told me you're a *stubido!*"

"You believe that son of a bitch?"

"Eh!—you got a mouth on you! I like you already! But, I'm telling you, this is real work. We start four in the morning and we don't quit till the sun goes down."

"That's all right. But I gotta get three-fifty a week!"

"You said three bucks!"

"For three bucks, you get only five days." Tony was thinking quick. "You want the Saturday, you get it for only 50 cents."

"Well–I guess I could live with that."

"Good. Cause I gotta get one day a week off. I gotta play on Sundays with Professore Siragusa's orchestra in Mulberry Park."

"*Va bene, okey-dokey.* You gotta meet me, Tony, four in the morning at Lorenzo's, the livery stable on Mulberry Street. You know where it is? Number 224. Don't be late! You know—the only reason you're getting this job is because I seen you was good with Fiorello, he likes you. Me, he hates. But remember!—don't be late!"

That night, the boy did not sleep at all, he was so terribly excited. It was as if someone, out of the blue, had given him a horse of his own. He could not stop thinking about Fiorello, and by midnight he had given up even trying to sleep. By that time Fiorello had become more legendary than Bucephalus and he himself an undoubted Alexander. He left the house at two in the morning, with everyone dead asleep, just to make sure he wouldn't be late.

That first morning, while Tony was hurrying back and forth in the pre-dawn dimness, pacing with anticipation, in front of the locked double-doors of Lorenzo's, Signore Domenico was slowly emerging from the shadows of a bad night's sleep into the glare of a foul mood.

Yawning, stretching and grumbling, scratching himself, blowing into his cupped hands, Domenico looked like a drowned dog dredged out of the Hudson River. He took one look at Antonio and said, "Ah!—you!"

Domenico had a key for the small door in the big door, and they stepped over the high sill into the stable. It was completely dark and they could hear a horse snoring. But Fiorello was awake. Domenico knew his way around in there without any lights by feeling along the horses' stalls. He led out Fiorello and handed the bridle-strap over to Antonio. Then he removed the long wooden bolt from the twin doors and pushed them open. "You take him out and I shut the doors."

Antonio and his glorious horse stood in the street until Domenico stepped out of the small door again.

Then began the longest day of Antonio's life.

Domenico started talking as if he were now wide awake and he continued talking whether anyone was listening or not. At first, Antonio thought he was talking to him, then he realized, no, he's talking to himself—but he would find out that Domenico talked to everyone, and no one, all day, without stopping, and that, probably, Domenico himself was not listening, either.

In the pre-dawn, unearthly quiet, with the city just opening one eye around them, they proceeded, with hooves echoing eerily on cobblestones, around the corner to the alley where Domenico kept his ice-wagon for the night, behind the four-story brick building where he lived. Then it was back out to Spring Street, where they turned right, to head west for the Hudson River.

Antonio rode on Fiorello, and Domenico sat on the wagon bench, with the reins limp in his fingers, while he counted all the money owed to him, as if the reins were rosary beads. Because he never wrote anything down, Domenico had to keep all his accounts in his head. As he drove to work he recited the litany of sums owed to him, and the thought of collecting it all kept him warm in the chill dawn. Meanwhile, he also instructed young Tony, in all the assigned tasks he would have to perform. Truly, his mind was like a locked cash drawer, with compartments. The clip-clop of Fiorello's hooves on the pavements sounded to him like coins dropping in a wicker box. The horse's hooves striking the trolley tracks as they were crossing Broadway—that was silver dollars being minted, with sparks flying.

"Let's see, Number 10, and Number 198, that's Baxter, now, not the other one, she owes me for two weeks—."

A sudden stab to his heart, as he remembered to castigate himself for having forgotten Signora Leandro yesterday—ah! He could not afford to lose a customer!

"Now, Tony, remember!—110 Lafayette—2nd floor—Leandro—we can't miss her today!"

Domenico explained to his new dummy-boy the answers to all the questions the boy did not know enough to ask, and he assumed his pupil would not forget anything, although he also assumed at the same time that he would have to repeat everything twice over again, today, tomorrow, and the next day, too, before he dared to ask, now, what did I tell you? And of course he's a bright boy and as outraged as I am myself with these no-good customers who *refuse to pay!* and who can blame him?

"Tony—look—listen to me—you know, you're gonna have to get down off the *bestia* and help me with the deliveries—if I didn't explain this before, I'm telling you now—and, of course, you can't carry a fifty-pounder or seventy-five, leave that, and the hundred-weight, to me—but you can carry the twenty-fives, I'll let you do that, it's nothing, like a feather to you, what's four flights up at your age? It's nothing! You run up those stairs—and don't forget, speed, *ragazzo*, speed!—you gotta be thinking every minute, that *ICE* on the sides of my wagon?–it's melting! Just because you can't see it, loaded on your back, that don't mean it ain't melting! It's melting! And you know what that means? There goes the money! Yeah! That's our inventory—that's what pays our bills and puts coin into the pockabook at the end of the week. And that's money slipping right through our fingers—just melting away! *Sonamabeech!* So you see why speed is so important? Eh? The faster we get the back of the truck emptied out, the faster we get back to the docks, or the icehouse, pick up another load—quick, quick, back to the route, pick up where we left off, all that time we spend-a just getting over there and back— all wasted time, the ice she's melting, and nobody gonna pay us for a puddle standing in the street in front of their building, that's for sure— we ain't safe till we get that block of ice into the Signora's ice-box, in her apartment—so you gotta hustle, my boy, hustle, hustle, you know how they say, move your *culo!*—no time for picking your nose on this job! And another thing!—don't even dare to think of cutting the ice! I'm the only one who knows how to do that! That takes a lot of experience, and if you screw it up—there's goes the money—in bits and pieces and dribbles and drabbles. If you take the pick to the ice the wrong way, you can shatter it into a thousand icicles!—no good to nobody— but for sure they melt a lot quicker! See—that's the thing! People think you gotta close it up tight to keep it cold— but the ice, if it don't breathe—then it's melting faster—it's that whaddycallit—hoomidity, or something or other—*condensation*—the schoolteacher told me. I ask her, you know, why's the ice always covered in raindrops, like she's sweating? Condensation, she says. The ice she's gonna melt faster if it's standing in water—that's why you see the wagon-bed, it's got slots between the bed-boards and the sides, to let the water drain out—and we don't close in the sides, let the ice breathe—but people they only think of their ice-box at home. That's the picture they got in their heads. They can't see beyond their own pockabook, you know what I mean? They don't know what it costs *me!* They think, you know, they think we make-a the ice for free, why it's costing them fifty cents a week! They don't think of where it came from, how long it took to get here, if it came by ship or by train, where's it stored?—you'll see, Tony! By the time I'm finished with you–!"

They were crossing Broadway now, in the half-dark, and Tony was holding up Fiorello to let an empty streetcar pass—*must be going back to, or coming from, the car-barn.*

"So, first of all, Tony, you gotta learn the route. We got a territory we cover, and we don't go in the other guy's territory. For instance, we don't go over to Sheeny-town, we leave that to the Yids. You and me we don't go north of Houston or south of Broome—we got about three hundred, three-hundred-and-fifty customers. Anymore than that, you can't handle it. We gotta get everybody on the route their ice three times a week. And the business is only good in the hot weather—that's when we make all our money—in the winter, they stick the milk bottle out on the windowsill or the fire escape and keep it cold easy—they don't need us—but in the summer, they're dyin' for ice—otherwise they can't keep everything from going rotten. And who wants a warm drink around here in summertime, eh? It's hard enough cooling off! These people are stuck behind four walls—they don't got no private beach down at the river, you know! And the barkeeps, if they don't have chilled beer—across the street goes the customer! Them, you gotta get 'em every day, no question about it. Now, in this town, that's another thing, people don't stop and think—there's only one supplier—and that's *American Ice*! That big shot Morse, he bought out Knickerbocker Ice long time ago, and ever since he gots the whole town sewed up tight. Nobody can make a move one way or the other or say booh or bah about it. He owns it all— every icehouse down by the river, and every barge in the river loaded with ice—we pay on the nose, and we pay him—he owns the soles of our shoes!"

They had followed Spring Street all the way to Hudson Street, and then turned south, and after several more blocks, they had turned into North Moore Street, heading west downhill to the Hudson River.

Tony had never been in this part of town, but he was amazed at how empty and vast it seemed— acres and acres of empty lots interspersed with warehouses and factory-type buildings. Some of the warehouses down by the docks were long and low—Tony was bewildered at how long they were, and he asked Domenico, who said, "Who knows, three or four hundred feet, but believe me, they got thousands of tons of ice stored in them things—and why they are painted all white and yellow? To reflect off the sun, keep 'em cooler. Meanwhile, down on the river, the ice-barges tied up at some of the piers—those, they're floating in the water, and the water keeps 'em cooler. *Cristo santo*, you got a lot to learn, kid!"

When they came to the tallest building Tony had ever seen, maybe nine, ten stories, at 27 North Moore Street, built out of red brick with tall, stately piers rising to Romanesque arches at the top, and thousands of windows glittering in the on-coming dawn, mingled with the glow and glare of the night-time city streets–that turned out to be the *American Ice Company*.

Domenico told Tony they had to drive around the back to the loading docks. There they encountered long queues of wagons, precisely like theirs, lining both sides of the access road, and then hooking round back into six or seven lines in the yard behind the building, which then looped around so that the open rear end of the carts and wagons could line up at the end of the conveyors. where 600-lb blocks of ice came sliding down, guided by men with poles. Domenico hurried off to sign the receipt, warning Tony to watch out and not get crushed by sliding ice.

It wouldn't do to dilly-dally around the loading docks—a hundred teamsters would be down your throat—but as they drove back the same way they had come, Domenico explained, "They're making artificial ice now, in the new building. They say some day it's gonna take over and there won't be no natural ice no more, but I don't know about that. If so, there goes my winter vacation." Domenico was laughing. "You don't think I stick around here in the wintertime, do you? I go north, all the way up to Maine! Yeah! That's right! For the ice harvest—it takes two months, from December to February, and then, it's over. But the pay is good. We got 1500 men working on the River Penobscot alone. And guess what—we sleep all day, and work all night! *Sonamabeech!*"

Domenico, for some reason, who knows why, liked this kid, and it amused him to think how the kid probably thought it was marvelous fun, a Carnival of Venice, to work all night and sleep all day, a fairy-tale, when to him, Domenico, it was a chore, just a chore, like all the others. *Oh, to be young again!*

The day began with their commercial customers. They only serviced the smaller cafes and bars in their territory—Domenico was an independent, but he could not carry enough for the high-volume *ristorante*. Those were delivered by *American Ice* vans. But still, the little guys all expected to be serviced between six and eight A.M. Some of them were just a walk-in hovel—some were even pushcarts or sidewalk pretzel and sausage stands. But *American Ice* handled the fish-mongers—the fish-mongers needed crushed ice, and much more ice than an operation like Domenico's could handle.

Tony soon found himself rushing back and forth on Fiorello's back to the loading docks on North Moore Street against a tide of ever-increasing traffic as the city started its day. Tony had his hands full. He had to lean on the horse's neck and keep him soothed while yelling people out of the way. He quickly began to understand why Domenico had seemed so temperamental that first day, at the accident-scene. It was maddening. Especially the pedestrians. Somebody's running for the trolley, not thinking or looking where the hell they're going, and there you go, another mishap!

After eight o'clock, they took an espresso-break at a café, but they stood out on the sidewalk by Fiorello. Domenico asked Tony if he wanted a Fatima. Tony said, "Sure." Domenico held out the rumpled paper pack. "I don't have time to roll 'em. Ten cents a pack. Or a penny a piece, in other words. Don't start on cigars—they'll stain your teeth. If I smoked one of them on the wagon, I'd never keep it lit, you know? This way, you smoke it, get rid of it."

"Now—what we pay at the dock for a 600-lb block, eh? A dollar eighty, that's what. And out of that, how many 25-pounders you gonna get? Can you add and subtract—in your head? You figure it out. Twenty-four. That's right. So how much we gotta sell 'em for, to make a profit? Twenty-five cents each?—sure, I wish. But these people—these no-good *sonamabeeches!*–they only wanna spend fifty cents a week on their ice—and they think the price should never go up!—they think it oughta be free! So we deliver 'em three times a week for fifty cents—that comes down to sixteen, seventeen cents a block—and outta that I gotta pay you three bucks a week—even though I don't get you for Sundays!— oh, no, three-fifty, come to think of it!–I gotta feed and water the horse, I gotta pay to put him up in a stall every night—*Gesù Cristo,* no wonder I can't make a buck! And they think the price was set by God!—it can never go up since the day Adam met Eve in the garden!"

"Now—it's already after 8 o'clock. We done the business customers. Now–between now and quittin' time, we gotta somehow deliver 150 more customers in apartments. Break that down—we gotta do that many 'cause we got 300, 350 on our route, and we gotta hit each one every two days, so we can only do half the route one day, the other half the next, and then we rotate back again—and listen to the belly-achin' from all the women! You got here late today!—all my food's spoiled rotten!"

Domenico's voice squeaked as he mimicked the housewife.

"Every one of 'em thinks I gotta hit her first thing in the morning, before everybody else. Well, how we gonna get to 150 apartments every day?—what with, we gotta go back and forth with all the traffic over to Moore Street and the time it takes cuttin,' and runnin' up and down all them stairs—we gotta deliver seven loads a day, Tony, *Cristo santo*, and we can't even break even! So, you see why we gotta hustle, hustle, hustle—you, me and Fiorello?"

"All I know is you must be getting filthy rich off of this business!" Tony had been calculating as fast as Domenico was talking.

"What? What? Whaddya got here, smart-guy? You been on the horse two hours, already you know better than me? Come on—*andiamo!*—we're wastin' valooble time here! Get up on that horse, and let's go!"

That first day, Tony thought he was going to die. Far from sitting on a soft seat on Fiorello while Domenico delivered a building, Tony found that it was his job to run up and down every flight, sometimes four or five stories in a brick apartment house, to check the ice-cards the people put out.

Tony was familiar with those from his own apartment door—they told the ice-man how much to leave today. For households, it was almost always 25-lbs—but if there was a heat wave, it might be the fifty. There were four numbers on the square card, which was divided into quarters with a big X—the customers flipped the card right-side up, and whatever number was on top, that's how much they wanted.

He had to race back out to the street and remember every apartment number and the quantity they wanted, memorized, because Domenico was waiting impatiently at the back of the truck-bed, already slicing and sawing 25-pounders ahead of time—lucky for Tony that's what most people wanted, and it made it easier to remember.

Then Domenico would start loading Tony up with blocks to carry into the first floor, to begin with—"And don't drop one—if you shatter it, it come outta you pay!"

They used cast-iron tongs to hook the cube on both sides and hoist it up on the shoulder. They had 12 and 18 and 24-inch tongs, but Domenico carried the bigger cubes. And they didn't want to let the wagon alone for too long, because all the kids in the neighborhood thought it was their birthright to help themselves, and they were armed with kitchen knives and forks and nails and files and all kinds of things for chipping and shredding shards of ice. "Good thing for us most of them are in school!" said Domenico. "Now if we could just match up, for sure, which buildings are in which double-session–!"

By noontime, Tony was stiff and sore, his shoulder ached, and his shirt was soaked—he had no leather vest, although Domenico found a scrap of sack-cloth he could drape over himself to absorb some of the water. They took a break for lunch, and Domenico bought Tony a *sangwich* of *zozzicce* from the man on the corner of Broome and Mulberry. Tony never tasted anything so good.

They sat on a stoop for about ten minutes, and then it was time to go again. The only real break Tony got all day was when all the ice was gone from the wagon-bed, and it was time to weave their way through traffic back and forth to Moore Street. That was his respite. He got to rest riding the horse. And he needed it—if he had not had those intervals, he would never have made it through the day, because by three o'clock in the afternoon, he had been going up and down stairs in tall buildings since eight in the morning, carrying 25-pound blocks of ice on his shoulder—which he couldn't drop. Every fiber of bone and tissue in his body announced its location. He had never been so tired, hungry, fed up and exhausted—and they still had another sixty deliveries to go!

At the end of his first day, Domenico stood there with his hands on his hips, laughing at him. "How you feel now, smart-guy! You should see yourself. Go home! Don't forget—4 a.m., sharp! Don't be late! You stick with me, Tony—by the time I get finished with you, you gonna know more about this business than anybody in this town!-except me!—Niccolo Domenico!"

This went on for about the next six or seven weeks. Every day the same. Just like the one before it. Young Tony could not say that he loved it with the passion of a Domenico—but he did love the money. Every week Domenico paid on time. Sure, sometimes he was hard to take—but, in the end, at least you could trust him not to screw you on your pay. He turned out to be a man of honor, who paid up, and he never did mind treating Tony to lunch now and then—although he swore that was gonna stop, absolutely, after Tony earned his first week's pay and had money of his own. Of course, he went back on that promise.

At first there was consternation at home. But what the hell could Uncle Eugenio do? By the time Tony was sneaking out of the house at two in the morning all the rest of the LaStorias and Castellanos were sleeping the sleep of the dead, worn out from racing all day. Then, when Tony got back after work, he fell straight to sleep on a floor-pallet, completely beat, and you couldn't rouse him even for supper. So when were you going to have a discussion of just exactly what he thought he was up to?

And then at the end of the first week, when Tony put $3.50 into Auntie Marietta's apron-pocket—well, even Zi'Eugenio had to admit, the money made up for a multitude of sins.

The Uncle reflected—*as soon as we climb one mountain, another one looms into view.* Should he call in the truant officer again? For he knew that Mr. Engel would not be pleased, and that he would hunt Tony down—and after all, Uncle Eugenio knew damn well from Enrico and Maria that Tony hadn't been in school one day all week. *Or should I just keep my big mouth shut, and take the money?*

Tony learned a lot from Domenico. He learned how to keep his nose to the grindstone. He tried not to let much slip by him. He was watching every move every minute. He memorized every catch-phrase Domenico used to get out of arguments with his lady customers—"Come on, Signora! Let's dance! No? Come on—make me a happy man! One little smile! Oh—oh—*che cosa bella!* No, no, no, *managgia*, I don't tell you husband! Whadda you take me for?–some kinda kiss-and-tell? *Ci vediamo!* I gotta run! Signora Zaffanella—she's a-waiting for me!"

Domenico summed it up. "Listen to me, Tony—one thing you learn in this life—in this wonderful life in this bootiful big city!—if you know your business, you can make a good buck—if you don't know your ass from your elbow, ain't nobody gonna help you figger it out! *Sonomabeech!*"

Chapter 6

L'anima Di Una Scarpa

Each week, Tony dutifully turned over his three and a half dollars to Auntie, not Uncle. She would let him get away with anything. If he wanted something for himself, he asked her first, and she would give him back however much he needed. It was never anything much. He was wearing out his shoes. He needed new underwear. He wanted to get a real haircut, at the barbershop. Six or seven weeks went by this way. The boys in the backyard complained that they never saw him anymore. *I guess you quit school, huh? What's it like, being loaded?*

Then one morning, early, Domenico was just climbing down from the wagon at the docks behind *American Ice*, when someone grabbed Tony by the collar from behind. "Hey!" Domenico yelled. "Whaddya think you doin'?"

Tony was being swept off his seat on Fiorello, neck first, by a strong hand. "You shut up, mister, or you'll find yourself in a great deal of trouble!"

Tony looked up, wrenching his neck around. It was Engel the Truant Officer.

"Good morning, Master LaStoria! You and I are going to take a little trip to see the principal at PS 130."

It was just as well, Tony decided. Domenico was killing him—he wouldn't live long enough to grow up.

The following Sunday, Uncle Eugenio was relaxing on a bench in Mulberry Park with his legs stuck out, his ankles crossed, the heel of one shoe balancing on the sidewalk, his arms spread out like wings across the back of the bench, his coat open, vest neatly buttoned, straw hat tipped back. "I'd like to know what you think you're up to," he said to Tony.

"Zio! I'm not up to nothing."

"You're always up to something." Zi' Eugenio stuck his lower lip out, lowered his chin, and inspected the buttons of his vest. "You give three dollars to Auntie Marietta, it only comes back to me, you know."

"I know."

"So, why bother?"

"I don't know."

"I had a visit the other day, from somebody trying to do you a favor."

"Who?"

"Who do you think? The Professore."

So. They're all in this together.

"You're back in school, no? Why don't you go see him, pay your respects?"

Tony could hear the orchestra in the distance playing from the pergola for the Sunday concert. "*Va bene*, I'll think about it."

"While you're thinking about it, your mandolin's gathering dust in my apartment. Why did you bring it across the ocean if you're not going to play it?"

"I can't play when I'm not in the mood. Besides, I been busy."

"There must have been some reason—I can't figure it out—why you carry that thing on your back all the way to New York—and then you just drop it?"

"What's it gonna do for me? It's not gonna make me any money."

"Soldi, soldi, soldi. Me, too. Always money."

"I'm a tailor, Uncle—like you."

"Yes, it's the family business, all right, that's true. But your mother—she wanted you to learn something. Well—all that money she spent on lessons for you? Poof!–down the drain! By the way—"

"I know, I know. I will write the letter."

A few days had to go by before Tony showed up after school at Signore Siragusa's orchestra practice. He took a seat at the back of the classroom. The Professore paid no attention at all to him. He did not appear to even notice anything was changed—or that Tony had suddenly returned, without a word.

When rehearsal was over, and all the suddenly noisy boys were putting on coats, getting ready— the cooler weather was coming—Tony was straightening the twisted strap on his bowl-back mandolin before slinging it over his shoulder when he became aware of the teacher standing there, behind him. He felt the eyes on his back, watching. He turned, and found the professor patiently waiting, arms folded, head tilted to one side, lips compressed.

"So–you've returned to the flock."

"Yes, Professore."

"Hmm."

Tony could not meet his gaze. He looked at the maestro, but then he had to look away. He had that acutely uncomfortable feeling of Siragusa looking into his eyes, deeply, and beyond, with a penetrating gaze, right down into his soul.

"Now I think I begin to understand you, Antonio LaStoria. No, you are not one of the convent boys. Not orphaned by his parents. *Meglio ancora. You* are the one who abandoned them."

Signore Siragusa's countenance sagged with the profound disappointment he had found in his student.

Tony could not find anything to say. Words failed him, but as he turned his back on the man, he felt stunned. And accused. He walked away, and the strap on his shoulder, the weight of the mandolin, was heavy on his back, like the weight of mountain boulders. He stopped in the doorway—then he thought again, that it was better not to turn around—he would have to simply put one foot in front of the other, and melt away.

Such moments made him feel as soft as the dough in the middle of the loaf, when what he wanted was to be as un-crackable as a walnut.

The boys at the clubhouse teased him mercilessly. "Mr Big Britches," they called him. "Signore Pant-a-looney!"

"So they dragged you back by the ear, eh! How does it feel, Naso!"

"Miss Bloomers!—I'm sorry I skipped so many classes! I won't do it no more!—I promise, cross my heart and hope to die!"

He shut them up with a trip to the soda fountain at D'Agata's Drugstore. All treats on him. They spent a whole afternoon gorging themselves on gelati and lime rickeys. He knew that this display of generosity would put them under obligation, and remind them that they owed him respect.

Then he found another job, this time rather easily, on a tip from Mousey, who heard about a couple of chiseling taskers who were doing contract work for the padrone over on Rivington Street. They were on the other side of the Bowery, stuck up an alleyway in Sheeny-town, on a stretch of the street with livery stables and welding-shops where nobody wanted to go.

Their shanty was at the end of a lane of back-buildings behind the brick apartment houses on Forsyth. The place was condemned as unfit to live in, much less operate a business. What it did have was electricity—which meant they could run faster and cheaper than home-taskers.

The two men running it, the partners, Pepe and Cortino, a pair of Calabrians, were stealing electricity from the meter next door to run their machines.

The retailers, such as Brooks Brothers, Bonwit Teller and Levy and Son, pushing their pencils in their prime locations on Broadway, sub-let the contracts to the padrone, calculating that they saved 3 cents per coat by farming out the work to the likes of Pepe and Cortino, who could do it for 45 cents a coat, as opposed to 48 cents for somebody like Tony's uncle and his wife and kids, at home, in their apartment, simply because, by working faster, they produced more. Foot-power could not run the machines as fast as power from the Edison Company. Electricity did not get tired. Electricity did not get cramps in the calves.

And Pepe and Cortino were even cheaper than 45 cents, since they were not paying for the electricity.

So, Tony went to work for Pepe and Cortino, for the same he got from Domenico, only a little less, three bucks a week.

Compared to these guys, Domenico the iceman had ethics, but—the Calabrians were in the garment-making line. That's where Tony wanted so badly to be. And he could work there after-school hours, after orchestra-rehearsal, Saturdays, too—perfect. He wouldn't have to worry about Mr Engel or Siragusa or his uncle or Domenico or anybody. In fact, if he took a tip from Domenico, as he did, it was: *know your own business, ain't nobody gonna help you figger it out.*

But Tony had miscalculated. Pepe and Cortino turned out to be a bad bet. Smoking and drinking all day in a wooden shanty with machines running, scraps of cloth piled everywhere, machine-oil slicking up the dirt floor, they would get beer and cigarettes from peddlers who freelanced the neighborhood. If they wanted to eat, they had food sent in, already cooked. They never left the shanty, and once Tony got there after school, they didn't let him leave either. Both bachelors, because who the hell would marry types like them?—or else they had wives and kids far, far away, back in the old country. So ignorant they couldn't even read. They had a couple of little Jewish school-girls from the neighborhood come in to read newspapers and stories to them while they worked, otherwise, how would they know what the hell was going on? They worked by electric light till ten or eleven at night. They chain-smoked, and tossed uneaten food in the corners, and drank beer from a pail with a ladle, and then went to sleep, half-dead, late at night on two folding cots they pulled out. It was too late for Tony to go home in the dark all the way to Mott Street, so he went to sleep on the cutting table, but he had to get up in the morning and get to school anyway, no matter what. There was no place to pass water or move your bowels or even clean up till he got to school. After two weeks wearing the same clothes six days a week, changing back home on Sundays, Tony had to quit. It wasn't going to work out. He would have to put it down as a bad job and try to learn something from the experience. Even he could see that.

When Tony went one day to Savastano's, the barber, for another haircut, where he got his hair cut the first time, weeks ago, while he was sitting in the chair, waiting for one of the three barbers, Savastano said to him, "What's with you, Tony—we ain't seen you for a while. Whatcha been up to?"

"I been workin' and goin' to school."

"Yeah—I know—we used to see you runnin' around with Domenico, the ice-man. What happened with him? You gave him the shove?"

Tony said, "No, not at all, what happened was this," and he explained about that bastard Engel.

And Savastano said, "So, now you're a gentlemen of leisure. Well. I might have something for you. Would you be interested in pickin' up an easy seven, eight bucks a week?"

Tony was skeptical. "You gonna pay me that much?—for what?"

"I don't have to pay you nothing at all. The customers pay you—and the tips are good!"

Savastano went to a tiny room at the back of the shop. It was a closet, practically, and all Tony could see, when he opened the narrow door, was a chipped and blackened, stained sink, and a telephone on a small shelf bracketed on the wall. Savastano pulled out a shoe-shine box with a built-in foot-rest, and slid it across the floor to Tony.

"This?"

"Yeah, this! Jesus Christ—I give you a gift horse, you gotta count the teeth!"

"I don't get it."

"It's easy. Let me explain."

All the time they were talking, Savastano had a customer tilted back in the chair, with a straight razor at his throat.

"You see these guys like Michelangelo here, they come in every day for a shave?—'cause they're too lazy to do it at home for themselves? No, seriously, now—you can't understand, you're too young to shave yet, but look at it this way—they would rather come in here and get the full treatment with the hot towels and everything, lay back and relax, and all, than to scrape their skin with a straight-razor in a cold-water flat, know what I mean? Am I right, Mike?"

"You're right, Charlie!"

"See all them mugs, kid, lined up?—over here, the mirror—every mug's got a name on it—that's my steady guys, come in every day for a shave, they got their own brushes, I keep 'em here for 'em. Twenty-five cents a shave!"

"Plus the tip," said Mike in his chair. "that's another nickel."

"So what! Mikey! You can afford it."

Savastano turned to Tony.

"Now, you kid—it's a nickel a shine—but most guys they're gonna give you a dime, minimum— once in a while, the big-tippers wanna throw you a quarter—maybe you can't make change—pretty soon, you're rollin' in it—I'm telling you, seven, eight bucks a week. And I know you're a good worker, I seen you operatin' with the ice-man and that hot-tempered horse of his—and you happened to be in here on the right day. My last boy just left me to go to high school—of all things! He's gonna become a doctor, he's joining that crew they got down on Broome Street, the medical corps, they're all students, they deliver babies. He was here with me five years. How do you think he got all that money you need to go to school for medical? Shoe-shine, that's how! You think he would stay here five years if he wasn't makin' it?"

Savastano started stropping the razor.

"Tell you the truth—he was getting too big for it anyway, too old. Guys wanna deal with a kid your age, your size—I don't know, it's crazy, but Filipo–he's almost grown-up, now, for Christ's sake—the guys want somebody they can pat on the head, you know?—so, whaddya gonna do, he's gotta go! So, whaddya say? We got a deal?"

"I don't know," said Tony.

"You're a *pazzo!* Now here—take this." It was folding money.

"Run down the corner and get us some coffee—and bring back the change! You start when you get back!"

As it turned out, they should have named it Savastano's gold mine, instead of barber-shop, as far as Tony was concerned.

He had never seen so much money in all his life. It was almost shameful, because he was able to make, by himself, as much money in a week as his uncle made running two teams of garment-taskers at home for six days—just by shining shoes!

Sometimes he wondered at his luck. He didn't need to skip school. The work was easy, compared to what Domenico put him through. He stayed in one place instead of pell-melling all over. He didn't have to sleep on a cutting table all night. He wasn't under the thumb of a put-upon uncle, or anyone else, for that matter.

The kind of men who came into the barbershop to lounge around, spending the better part of a day, with plenty of time and no-place special to get to, these were not the men who were getting dirty in a hole in the ground, struggling to dig sewers up on First Avenue, or unload ships over on the Hudson.

These were prosperous men who smoked cigars and carefully trimmed their beards and moustaches and liked looking at themselves in the mirrors all over the walls, because they were well-dressed and had coin jingling in their pockets. Tony couldn't believe how they threw money around. Where did they get it all? And they loved Tony, as they got to know him. He became a kind of a neighborhood mascot.

They could count on him being there every afternoon sitting in his corner with his shoeshine box and his books.

Tony had found out that he could do his schoolwork while on the job, easy, it was a snap. Now he enjoyed school more, once he knew he didn't have to spend the rest of the whole day slaving away lugging 25 pounds of ice up four flights, or watching the Calabrians swill beer while he had his head down pushing the sewing through the deafening electric-powered Singer sewing machine, or—yes, it must be said, he knew he ought to be more grateful to his Uncle, but pushing out twenty coats a day on the sweating system, before, and after school, too—and no money in your hand at the end of the week? *Whaddya call that? Slavery?*

He had discovered a new friend at school, and it turned out to be one of the teachers—a kindly lady named Miss Morgan, who ran the library after school.

One day he wandered in, and she asked him what he was looking for. "Something good to read. That will last a while. And help me improve my vocabulary."

Miss Morgan told him about an author—there was a word!—called Horatio Alger—who wrote books, she said, for boys just like him, who wanted to get ahead in life.

The first book Miss Morgan loaned out to him was called *Strive and Succeed*. It was a thrilling story about a boy from a poverty-stricken family. This boy happened to be both very brave and very honest, and, to Tony's utter surprise, seemed to know a lot of Latin, which Tony had only heard in church—and this young hard-working boy, who was named Walter Conrad, even knew a lot of Shakespeare, and even the ancient Roman Cicero. Walter—in the story–found a stolen watch, and, being honest as he was, he sought out the elderly gentleman who owned it, who turned out to be, in addition, by the way, very wealthy, and who in turn, helped Walter by taking him into his home, rescuing him from his cousin, a snobbish youth, and his uncle, a kind of an evil squire who more or less just spent his life being rich, but did nothing for his impoverished nephew, Walter. The kindly old gentlemen, however, found Walter a position as a clerk in an office which raised him up from the slime, up to the realms of '*Spectability,*' as Walter called it.

Now that was something young Tony could understand—Respect.

After *Strive and Succeed*, he read also *Sink and Swim*, and *Slow and Sure*, and *Strong and Steady*, and *Try and Trust*, and *Luck and Pluck*. He could rip through an Alger novel in two days. Once he started he couldn't stop. After he read the whole series, which, he found out, began with *Luck and Pluck*, he then discovered *Ragged Dick*—who turned out to have been a bootblack, right here in New York—a kid more or less just like Tony himself.

Even though all the books seemed to tell the same story over and over again, Tony never got tired of them. When he finished a whole bunch, he just went back and read them over again. He'd lie awake at night thinking and dreaming and planning and scheming so as to make sure his own life would turn out just like Walter Conrad's. He blessed the name of Miss Morgan, who had opened up this whole world to him that Tony never knew existed, and he began to look forward even more to school each day, because he knew he could see her again, and she would talk to him, and encourage him, and try to help him, and seemed to like him—even if he was just a street urchin from one of Alger's novels.

Meanwhile, real-life continued at Savastano's Barbershop. Tony began to view the adults around him as potential benefactors, and he strove to please them with good service.

And when he began to hang around in the barbershop, he began to see himself, in the multiple mirrors covering the walls, the way others saw him.

First of all, it was his shock of silky, fair hair, which flowed straight back over his head from temples carved out of soft and malleable, youthful, blooming marble. Because it was perfectly straight hair, and as fine as silk, he never wanted to cut it, but neither did he want it unkempt and overly long. Auntie Marietta had taught him to part it in the middle, and nowadays, he was able to keep it carefully combed back over his ears, straight back, flowing, just like a lion's mane. Now that he worked all afternoon in an emporium full of mirrors, he was learning, without realizing it, to admire himself, even to take a little more care over his appearance. Auntie Marietta, whenever she was brushing his hair for him on Sunday mornings, for church, would coo over him. And it made Tony remember that his mother used to do the same thing, to marvel over his fine head of hair, and to explain to him, though this he did not himself remember, that he had been born a blond, just as she had. "Yes, that happens," Auntie Marietta would say, "and then, as you get older, it darkens a little."

Tony also decided that his nose was really not too big at all—it was merely prominent, that's all. It lent a great deal of nobility to his visage, in fact. Now that he was making money, he'd gone to the Banco Malzone downstreet and converted small change into an eagle-backed silver dollar, which he kept in his pocket, without spending it just to have something to hold onto, and this inspired him to feel, as he looked at it, turning it over and over in his hand, that he boasted a profile as noble as the American Eagle's on the silver dollar. *Visage*, that was one of his new vocabulary additions. *Profile*, too. He now inspected his visage and his profile in the mirrors on a daily basis. He began to dress a little better, because he had more money, and he got himself a celluloid collar, because you could keep it clean every day with just a wipe, and it always looked fresh, and it made him look more grown-up and distinguished, he thought.

His patrons exceeded their previous generosity, and he became known around the neighborhood as the gent's shoeshine-boy. He was always attentive and interested and did a good job and was never obsequious or fawning—*eh, he's one of us, just smaller.*

And for a kid his age, good-looking– which somehow always made people feel better about themselves. As for the grown men who frequented Savastano's, it was as if Tony proved to them that humanity, despite what they saw every day, *che brutto*, could also soar up there, with Michelangelo, to the ceiling.

They adopted him, and he became their *Little Prince*.

Nowadays, Tony was able to give Auntie a steady three bucks every week, sometimes four, if he felt like it, and keep plenty for himself.

It seemed like there had to be at least a hundred and fifty Nickleodeons between their neighborhood and the East River, so he was able to treat the boys from the backyard to all the shows they were dying to see. Penny candy at the caramelle shop was no problem, lime rickeys at the soda fountain in Pirone's Drugstore–you could get a Hooten's Bar loaded with chocolate and peanuts for 5 cents!

Christmas was coming, and Tony asked Auntie if he could get a doll for Maria, and something for Enrico, maybe a deck of cards or a spinning top or some aggies, he might like that, something for little Luigi, like alphabet-blocks he had seen at the toy-vendor's pushcart. Little Angela, she was still a baby, he didn't know what to get her, maybe something to wear, or a blanket. But Auntie said she didn't want Tony spoiling the kids, they had enough of everything, "it would only make them want more things than we can afford," and besides, she was knitting winter caps for all of them for their Christmas presents. Tony said he didn't feel right not sharing his good fortune with his cousins, and, as usual, he got his own way with Auntie, she couldn't say no to him.

Normally he was all finished at the shop by seven at night, but on Christmas Eve, Savastano locked up early, and Tony went to the drugstore and got some cotton balls and a jar of honey. He smeared the honey on his face, stuck the cotton balls on for a beard, put a sock on his head, and used a burlap sack for the toys, and went home to play Santa Claus for the kids.

At the barbershop, he had seen a discarded newspaper, with an article that got re-printed every year about this time, with the headline

Yes, Virginia, there is a Santa Claus!

Then came the New Year, 1900. It was the biggest celebration the city of New York had ever seen. Savasatano opened his shop for all night, threw a big party, and absolutely everybody came. It wasn't just his customers—it was the whole street. In and out they went, in shifts. There wasn't a sober man within a mile of the place. Pretty women weren't safe outside their bedrooms, and not there, either.

Even their married sisters and maiden aunts discovered they were somebody's fantasy. People were marching up and down in the streets banging every pot and pan they owned, laughing like hell, making as much noise as they could. Drunken discussions of the great new inventions that were sure to come about in the new century were seriously conducted under every gas lamp by inebriated revelers. They decided the whole shebang was going to be electrified. Steamships were going to cross the ocean in four days from LeHavre. Maybe in the not-too-distant future they'd fly across the ocean. Impossible! You—you're the biggest hot-air balloon in this whole town! *But how do you know?* I hear they're gonna dig a train line underground all the way up Second Avenue, all the way to the Bronx! No! At Savastano's they had one guy dressed up in a top hat and cane playing Father Time. When midnight arrived, at the stroke of twelve, they carried him out the door in a casket, while the New Year came in the door, with a bare-foot, bare-chested, guy wearing a sheet wrapped around his torso, playing the Big Bambino in his diaper, sporting a big blue ribbon draped diagonally across his hairy chest, embroidered in gold-lettering, saying *Happy New Year, Anno Domini 1900!*

Tony would never forget that night. He was having the time of his life, smoking cigarettes, drinking wine, and running around the shop and the street outside. Nothing could stop him, till he bumped into Nicky Domenico, and when he asked him if they could go to Lorenzo's Livery Stable to visit Fiorello together, the man had to tell the boy that the horse had been destroyed.

Tony was devastated. He loved that horse. How could he be gone?

"It was an accident," Domenico said. "Remember that snowstorm we had, the first one, back in November? And the week after, all the streets iced up? Well. Fiorello slipped on the icy cobblestones, and went down—but he didn't break anything—he just kinda knelt down. We got him up again—it was a struggle, but we got some ashes out of the ashcan, and spread 'em around to help him get his footing, and eventually, we got him up on his feet again. But, then—we had that storm two weeks ago, before Christmas? Well, this time he wasn't so lucky. We had to put him down, Tony. He broke his leg and there wasn't nothin' nobody could do. We called the cop over from his stationary post. The one they call Dead-Eye Dick. He stuck his gun up to Fiorello's head and he put him away. Dead-eye Dick. It was better that way, Tony. He was out of his suffering."

Young Tony LaStoria began the new century drunk, sitting on the ground in Lorenzo's stable, with his back up against the door of Fiorello's stall, asking God and his mother, the Blessed Virgin, asking his patron, *Santo Antonio*, asking his own mother, *asking himself,* why, why, why, did he have to lose his best friend, his beloved *Fiorello,* until the tears came, and crushed all the spirit out of his body, the way you crushed all the sweet juice out of an orange or a grape, and the hot, cast-iron ice-tongs of grief gripped his temples in a searing, scalding vise, a headache so intense it caused him to squeeze his eyes closed, whereupon his throat choked, his nose filled up and overflowed, his chest heaved, he couldn't breathe, the sobbing racked his convulsing shoulders, and he cried helplessly, the water gushing out of him all over the hands he buried his face in, while over and over he accused himself, saying, for this horse you blubber like a baby, while for the loss of your own mother, you felt *nothing, nothing, nothing!* And this was the worst grief of all, that he knew– *himself–* and forgot not one instant of his own life nor one injury anyone had ever done him, and yet, and yet, and yet, *he comprehended none of it, he understood nothing* . . .

Finally he fell asleep in a heap from all the wine, all the weeping, with the hot tears dried on his face like sticky, sour lemon and his heart lying in the gutter like a discarded cheese-rind.

Nicky Domenico stayed with him, to make sure no harm came to him. The iceman had to get his new horse going at 4 a.m., in any case, so, *what the hell.*

Tony woke the next morning with a vicious hangover, but that was gone by nine o'clock. His grieving over the death of his beloved horse lasted longer.

But the new century at Savastano's was not waiting for a boy to get over his love for a horse, unless the horse raced around a circular track and you could place a bet on him.

Savastano wasn't just making money curling moustaches. While they were shooting the breeze in his place, his customers appreciated the convenience of placing a bet or two on the ponies, or playing the numbers. When that telephone on the bracketed shelf in the sink-closet rang, Savastano was the only one allowed to pick it up. He got the race results from the Harlem Speedway and Belmont phoned in, and then, about four o'clock in the afternoon, he would write the number on the mirror with a cake of soap. You could see the number 6 up there through the front window, and people going by would stop to look in. An hour later, he would get another call and put up a number 2. Then the next number might be a three, so 623 was the winner for the day. People came in and out all day long just to play the numbers. They sent their kids with nickels and dimes.

Lately, Tony had taken to always wearing a white shirt with his collar—it went with the collar and it went with the white coats the barbers wore. Everybody got used to seeing the boy with the white shirt and the celluloid collar going in and out of the barber shop and down the street, all afternoon, from time to time. Savastano would send him to collect bets or pay off people who won, if he knew they couldn't get down to the shop themselves. And Savastano knew his business well, same as Domenico. So Tony became his runner.

Tony didn't mind. It was no big deal, everybody played. Tony started playing himself, once he got past Christmas and the few new things he wanted to buy himself. If he hit, he hit—if he didn't—better luck next time. He knew enough not to bet the house, so he never let it get out of hand. He took care of Auntie and the kids at home, his friends from the clubhouse, so why not? If he hit, maybe he could splurge.

He didn't place bets on the horses at the track, because for that, you had to know a lot more. You had to study the green sheet, get to know the ponies and jockeys and all their histories.

Savastano's clientele taught Tony all he wanted to know about that, and more, simply from eavesdropping on their constant discussing and arguing. Horatio Alger wrote a thrilling book but he could not argue jockeys like Savastano's customers.

But the numbers, that was just a guessing game. That was plain luck.

Nobody worried about the cops. Savastano knew they were good guys, too, so he took care of them. If there was ever going to be a raid, it would happen because some over-zealous Tammany Hall social-climber, or a local police captain, had suddenly gone off his rocker with a fit of morality. Or maybe he was just getting pressured by the press or the Settlement House do-gooders. It always blew over, and nobody ever went to jail for more than thirty seconds, or maybe a couple of hours. And if they ever came in his place, all Savastano had to do was wipe off the mirror with a towel, and there goes the evidence.

Every week the barber would collect from Tony, too. First, he took a buck for letting Tony operate in his shop, and then he took a buck for the Black Hand, so they would continue letting Tony operate in his shop. It didn't bother Tony, or anyone. Those guys had to make a living, too. Nobody was afraid of them. Once in a while they broke somebody's windows or a wagon-axle, or maybe poisoned a horse, but, what the hell, that was just life. As long as everybody minded their own business and everybody was making money, everybody was happy, and nobody had any problems. So, to Tony, if he made nine bucks that week, with all his tips, and he had to give back, say, two—that left him with seven—and that was a lot more than he was making at Ferrara's, when the old bastard got around to paying him, which he never did, or with Domenico, for that matter—a helluva a lot more.

Eventually, things were sailing along again, and Tony was wearing his special smile for his customers, when, one afternoon, somebody walked in, and the atmosphere changed.

Waiting customers rose slightly from their seats to tip their hats. Somebody said, *Don Serafino, how are you?*

Then another one said to this well-dressed personage, "No, no, you go right ahead, Don Serafino. I'll wait."

The Don seated himself for a shave in the chair operated by Savastano himself, and tilted back, exchanging pleasantries, compliments, commentary on the weather, and so on, and finally complimenting the master barber on his general hospitality and his particularly hot towels.

Then it was Tony's turn. The Don seated himself and lifted one foot onto the instep of the box. All he said was, "Make sure you do a good job if you want a good tip."

The Don tilted back his head, lowered the brim of his Panama hat over his eyes, which narrowed to slits, and appeared to sleepily observe Tony's every move.

It was all a show he was putting on and Savastano's customers were his audience.

It was a little bit unnerving. But Tony proceeded to pry the cap off the tin of brown polish, and he got busy with his brush on the Don's left shoe, the one he had presented first, and he perhaps dabbed on a tadge more polish than he might have, usually. But he put that aside, and bent to his work with his buffing brush, which vibrated back and forth expeditiously in his practiced fingers—meanwhile whistling a tune noiselessly between his lips—and then he looked up at the Don and flashed one of his lamplight smiles. Then came the soft cloth—around the heel—along the sides, flapping just so—over the toe—there, done to perfection. He looked up, beaming. The Don did not take away his foot. Slowly, he said, "I think you forgot something."

Tony looked at him, puzzled, but the Don lifted his toe slowly, while keeping the heel planted, thereby gradually exposing the bottom of his foot.

"Aren't you going to polish the sole of my shoe?" said he.

Tony hesitated, not understanding. But in his ears he heard laughter. The men in the barbershop were tittering with amusement at one of the Don's little jokes. When nothing happened, and Tony glanced up at Don Serafino, he saw the big man in the Panama hat glancing sideways out of his narrowed eyes, which were twinkling with merriment at some shared glee over the squirming little fish he had on a hook. Tony followed the Don's eyes, first left, then right, then behind him, over his head, and in the mirror on the right, Tony saw one grownup's face twist into a grimace of a clown's mask, and in the mirror on the left, he caught another adult bellow out a loud guffaw that he just couldn't keep in, which distorted his face into a mean caricature of evil-spirited mockery, and—it dawned on Tony—they were all laughing at him. And he seemed to be trapped in a circle of distended faces, which all multiplied in the mirrors surrounding him, till the room began spinning in a grotesque whirlpool, full of faces of cruel scorn, all aimed at him; and the laughter spread from throat to throat, getting louder and louder, till his ears rang with hot red funhouse shame.

Tony jumped up, insulted, and threw his shine-cloth to the floor, and there were flames spitting from his eye, as he told the Don, "Polish it yourself!"

For a moment, nothing moved—but then, the Don started to erupt with laughter—and the whole shop followed suit.

Sizzling blood rushed into Tony's cheeks, and he looked left, he looked right—they were all laughing at him!—splitting their sides!

Incensed, he put his chin down on his chest, and attempted to rush out the door—and only Savastano's hand on his arm impeded him. But Tony persisted, and quickly he was out in the street, his back turned, storming away as fast as he could.

With his eyes, the Don told Savastano to go bring the kid back. Savastano rushed out and caught up to the boy.

"Tony!—Tony!—stop!—you forgot your tip—he's got a special big tip for you—he wants to make it up to you!–what are you doing?—don't you know who that is!"

Tony whirled. "I know who it is. You tell him for me, I said *Ba-fun-goo!*"

Stalking off, leaving Savastano standing there empty-handed, Tony found that he was trembling with anger.

He stuck his hands in his pockets, and he took himself home to Mott Street, and the whole time he was thinking, *what the hell am I gonna do now?*

Chapter 7

Wrong Turn On Rivington Street

By the time Tony showed up in school next morning, there was nobody who hadn't heard, *Tony told the Don to go polish it himself!*

The rest of the week, Tony was off his stride. Nothing rang right anymore. The whole world was out of square. After school, each afternoon was empty, with nothing to do, nowhere to go. Self-disgust was making him choke on his food. *If only I didn't get so mad! Why do I have such a temper? What's the matter with me? It's out of control!* And yet, he argued with himself, *I couldn't do anything else!* Never, never, never, could he let himself be treated as an object of scorn like that. *It's all the Don's fault. He did it to me. I show him respect and he treats me like dirt under his feet!* By the next Sunday, when it came time to play in the orchestra at the park, he was in no mood. Children in the park, five years younger than he was, caught up in their imaginary pursuits, mothers minding babies in baskets, the old men playing bocci-ball, even the dogs running free—the very thought of life going on, taking no notice, offended him. When he saw his friends, he wanted only to pick a fight with them. Mousey, Knickers, Long-johns, they moved away a little on the bench. Il Gatto said to him, "What's the matter with you today?" He received a one-look answer. The sight of the uptown swells in their gigs, the mere presence of the Fifth Avenue stages, made Tony want to kill someone.

"Let's get outta here," he said to nobody, as he gazed broodingly over the scene in Mulberry Park, rejecting everything he saw.

When he stood to leave, Auntie Marietta gave a glance of alarm to Zi'Eugenio. Tony was handing his mandolin to her, saying, "Hold onto this for me." No *per favore*, no nothing. Her husband waved away his wife's dismay with a gesture of his palms turned up, empty, as if to say, *whadda-you want from me?* He was loath to forbid his nephew, figuring that would just start an argument in front of everybody. He didn't care to embarrass himself or cause people to stare at his family. The boys all stood up and followed Tony obediently. He stalked along, head down, they stalked along with their heads down. He put his hands in his pockets, they thrust their hands in their pockets.

Knickers said, "Where we goin', Tony?" Mousey said, "Whadda we gonna do?" Tony turned on them. "I don't know!"

After a while, Il Gatto said, "Hey, Tony, we're gettin' out on a limb here. This ain't our part of town."

"What are you guys so afraid of? You never been anywhere in your life. East Side, West Side, all around the town—and all you guys can think of is to stay stuck in the gutter on one lousy street." After that, nobody said a word.

Tony plodded onward. His mood was darkening. They were now crossing the Bowery, heading for a neighborhood where, everybody knew, they didn't belong. Through gaps in the apartment-house skyline, they could see the Brooklyn Bridge peeking over the rooftops from a distance.

Long-johns said, "I don't like this, Tony. We don't know nobody in Sheeny-town."

Tony said, "Well, I do."

"Who?"

"Mousey knows. He's the one sent me there. I owe you for that one, Mousey."

Mousey wasn't sure exactly what that meant. *Was it good or bad?*

But now that the thought occurred of those two Calabrian *pazzi*, Pepe and Cortino, Tony figured *might as well get there as anywhere*. "Don't you wanna see where I used to sleep all night on the cutting table?"

"What for?"

"We came to hear you play on the bandstand, like always."

"To hell with that. I don't feel like it today." Tony was taking a certain perverse thrill in their discomfort. If he had to feel miserable, twisted and engorged with rage that he couldn't stifle—why shouldn't they?

The streets were crowded. Tony was oblivious, but the others were nervous, sensing a change in the atmosphere. People were looking at them differently. It was not hostility, but a guard going up. On their own streets they would have blended in without notice. Here they were conspicuous, or thought they were. Heads turned as they went by—or did they? Suddenly they were feeling vulnerable, as outsiders always do. They clogged together without being aware that they were clumping closer, and that only attracted more looks.

"Tony, I don't know about this," said Il Gatto.

"Look—we're just out for a Sunday stroll. You guys ain't never seen the El that runs on Allen Street, have you? Don't you wanna see something before you die? You ever stood under the Brooklyn Bridge? Huh? I'll bet none of youz ever even seen the East River, have yez?"

They were just rounding a corner onto Chrystie Street and beginning to approach Tony's old haunts on Rivington when Il Gatto, now as nervous as his namesake would be tiptoeing on a hot stove, noticed a boy their own age, all the way on the other side of the street, walking parallel to them, in tandem, almost, stride for stride, and that this boy kept glancing sideways at their *gruppo*. "Tony—you see that kid?"

"Yeah. So. What about it?"

"How long's he been there?"

"I don't know. Who cares?"

Long-johns spoke up. "He's been there awhile."

Knickers was next. He said to Tony, eagerly, "I think he's followin' us."

"Let 'im. It's a free country, ain't it? We can go wherever we want. We ain't botherin' nobody."

The next thing you know, the kid started to run on ahead of them—on the other side of the street.

Now Tony had to take notice because there was another kid waiting at the next cross-street.

Tony watched—all of them did—as they kept walking onward, but a little slower.

The second kid turned and ran up to the next corner, where there was yet another kid. They were running a relay—sending a message on up ahead.

Tony was not worried about the grown-ups on the street. It was Sunday, and everybody was out with their families for a stroll, or sitting out on the stoop—just like in their own neighborhood. He and his boys were innocently weaving their way down the street, affecting nonchalance.

The Big Kids wouldn't bother them because it would lower their status to take the least bit of notice.

It was kids their own age you had to worry about—and that was exactly what the relay runners were—eleven, twelve-year-olds, like them. Maybe eleven. Maybe as much as twelve, no older.

Tony knew now that trouble was brewing. He felt it. It matched his mood the way grey skies match thunderclouds.

He welcomed it. He was wound up like a top. He wanted to blow off some serious steam.

Anyways, it was too late for him to back out now. He would have to get them all out of this, just like he got them all into it—but what were they getting into?

He figured that if he could get them as far as Pepe and Cortino's alley off of Rivington–. But they didn't make it that far.

They rounded the corner of Chrystie and got onto Rivington going east, all right, but there were fewer families and little children out in this disreputable section of the neighborhood, fewer people at all, and a quick scan told all of them that they had unwittingly entered upon a sort of deserted place—perfect for a little fun, if that's what you were after. They hadn't lost their company on the other side of the street, either, except that now there were four instead of three—and up ahead, blocking the sidewalk on this side, were two more kids, a tall one leaning up against the post of a gaslight, and the other one, shorter, lounging on a black-iron railing opposite.

Then the boys on the other side of the street crossed over to join their friends, and grouped themselves behind the first two, so that, now, the sidewalk was blocked.

They could have crossed the street, to evade these boys, but not even Il Gatto or Mousey wanted to go that far. They would have ended up looking bad, looking scared, getting chased, being forced to run away—so, now they were stuck.

The tall boy said to his pals, "Whadda we got here, gentlemen? Looks like the altar-boys, come to pay us their respects."

They all sniggered, and one said, "Where's your red skirt, missy?"

"Up your ass, Jew-boy!" Tony spat out. He had prepared himself for trouble, and trouble was here, for sure, but—the altar-boy thing really caught him off guard—the sewing-needle had found the soft flesh under his fingernail—and he reacted.

"Now that's not very polite," said the tall one.

The two groups spread out a little, as tempers flared and neither side wanted to be caught unready. But the tall boy stood up and took over.

"I think you come over here lookin' for trouble," he said, addressing Tony alone, face to face. Tony said, "We're mindin' our own business."

"You got no business here—this is our street."

"So just move over, and let us by."

"You gonna make me?"

The tall boy shoved Tony with both hands in his chest.

Tony took a step back and repeated, with as much menace as he could muster, "You don't wanna fight me."

"Whatsa matter, scared?" He shoved Tony again. "Look, boys—the little dago's pissin' his pants!"

Tony could feel his leg shaking violently, as blood rushed through his body. "How do I know you're gonna leave your boys out of it? You gonna make somethin' out of it, you make it just between you and me."

"Down the alley," said the tall boy. "I don't want nobody interrupting me while I rearrange your face. And no knives. I know how you Guineas like to stick people."

Tony recognized the opening to Pepe and Cortino's alley, and the tall boy noticed. "You don't work with your wop relations down here no more—that didn't last long—so now, you got no business being here at all. I know those two *jamolkas* down that alley—Benny here, his sister used to go over and read newspapers to 'em."

They were in the alley now, in the little scrap of open space between all the rubble and refuse, the alley Tony remembered so well, the ashcans and the discarded oil cans and everything that people in the second-floor apartments on either side threw out their windows, from half-eaten food to the contents of chamber-pots. Down at the alley's rear end was the entry to Pepe and Cortino's little shanty, with the door closed. And no indication whether they were there or not.

The two groups rounded off in a circle and spread out their arms to form a makeshift boxing-ring. They let Tony and the other boy into the circle. The tall boy said, "Okay. Come on. Let's go then."

Under the fighters' feet was nothing but the dirt floor and strewn debris of the alley. The tall boy circled, he was taunting Tony, and all his friends were laughing. It was over before it began when he socked three quick jabs into Tony's nose, which stung tears into his eyes. Everyone was laughing— except for Tony's friends, who just looked dismayed. Without thinking, without a plan, blinded with rage, Tony lowered his head and shoulders to bull-rush at his opponent's stomach. He got his arms around the tall boy's waist, and thrashed him back and forth, with a strength he didn't know he had.

The other was laughing. "Whaddya wanna wrestle?"

But Tony held on fast. The other one threw a headlock around his neck and used his length and leverage to trip him over his stuck-out foot. Tony was still holding on tight to him, so they both went down in the dirt. Tony seized the other boy by the hair on top of his head and threw him off. Once he was on top of his opponent, he lost all sense of control and started choking him viciously, with all his might, trying, for all he knew, to kill him.

They had rolled together in a heap on top of the fancy brick border edging the basement-window-well of the building on that side of the alley. Bricks were planted in the dirt like slanted pottery-shards. Tony was grinding the other boy's face into the bricks as if they were a cheese-grater—the boy howled "Hold it! Hold it!"

Tony rolled off him and sat back breathless, his legs spread out fan-like and limp, utterly exhausted.

The other boy gasped, "What the fuck was that? You trying to put my eye out?"

Tony said, "I think you broke my nose!"

"I hope to hell I did!"

Tony heaved one big breath, at last. "Fuck you, you asshole."

"I think I'm bleeding to death."

"I hope you do!"

"You're a fucking animal!"

The other boys in the alley, thrilled, on both sides, with fight-fever, were jumping up and down. "Oh, my God! What a fight!" But they were relieved, too, that it was over, and it wasn't their faces ground into bricks, because they could sense that what started so one-sided had blown completely out of control.

Now that everything was all over, that was when Pepe and Cortino emerged from their hovel. "You boys shoulda not-a fight like dat," said Pepe, in his halting English.

Cortino said to Tony, *"O, sei tu, piccolo bastardo!"*

Tony's opponent, slumped against the wall, after wiping his left cheek, was looking at the copious red blood that came off on his right hand. "You cut my face wide open! I'll be lucky if I ain't scarred for life!"

Tony was looking at Mousey, with surprise at his own ferocity, while he tried to calm down his heaving chest.

The grown-ups, Pepe and Cortino, were now stepping in between the two sides to make sure they didn't start up again, while the tall boy's friends started arguing with Tony's group over who won.

From his seat on the ground, the tall boy settled the matter. "Hey! Shut up, everybody. The kid won, fair and square, 'cause he fought dirty, alright? It's over!"

Pepe and Cortino then pulled the two opponents to their feet, and Cortino said to Tony, "Why you come around here making trouble, eh?" Pepe dragged him by the arm inside the Calabrian's shop, and Cortino got busy shooing all the rest of the boys from both sides out of the alley.

"Go home. Go home," cried Cortino, pushing and shoving at both groups, while he pulled Tony's opposite inside. "No come back here no more, make-a da trouble."

Once inside the shanty, Pepe applied some linty scraps to the tall boy's cheek, pressing with his fingers to stop the bleeding, and then examined Tony's face, where the eyes were discoloring already. Pointing at Tony's eyes, with forked fingers, Pepe told him, "You gonna have coupla nice shinola over there."

Now Cortino came back in. *"Va bene,* I get ridda da rest. Now, you two—get out and *no ritorno!"*

"Don't worry, I'm leavin,'" said Tony.

"Already one time we get ridda you, now you back, you no-good?"

"You didn't get ridda nobody," Tony told him. "I quit!"

"Out! Out!"

The two boys found themselves shoved back out into the alley with the door slammed in their faces by an angry Cortino, while the solicitous Pepe could only shrug.

So the two combatants were left standing there looking at each other.

Slowly, they turned and headed back down to the mouth of the alley.

Once or twice, they stopped and looked at each other, not knowing what to say.

But when they got back to the street, and looked up and down the sidewalk, everything looked deserted. Their erstwhile faithful followers, saving themselves, had left them to their own devices. The only thing looking back at them was the motley street of nondescript warehouses and junk-dealers gone-out-of-business.

"Well, how do ya like that?"

Tony looked at him, holding up to his cheek the scrap of muslin Pepe had given him, with blood oozing out between his fingers.

And the other boy said, "I suppose you're gonna run out on me, too."

"What are you talking about?"

"Damned if I know."

"Look, I don't know you, and you don't know me, so let's just leave it that way."

"Sure—after you scar me for life, you just wanna walk away, is that it?"

"That's right," said Tony. "I'm takin' my little Sunday stroll down to the East River, like I was startin' to, before you came along and tried to make somethin' of it."

And he turned and started to walk away eastward, but the other boy went right along with him.

Tony wheeled on his antagonist, who said to him, "What? What? I live down this way." In a few more steps the tall boy added, "And I'm not crossin' the road just to suit you, either. I got as much right to this sidewalk as you do—more."

After they walked an entire block in silence without saying another word, and came to an intersection, Tony stopped dead and turned to him. "So—what are we doing here?"

"You wanna come over my house?"

"No, I do not."

"Why not?"

"What for?"

"To get that crooked nose slanting across your face looked at."

"I said no."

"What's the matter—you never been in a Jew's house before?"

"What?"

"Why not?"

"I never even seen a Jew before I come to New York City."

"See, that's why youz hate us—all youz guineas are ignorant—you don't know any Jews—you don't wanna know any Jews–."

"How can I go over your house after what I done to you?"

"I'll live. Maybe. If I can get this bleeding stopped. Anyways—you gotta come over. You can't say no."

"Why not?"

"Because I said."

"Forget it."

"On top of killing me you wanna insult me, too? Go ahead, spit on my dead body."

"I don't know you!"

"I don't know you, either, but we're enemies now!"

"Well, I ain't going."

"Whaddya expect out of a dumb *goyisher!*"

"A what?"

"Listen—you owe me a chance at Round Two!"

"I don't owe you a damn thing!"

"You owe me respect."

"Why? Because I beat the shit outta you?"

"Because I let you."

"Ha. You let me."

"Come on—I had you and you know it."

"Look—I don't know you—and I don't wanna know you."

"Harry Spritzka. Now you know me. Well—you gonna tell me your name?"

"What for?" They were standing at an intersection, waiting for the traffic to let them cross. "Tony." He said it warily, grudgingly, without making eye contact with the other, instead, sticking his hands in his pockets.

"Goddamn. It's like pulling teeth. Tony what?"

"Tony LaStoria."

"Look—can we go now?—*Tony?*–'cause I'm bleeding."

"Go. Nobody's stopping you. *Harry.*"

Harry Spritzka stepped into the street. But he stopped to look back at Tony, still standing on the curb. "You coming?"

Chapter 8

A House Made Out Of Chocolate

The plush dry goods store at the corner of Division and Allen Streets, in the heart of the Lower East Side's shopping district, stood out amid its surroundings. The signage which wrapped around the corner above the plate-glass windows read *Vilna House of Style Fine Apparel for Men, Hats, Gloves, Neck-ties, Cuff-Links, Ladies' Evening Wear and Dressing Gowns Vilna House of Style.*

When Harry pushed the door open, Tony said, "Why are we goin' in here?"

"I live here," said Harry.

"You live here?"

"Not here, upstairs."

The freshly-folded smell of fabrics rushed up into Tony's face, erasing the odors of the street outside. Everywhere he looked he saw discreet islands of cloth, draperies, curtains and table-cloths, and bolts in every texture and color from navy blue to grey and black, and the smell of woolen serge pulled at him seductively.

"Mama!"

Harry rushed off, leaving Tony standing there, surveying with widening eyes the rows of ready-made three-piece suits and men's overcoats lining the back and side walls, with counters and tables full of men's work clothes and undergarments guarding the approach. Tony took wondering note also of a smaller section of ladies' apparel for day-wear and bedspreads and sheets. When he saw a well-dressed man with a yellow tape-measure hanging around his neck, patrolling the aisles, it brought to mind forgotten images of his own father.

Drinking this all in, in a rush, he felt as if he had just passed through a doorway from one world into another.

Harry was waving furiously for Tony to catch up to him where he had halted beside the woman he had called to, who must be his mother.

But she was not a woman, she was a lady, the lady who belonged to this shop, and she looked, and played, the part, wearing her ash-blonde hair rolled in a soft, silky pompadour.

She seemed to Tony a vision in that voluminous, poofy coiffure, loosely pinned near the nape of her neck with a tortoise-shell clasp, and trailing wispy strands of stray, curling split-ends. She was dressed in the height of Edwardian fashion and resembled nothing less than a Gibson Girl just stepped down from a billboard to grace this real life where mere mortals dwell.

She was the lady who belonged to this shop full of fine apparel. To Tony, she was the princess in a fairytale; or, in the annals of a king, the queen.

Suddenly self-conscious, ashamed to be wearing rags, Tony felt painfully that he did not belong in this setting of munificence; wincing from the soreness in the center of his face left over from the blows of doubled-up fists, afraid his eyes were now puffing up, making him look ugly and even more out of place; nevertheless he dare not refuse to approach, at a queen's command and stern look.

"Did you do this to my boy?" said Harry's mother, as she knelt on one knee, pinching Harry's chin in her fingers, twisting his face to show Tony the bandaged cheek.

Examining the floor at his feet, Tony lowered his eyes and forehead, ready to receive blows from her lips. This was the most gorgeous creature outside a newspaper advertisement he'd ever seen, and her pretty brown eyes were even darker and stormier because she was angry at him.

"Who is this *yungotch?*" she demanded of her son Harry.

And Tony searched the floor for some way to sink into it and disappear. "That's my friend!" Harry protested. "His name is Tony!"

"He's a *shagetz?* He's your friend, so he beats you up?"

"We had a fight, that's all. Boys like to fight, you know? But Mama—*er badarf a doktor!* I think I broke his nose!"

"*Oy vey!*"

Then the handsomely-attired man with the tape-measure around his neck, who had just come up, put in a word. "Mama, you should have given me girls. So much less trouble. You gave me two sons instead. What do you want from me?"

This was Harry's father. Harry said, "Totti!—can we get Doctor Wolfsheim for my friend!"

"What's wrong with him?"

Harry said brightly, "I broke his nose!"

"Good—he looks better!"

Harry's mother looked with exasperation at Harry's father, and she told Harry, "Your Totti will talk to you later. Right now you need to get that cheek of yours attended to. Meanwhile—oh!—careful, Harry. I don't want you bleeding on my dress, for goodness sake. You get upstairs to your Bubelah—*atsind! Haynt! Nu! Gay shoyn!*"

This time Harry, wary of leaving his new friend to the dispositions of his mother's wrath, or the vagaries of his evident fascination, made sure to pull Tony by the sleeve along with him. While Tony, mesmerized, turned round and round, gazing at the lovely apparition with the strands of pin-curls dangling delicately round her tender earlobes, and the flashy diamond engagement ring on her hand.

Tony let himself be dragged away while he drifted in a daze where he was memorizing every fold, crease, pleat and button-hook of Harry's mother, glancing back over his shoulder. He had to look back, one last time. She did not merely wear a dress. She modeled an exquisite taffeta frock, cinched into a narrow waist beneath a lavender bodice, and her shoulders were blossoming in puffed sleeves of royal violet silk organza. Her slender white neck was caressed by a high white lace collar, and her long dress flowed down to the toes of her high-top boots. Her heels gave her a dainty and diffident posture, when she straightened up, but when she had knelt down beside the boys, Tony had been granted a glimpse straight into the purple sunflower patterns woven into her bodice, which was decorated with stems of faceted glass beads.

Her scent had filled him with a heavenly sensation of warm tenderness. It was like bringing rose petals cupped in the hand slowly to your nose and breathing deeply in. He was so enchanted by her spell that he almost tripped over himself as Harry pulled him along, and he felt no pain in his face at all.

To reach the back stairs, they had to leave the storefront through a doorway without a door, only a beaded curtain to be swished aside. Tony caught a glimpse down the passage of the workshop in the back of the building where tailors busy at their work glanced up briefly, but, seeing it was only young Harry, took no real notice. Then Harry, at a run, shot up the stair, which was enclosed in a narrow walled-off hallway trimmed with vertical-slatted wainscotting to a height of four feet. Breathless, he hovered at the top, calling down, with a wave, "Come on!"

Hesitating, Tony went up, running his left hand admiringly over the smooth, solid oak cylinder of the handrail fastened at intervals to the wainscotting with black iron brackets, arriving on the landing above at an open door giving way to a kind of sitting room. Within, he saw a tiny woman seated on a sofa by herself.

She could have been a butterfly resting in a tulip, an immensely ancient butterfly, who flew no longer. Tall windows with drapes cosseted in bell-ropes let in ample light from the sky, which shimmered on her in a silver sheen, so that she seemed to be balanced on a throne-cushion.

"Bubelah! This is my friend, Tony! We had a big fight! I gave him a broken nose, I think. And look what he did to me!"

"Oh, my darlings, come here, come here—tell me the whole story! But first, fetch me my medicine chest, like a good boy." For such a small person, Harry's Bubelah had a very profound voice, which came from deep down inside her, a creaking door-hinge, with rusty iron in it. When Harry brought back her box of remedies from the hutch in the corner, he tried to squeeze himself in between the arm-rest of the sofa and his grandmother. "Careful of my hip, darling!" She moved over slightly, and Harry apologized. "It's all right—you won't break me, I'm not a teacup, you know—you're simply too excited, I can tell. And, Harry—I'm so happy for you! You have a friend! But I thought you had lots of them."

"Oh, I do, Bubelah, but they're just neighborhood kids—they don't count. Tony—he's different. He's from the other part of town—if you know what I mean."

"Oh, I do, I do! I'm so happy for you." She turned then to Tony. "And you, dear child, you come sit down right here on the other side of me, and both of you—tell me the whole story! But, you know, Harry, my dear boy, I'm—hold still—I know, it stings." She was cleaning out the groove of the cut in Harry's cheek with cotton balls soaked in alcohol. "There—give me my scissors—I'm afraid you're going to have a beautiful scar out of this, dear Harry."

"Will it make me look like I was wounded dueling with sabres, Bubelah?"

"Oh, you foolish thing, what imaginations you boys have!" Her voice was a syrupy gravel poured into the boys' ears while she carefully cut an oblong patch of gauze bandaging, in two or three layers, to cover Harry's cut, plus strips of tape to fix it on. "Now keep your hands away, Harry, even if it itches. I don't think you will need stitches, but if you pull the bandage off, it's going to start bleeding again. Now you boys were going to tell me the whole story of whatever possessed you to be fighting like this."

Harry, with relish, began, explaining how Tony had provoked the entire affair.

"Did not."

"Did so."

He ended by explaining how he won the fight and beat Tony, fair and square. "Did not."

"Did so."

Tony saw that he wasn't going to win this time.

Sitting next to Harry's Bubelah, Tony was astounded by her diminutive size. Seated on the sofa, her feet did not reach the floor. Tony wondered if he himself was actually taller than she was. Her grandson towered over her, even when sitting.

Bubelah, like Harry's mother, was also fashionably dressed. Tony wondered if it was because this was Sunday. Could it be that they dressed this way every day? His own Auntie Marietta had to make do with a single flimsy cotton house-dress and try to keep it clean through the whole week.

Everything about the store downstairs, Harry's parents, this upstairs apartment they were now sitting in, the shop in the back of the first floor, spoke of money, and the things money can buy.

Here, a boy could breathe, and stretch out.

It hit Tony like a fish slapped down on the ice in a push-cart, the difference.

"Bubelah—can we get the doctor to come over and look at me and Tony?"

"Why, of course, my darling. You run downstairs and tell one of the men that I said they should run down the street and send for Doctor Wolfsheim to come over, right away!"

"But don't do anything till I get back!"

"That will give me a minute to get to know your young friend."

"I don't want to miss anything!"

"Oh, go now, be a good boy."

When Harry was gone, she turned to Tony expectantly.

Tony thought she was waiting for him to say something, but all he could think of was to blurt out, "You speak very good English."

She laughed, heartily. The laughter shook her so much that she rocked away, in danger of toppling over. "And why not! I had very good teachers!"

"Where?"

"Vilna. Do you know where that is?"

"No."

"Far, far away. In another lifetime. Another world."

When she looked away, toward the drapes and the bell-ropes, where the sun faded in the window with a gossamer of pale gold, she fell silent, and seemed to be content with the pleasure of a boy's company, wherein nothing need be said, because nothing could be said that was not already understood between them.

When her grandson returned, the old lady said, with a demure smile, "Your friend thinks I am strange."

She turned back to Tony and gently explained, with grave courtesy, "I am not strange, young man, just different." She tilted her head, raised her eyebrows, pursed her lips, making the sort of funny face a kind old person would make to amuse a child, and then her eyes drifted off to the right, to a far-off place. "This world has many strange and different things in it, Tony." She patted Tony's knee. That was to be the secret they would share. "May I call you Tony? You don't mind?"

"That's the name I like, yes."

"I would like to call you by your first name, because I think we shall be great friends, and great friends should go by first name with one another."

"So–." Tony did not know if he should ask this or not. "What is your first name?"

"You may call me Lily."

Tony was thankful to clear that up because he could not very well call her Bubelah. 'Lily' was a nice flowery name, which had a singsong sound that seemed to suit her.

"And now, young man, you must tell me all about yourself. For instance—where are you from?"

"I'm from Mott Street."

"That is here, in town?"

"Not this part of town—on the other side of the Bowery."

"Oh, yes. Little Italy, they call it, I believe. And you live with your family?"

"With my auntie and uncle and my cousins."

"Where are your own mother and father?"

"Back in the old country."

"Hmm," said Lily—and then, "You miss them, I suppose."

When Tony hesitated, and did not seem to know what to say, Harry's grandmother did not press him. But finally Tony felt a memory triggered, not of his parents, whom he did not like to think of, much less discuss, and he thought of a small, remote mountain town, on no one's map of the world, a place called Alta Villa, where he came from, and impulsively he said, "I miss the little town where I come from."

"And where is that?"

"Near Avellino. It's called Alta Villa. Alta Villa Irpina."

"Hmm. Pretty name."

Tony wanted to change the subject. "Will you tell us, Lily, about Vilna? Is it a big city?"

"Do you really want to know?"

Harry had kept silent for a time, watching the other two. He had a plan to invite his new friend to stay overnight, and he wanted his Bubelah to like Tony, and approve of this, which would smooth things with his parents. Mama and Totti often could be swayed by Bubelah's wishes, and usually wanted to indulge her; whereas, with their boys, Harry, and his older brother, Robert, they felt it was put upon them, in the parental role, to be the ones to enforce the rules.

Now the two boys looked at each other, in unison, and agreed, with a nod, *yes, we want to know, really we do.*

Bubelah was prepared to smother them with attention. "Well—if you promise to be very, very good boys—." This was her way of getting boys to behave. "And very, very good friends to each other–."

Lily leaned back against the cushions of the sofa, and she reached out to both of them. "It was such a long time ago."

And circling their shoulders, she drew them in, to herself, so that they both leaned gently against her; after all, they were three people equal in size; and she cuddled them, as if they were much younger, more innocent children than they were, and certainly not the pair of brawling bruisers they would have liked to think they were.

"When I was a child—a very long time ago—Vilna was a very great city, indeed—it was the biggest city in our whole country—like New York—and it stood on both sides of the River Neris—and it was the capital city of our country. Imagine that. To grow up in such a place. But we had our own part of town, and in our town, there was a kind old man, very kind, who lived all by himself, whom all the children loved. They adored him, and he loved them, too, and because he had no children of his own, or grandchildren, either, because you see, he was very old, so–he used to have all the children in the town come over to his house for chocolates. And he would give them one piece of chocolate at a time, because, you know, if you stuff yourself with them, you can get sick—and he did not want for any of the children to get sick, he wanted them to come back, to see him again. And they did."

She paused, dramatically, to look at both of them, tucked under her arms, back and forth, from one to the other.

"Well. What do you think happened then? Well, the old man was so happy that he wanted to make the children more and more happy all the time, so, he decided, at the end of one summer— because the summers were hot in Vilna, in those days—that when September came, and things cooled off a bit, it would be the perfect time to build a new house, even larger, and bigger, to fit more and more kids in. But he decided, this time, to make the whole house out of chocolate! Wouldn't that be wonderful! Imagine! The children would be so thrilled! And so he did. And when it was all finished, he moved in all new furniture—but the tables and chairs and even the sofa were all made out of chocolate! Oh, the children were so happy! And they came all the time, over and over, and so, September turned into October and then finally November came and it was beginning to get very, very cold, so one day, when all the children were there, the old man noticed that they were shivering in their boots, and he felt so bad, he took pity on them, and so, to keep them warm, he built a huge, roaring fire in the fireplace— and what do you think happened then, to the house made out of chocolate?"

"It melted!" cried Tony and Harry, simultaneously.

"Oh, you are such good boys! And so clever! And I love you so much—both of you! And I hope we will always be friends, just like this. Oh, I'm so glad that Harry has a friend, at last! Now, Harry, do something for your guest—go over to the sideboard, and fetch me my sewing box."

Harry brought back to them an old-fashioned-looking birchwood box with a lid decorated with borders of white ceramic inlay alternating with dark walnut blocks, in a trim resembling a chessboard, laid out in a rope which encircled the rectangular lid. And in the center was an oval photograph under an amber-colored, hard convex lens, embedded in the birchwood, an obviously browning old picture of Lily as a young girl of seventeen or so. When she opened the lid, there were no compartments inside, but nevertheless, square and round chocolates were packed in tightly, nudging one another.

"Now, here, Tony, you can have a real piece of the old man's sofa—a chocolate that I chipped off the cushion, or the arms, or the back—that I saved from the fire—and I have kept it for a special occasion, such as today, for all these years. Which one would you like? And Harry? You pick one, too."

Chapter 9

The Thread In The Spool

Tony's Uncle Eugene found out the landlord had sold the old two-story clapboard shipwreck, 193 Mott Street, to a second cousin, who intended to tear it down, yesterday, and put up a brand-new four-story brick, tomorrow. It was happening all up and down the street. "Where there's a buck to be made," he said. When he was saying goodbye to the Castellanos, all he could do was to shake his head. "Everybody's got a second cousin but me." So the *famiglia LaStoria* packed up and left in the middle of the night, piling all they could on a hired wagon.

Zi'Eugenio had heard that there was a whole street uptown with people congregated on it who all came from the same place they came from, back in the old country. The Avellinese were moving in on the Upper East Side, from around 62nd Street up to 65th, between Second Avenue and the river. It was another Little Italy, just south of the enclave of Polish and Russian Jews, in the Seventies, and Germantown, up in the Eighties. Castellano told him they were finished with New York, and instead, were going to head for a farm in a place called

Metuchen, in New Jersey. "Don't tell me," said Eugenio, "your second cousin, eh? I knew it."

Nephew Tony, when he finally went to Mott Street, to check in with them, and let them know he was all right, found them all gone, and the house under demolition. He had no idea where they were. He hadn't been home, or to school, for a couple of weeks, because he didn't care to have to start explaining two black eyes. None of his friends knew anything, either. Everybody said that probably Uncle Eugene had run out on the rent, because that's what everybody did, *so that's why he didn't leave no forwarding address, you know?*

It didn't bother Tony. They must be someplace. They might even turn up. He just hoped they had taken his *mandolino* with them. Meantime, he was more than happy to stay over with his new friend, Harry, who had a chest of toys. Harry might be bored with them, but sprawling on the floor upstairs to play toy soldiers, for Tony, was a novelty, and playing soldiers, or checkers, or chess, which Harry was teaching him, or else jacks or dominos or tops, occupied them for whole afternoons, while Bubelah was minding them.

Harry Spritzka idolized his big brother Robert. In age, they were seven years apart—so they had never been playmates. Robert to him was polished, distant and dazzling. Harry wanted very much for Robert to like his new friend Tony.

Robert had come in to find them sprawled on the floor with Napoleon's Grand Marshalls spread out, re-enacting Waterloo, which Harry seemed to know by heart. "Who's this?" said Robert, immediately.

"Oh, that's just Tony!"

Robert said to his brother, "You've been slumming again."

"Robert, please be nice. This kid scarred me for life. Look at my cheek. So don't get him mad."

"And that made you somehow the best of friends?"

"I knew you wouldn't understand. Neither does Totti."

Robert bent over and said, "Are you sure you have Marshall Ney's brigade positioned on the right hill?"

"Oh, Robert! Quit it! You know Marshall Ney wasn't there that day! And he wasn't a brigade commander, either!" Harry protested to Tony. "A brigade commander! Marshall Ney!"

Tony LaStoria soon became accustomed to bagels and lox or even a blintz to start the day, with coffee, or tea, golden-brown sugar, and cream, not milk. He even became accustomed to older-brother Robert. Harry's mother, Miriam, he found spellbinding. The fact was that Tony did not tire easily of looking them all up and down—casually, he thought—after all, he was in their home. The Spritzkas were quite amused and mildy annoyed. But Tony simply drank in the aura of the lady of the house. Her husband was another matter. If anyone among these rich people was going to step in between him and Harry, it would be Louis Spritzka. Fortunately for Tony, the man of the house had more on his mind than two little *kletsers* like Harry and Tony.

"Abba—I found us a good place to go," said Robert to his father, one evening when they were all at the dinner table. "For the big move."

"I should be so lucky as to find a good place to go."

"Everything these days is moving up to 34th Street and that neighborhood."

"The world is moving up in the world, yes, I understand. Me, I'm just a poor *putz* destined to be left behind in a thriving business at Number 68 Division Street."

Robert was talking to his father, but his father was answering him to his mother, so Robert replied to her. "Mother—we need space!"

Miriam was Lily's daughter, so Tony took note of how Harry's Bubelah discreetly stayed out of the sparring. After all, it was dinnertime, and the Spritzkas were nothing if not practitioners of etiquette. Bubelah quietly took note of Tony taking note. *Clever child.*

"Up on 34th Street, they have lots of space," Miriam's husband explained to her. "You are the proud mother of a son who's going to find space in the garment district." To his son he turned next. "To you I say, *goyisher tov.*"

Tony was drinking in every word, Yiddish or not. He had his own stake in this business. Eyes and ears open might keep him in the lap of luxury, but if he relaxed his vigilance, he might find himself sleeping in the park.

"Abba," said Robert, patiently. "You have to own the building where you carry on your business. Real estate is the key. Real estate is everything. This is New York! We're in a new century now!"

Tony was consumed with curiosity. The Spritzkas to him were endlessly strange. As soon as he had a chance, when they were alone, he asked Harry, "Why do you call your father "Totti"—but Robert calls him "Abba?"

"I don't know—ask Robert."

"And what's it all about?"

"I don't know—let's play!"

They were spread out on the floor with their two armies contending, and, as usual, Bubelah was perched on her sofa, observing with perfectly feigned excitement the to-and-fro of battle, wishing them both victorious, ever-ready to console the defeated.

But the boys were still only twelve, going on eleven, and they quickly got bored. Bubelah would say, "No mischief now," but she left the actual forbidding to Louis and Miriam, and the boys would frequently leave her abandoned, without a second thought, to pursue their other interests, outdoors, in the big city, which offered enticements to trouble they could not have dreamed up on their own.

Sometimes Harry felt like having an egg cream, so they went over to Auster's candy shop, at the corner of Third and Division, where the *kibitzers*, Harry called them, were regularly standing around inside the shop, and out on the sidewalk, sipping their egg creams. You could spend the whole afternoon there getting an education while you sipped. Other times they went for a dip in the East River under the Brooklyn Bridge, or sometimes way up to where the barges were, although they had observed people they called bums defecating in those waters, typically, furtively, between two barges, with their pants down around their ankles, eyes darting. Nobody cared. Gangs of kids would strip down to their underwear and plunge in irrespective. You had to share the river with amphibious rats anyway, so what difference did it make? Sometimes they even went further, all the way up to what people called the Dead End, the area where East 59th and East 60th came down to the river, which was populated by big rocks interspersed with three or four isolated apartment buildings where the Irish lived. Harry and Tony loved exploring the city and finding out how things worked and where everything was, especially things and places they had only heard of, which were precisely the places with the most allure.

The 2nd Avenue El had a railroad engineer called Red Mike Hyland, who was famous, so they went over to Allen Street to buy tickets.

"I'll get my own," Tony told Harry.

"You got money? Where did you get money?"

"None of your business."

"Come on, give."

"You don't have to know everything about me."

"You wanna be that way?"

"I got it shinin' shoes at Savastano's."

"Where's that? What's that? You gotta take me there."

"In a pig's ass."

The noise of Red Mike Hyland's steam locomotive running so close between apartment buildings on the El was ferocious. From the train, you could see the smoky grey window-panes in people's flats shaking. Residents kept windows closed even in the hottest weather so that cinders from the train's stack wouldn't set the apartment on fire. Everything was shaking. The boys bought tickets, and rode back and forth to the end of the line all day. You thought you would be rattled till your bones came apart. Even though they went back day after day, they still hadn't met Red Mike, so one time they decided to stay on the train all the way to the roundhouse, and lay in wait for him. When he stepped down out of the cab, finally, with a lantern in his hand, he didn't seemed surprised to find the boys.

"Why do they call you Red Mike?" said Harry.

"You see this nose?"

On occasions like this Tony let Harry do the talking. That way he found out more without having to lift a finger.

"How'd your nose get so red?"

"This is a whisky nose, son. So leave whisky alone and you won't get one. Wanna carry my lantern?"

Red Mike walked them back to the station and made certain they got on another train home. He stood on the platform waving to them as the train departed.

Harry Spritzka did not really need to collect coal in the street like the poor kids did, but somehow he and Tony still delighted in showing up black and filthy at the back door of the sewing room in the rear of the family store with their paper sacks of coal.

On the cobblestone streets, all you had to do was follow the wagon with the cannel coal, wait for the inevitable bump and lurch, and lumps of coal would fall off the back. As long as you stayed well back, and were fast, the boy with the stick, who had the same job Tony used to have on Domenico's ice wagon, couldn't catch up to you.

Miriam Spritzka would yell at the hired help, "Don't you dare let them in like that!" She would send them off to the public bath-house.

You could go to a bath-house on Monroe Street for two cents, and that got you a towel and a piece of soap. There was an eagle-eyed attendant all dressed in white, with white shoes, who had a watch in hand, and somehow, he knew it if you went over your five minutes under the shower nozzle, even though he'd let in twenty at a time, slipping, sliding, yelling, pushing, shoving, laughing, cackling kids and grown-ups, awash in soapsuds, under the shower. So you had to rush, or pay another two cents. Sometimes they would go over to the

Rivington Street baths, where they would find a hundred kids lined up out the door and onto the sidewalk, waiting. One time they were in the shower, and somebody said, "Look—he's not Jewish!" That was how Tony found out about the *bris*. He had never imagined such things.

Neither one of them had stopped going to public school, if not always, at least, usually. The do-gooders and the truant officers had not given up their campaign of tormenting kids. Tony never did go back to PS 130 on Baxter Street, as he was no longer living in that neighborhood; he simply went with Harry to PS 114 on Henry Street. But Harry had to go to *cheder* five days a week also, after school.

"There's an old man with a red beard and a stick. And he has six or seven students in the class. You go to his house, and you have to read the Torah—we take turns. You have to pay him a dollar a month. And for that, at the beginning of class, every day, he starts out everything by saying, 'Who wants a whack today?' Then he picks one out, and says, 'You haven't had one for a while. Come over here.' Then, when you come, he calls you a *dummkopf!*"

"What's a dummkopf?" said Tony.

"What does it sound like? A blockhead, you dummkopf!" Tony shoved his shoulder. Harry shoved him back.

Harry's mother had told him that babies were delivered by the cabbage man. Every day you went out to the cabbage wagon and you picked out a nice one. And then one day when you brought it inside and unwrapped the paper, instead of a cabbage, there was a baby inside. Long ago, Tony's mother had told him they baked them at the bakery. When you wanted one, you just went down the street. Babies were just like a loaf of bread—same size—warm and good-smelling, and, like bread, you can carry them home in the crook of your arm.

Tony did not really believe this anymore than he had believed the stories of Santa Claus he had cheerfully told his little cousins. But still he did not know what to think. Nobody ever told you anything. Not even Harry's older brother, Robert, who should have. All he would say was, "When the time comes, kid, when the time comes. Just don't talk to Abba. Come to me. I'll give you the straight dope—without the whitewash."

So the boys resorted to the bath-house. When they were tired of Monroe Street or Rivington Street, and they didn't want to pay a whole dollar, which is what it cost you at the fancy-schmancy places like the Second Avenue baths, they would go to the place with the ritual baths that everybody called Schmoolkie's Palm Garden.

There, for 3 cents on a Friday afternoon you could get a tush and a dip in Schmoolkie Schmulowitz's two-by-four-foot pool, which was as brown as the East River. That's where the boys found out, "Babies come from kissing. When the Mama and the Papa start kissing—watch out."

The following week, when they were back in the palm-garden pool and they repeated their discovery, somebody overheard them, and said "Whaddya talkin' about?—that's crazy. Look. This is how it's done." And he made a circle with the forefinger and thumb of his left hand, and he put the forefinger of his right hand in and out, several times, back and forth. "See?"

When the time came that Tony had stayed away much longer than he ever intended to, he finally dropped into the barbershop. Sure enough, Uncle Eugene had left word with Savastano, figuring that sooner or later, Tony would show up.

He found them at 410 East 62nd Street, which was a four-story brick building like all the others in the block between 2nd and 3rd Avenues, although a few were brownstones, with a dozen or more stairs, ample balustrades leading up to the front door, and stairs going down either side to basement flats.

The building where the LaStorias settled in on the top floor was not as pretentious. It was plain and pragmatic, but, being much newer, it was still a far cry from their ramshackle place on Mott Street.

Tony simply reappeared one evening, at suppertime, and he was welcomed with such fervor and relief that he wondered how he could ever have stayed away. Nor did he intend to skip any meals. Auntie Marietta's home-cooking, the simmer of garlic, and the tang of pork rind, made him feel like himself again.

His disappearance, and reappearance, again cloaked him with an air of mystery, even glamour, to his cousins, but also to his aunt and uncle. Somehow his misadventures provided an escape from the awful thought, *is this all there is? Will our entire lives be nothing but drudgery?*

"And what do they eat, the yids?" Uncle Eugene wanted to know.

"Well, they don't have farina in tomato sauce for breakfast!" Everyone laughed. "I don't know. How can I describe it? Everything tastes like cardboard. Maybe that's why they put cream cheese on everything."

"Cream cheese is good!" they all chimed in.

"Si, certo, but not on pickled herring! That they eat every day. Every single day. You can go down to Hester Street and what do you find? Every Jew in the street's got his own little shop—they don't work for other people, you know. They all gotta have their own business. So, you go down to Hester Street, and you can find the pickle store, the herring store, the bagel shop, the shoemaker, the bakery, the barbers, the drugstore—"

"It's another Mulberry Street," Uncle Eugene put in.

"Then on Friday, that's the only day Mrs Spritzka—oh, Auntie, you should see her, the dresses!—."

"What's their name?" said his uncle.

"'Spritzka' is their name—but their dry goods store has a fancy name—*Vilna House of Style, Men's Fine Apparel, Hats, Gloves, Neck-Ties, Cuff-Links, Ladies' Evening Wear and Dressing Gowns!*"

"What kind of a name is that?"

"I don't know. They're Lithuanians, Zi! They're Lithuanian Jews, from Vilna."

"Jews, Jews, they're all the same—don't matter where they're from. We got Jews, too, back in the old country, in case you didn't know."

"Anyway, I was telling you, on Friday, that's the day they go to *shul*. That's like church to them. There's an old man, in the shop at the back, he's a tailor—Litvak is his name—every Friday, exactly at 5 o'clock, down goes the needle and thread, and he puts on his coat, off to *shul*. But Mrs Spritzka, that's the only day, Friday, that she doesn't work in the shop, out in the front part, waiting on customers—I think Mr Spritzka—his name is Louis—she's Miriam—he believes that *she* brings in the trade. Because the men, they like to look at her, and also, she's there for the women shoppers, you know, one of their own kind, because expensive ladies come in trying to fit their husbands. And they stay because they find plenty of things to buy for themselves. So, on Friday, the Mrs goes upstairs, and she cooks, she cooks all day, all that special food they gotta eat on Fridays, like, she bakes *holley*, and she boils noodles to make *rugelach*, she makes the herring-."

"They can't eat pork, you know."

"Yes, yes," Tony agreed, "that's against their religion—everything's gotta be *kosher*. So, I guess, potatoes must be kosher, 'cause those they got them comin' outta their ears! Morning, noon and night, potatoes!" He turned to his cousins. "Where we have macaroni—they got potatoes! Where we got salami, they got pastrami—it's another world!"

"What I wanna know," said his uncle, "is how the hell did you ever get them to take you in like that?"

Uncle Eugene had tried selling shoelaces on the corner and at the trolley stops, and then started peddling paper sacks to the grocers and shopkeeps, which was a little better. But the Singer sewing machines stood idle in the new apartment. "Eh—I'm a very long streetcar ride away from the *padrone* now. Can't carry bundles home and get them back the next morning, like I used to. I don't know what I'm gonna do. I lost my boarders, too. We got a letter, Antonio."

His heart jumped—his mother!

"From the truant officer."

"Mr Engel?"

"They got another one, up here in this neighborhood. His name is McSomething, I don't know how you say it. They're gonna assign you to a new school—PS 37, on 67th Street."

His cousin Enrico said, "Truant School, Tony."

"That's right," said his uncle. "They got a special school for kids like you."

Every day Tony went to PS 37. It was not like his old school on Baxter Street, or the one on Henry Street he attended with Harry. The other students were older than he was, many of them, but they were in his grade. They did not like each other, let alone newcomers. But if you were weak, you got picked on all the time. Tony was having to fight every day now. Otherwise, they would take your money, or your lunch.

He was miserable at school now. There was no school library, and the teachers were all men— they were veterans of the Spanish war, and all they wanted to do was beat you up. If you wanted to borrow books, you had to go to the 67th Street public library. But you didn't dare bring them to school, because the other boys would laugh at you, or call you names, like "Aristotle," or say something like "Look, he thinks this is a school! He doesn't know he's in jail!" Tony stopped trying altogether. He did not want to get promoted. He wanted to stay back, and let the others get promoted. How else to be rid of them?

Sometimes he longed for his old friends in Little Italy, Mousey, Knickers and the others. But would he ever see them again? It didn't seem that his life now would cross paths with his old neighborhood. It began to sink in to Tony that his only refuge was at the Spritzkas' storefront home. But Harry was jealous of every moment away that Tony spent apart from him. Every day was an interrogation. "Where have you been?— what'll we do today? How come I never see you any more? I was counting on you. Don't let me down, Tony."

Sometimes Tony grew weary. His life now consisted of living part-time in both houses, and neither one was his, in neither one was he free of the traps of obligation, he had to watch his every step, his life wasn't his own, where was he going to get money, the money to buy his independence with?

And yet, in his own calculations, he was loath to let go of the advantages he thought might just be within his grasp at Harry's house. Certainly Uncle Eugenio was in no position to grant any largesse to anybody. Still, what was he really after? He didn't know.

ARRIVEDERCI NEW YORK

When the boys were not indoors in the apartment upstairs, at the corner of Division and Allen, or the store in front, or the shop in back, they were down at the river; or up in the garment district, or riding the trains all the way up 2nd Avenue, or going to gawk at the niggers over in Niggertown, by Washington Square; or pinching fruit from the pushcarts in Hester Street, or Mulberry Street, or collecting cannel coal, or sipping egg creams at Auster's, or chasing the ice-wagon, or playing stickball with Harry's old pals on Division Street, or playing in the brand-new gymnasium the Settlement had opened at 299 Henry Street; when they were not in hot pursuit of any of these places or pastimes, they would be listening to the orators in the street.

It sometimes seemed to them these days that the entire Lower East Side was a mass demonstration. A lot of it was tied into politics, socialists, union-organizing, anarchists, Tammany Hall elections, but the rest was the local gangsters who ran bookmaking, pimping and the protection-rackets, who had wars from time to time with their rivals. If the boys felt like a fight, there was no shortage—all they had to do was pick a side. There was always brawling to be had. It came in the form of riots and demonstrations and pitched street-battles.

You might go down to East Broadway outside the building where the Jewish daily, *Forvitz*, had offices, and on every one of four corners, a competing orator would be haranguing an audience from a soapbox. That's where the boys heard the likes of Morris Hillquit, Judge Panken, Vladeck, or Joseph Barondess.

The soap-box men were popular among the Jewish immigrants of the Lower East Side. They were considered local leaders, if not actual neighborhood heroes. They were strident, emotional, rabble-rousing speakers—and their entertaining histories were written up daily in the wildly popular *Forvitz*. Bubelah used to pull the boys onto her sofa to read them articles, translating from the Yiddish as they went along.

One time they were down on East Broadway standing at the back listening to Vladeck berating the audience when a fight broke out down front. They stood on tiptoes to see, but they could not tell what it was all about. Then a surge of bodies took place, threatening to roll over them, and they ran. When they got to the other side of the street, they stopped to watch.

The next time that happened, they didn't run. It seemed that there was a picket line outside a factory down near the Williamsburg Bridge, and on one side of the street was a gang throwing rocks and bottles at the picketers; while a bottleneck of bodies from their side, at the mill building doorway, tried to prevent a phalanx from the other side from entering. It looked like a great show, a real-life nickelodeon, a chance at some fun for a change, and it also looked like they could join in with impunity. They knew they could always run if they had to, and no cop had ever caught up to them yet.

So the two boys started hurling bricks and broken cobblestones at the picketers, too.

Then the police came down the street on horses, and on foot, and not wanting to get caught, Harry and Tony retreated to a safe vantage point. To their amazement, the cops seemed to join in the fight—on the side of the ones attacking the picketers. They ended up clearing a path for the ones trying to get in the mill building doors. Tony and Harry looked at each other. *That wasn't fair.* Especially as most of the picketers were women.

They didn't have to wait long for their next chance to choose a side, and they had made up their minds for the underdogs. This time they joined in on the side of the union picketers with just as much fervor as they had put to work for the opposite side the last time.

All of the women on the picket line were older than Tony and Harry, but some were not that much older—many were young and pretty and the last young ladies you would ever think to be found rioting in the streets—nicely-dressed and quite dainty, like schoolteachers. Little did the boys know. Out of those pretty little pink faces under their kerchiefs and potted hats came ferocious shrieks.

"Youz lousy stinkin' scabs!"

"Can't find a husband?"

"Get outta here and go home, ye dirty rotten no-good *koorvah!*"

Harry started laughing, and said, "We gotta help these girls."

The girls, however, were equipped to help themselves—with sewing needles, sharpened hair-pins, and lead-filled umbrella handles.

The boys went home that night flushed with victory, but along a dark street, lit only by gas-lamps, a grown-up man and a couple of others stopped them.

"Who's youz two *meshugganahs?*"

Harry stopped short. "Nobody."

"Listen—I seen yez before."

"We're just minding our own business."

"I don't know about that. Youz were both seen a week and a half ago throwing brickbats at picketers. Now, I'm telling you, for your own good—it's one side or the other. What's it gonna be? Ya can't have it both ways. Ya got it?"

"We got it, we got it."

"You know, kids your age oughtta be home readin' their Torah this time of night! Now, get outta here!"

When they were a safe distance away, Harry said excitedly, "You know who that was? That was Dopey Benny! Ya gotta watch out for him, Tony. He's like the Gomorrah. He breaks heads, he breaks legs. He'll shoot you! He's nothing to fool around with. He'll shoot a scab in the leg for 60 bucks. He'll wreck your shop for 150, 200! For murder, he only charges 500! Between him and Yushke Nigger and Monk Eastman, they got this whole part of town all sewed up! Don't let those sleepy eyes fool you—Dopey's a menace, if you cross him!"

Of the three, certainly the most notorious was Monk Eastman. At that time, Monk Eastman was just coming of age, just gaining his stride. Most of the Yiddish Lower East Side were perversely proud to call him their own—but in reality, no one could be certain that he was even Jewish. He did not live in their part of town—he lived down on East 5th Street, only a couple of blocks from his biggest rival, Paul Kelly, who ran his gang out of the New Brighton Social Club. But Monk had his pet shop, where he sold mostly birds, including his prized pigeons, on Broome Street, in the Jewish section. And his gang associates were all Jews. They called themselves the Allen Street Cadets. They swore he was Jewish, and as proof, they said that Monk was circumcised. Whether he was Jewish or not, he certainly liked an Irish name for an alias, or two. He had been arrested for larceny as William Murray, and both William "Bill" Delaney, and Edward "Eddie" Delaney. And he was quite thick with Tammany Hall, who found him useful, recruiting him and his cohorts as repeat-voters and strong-arm men at the polls. He got acquainted with the politicians at the infamous saloon, Silver Dollar Smith's, not far from his pet shop on Broome Street, where they employed Monk as their "Sheriff." Although he was only five-foot-six, and built like a fire hydrant, his appearance was intimidating—he had an unruly mass of wild hair sticking out from under a bowler two sizes too small, and he liked to go shirtless, or in torn jackets, always parading his pigeons—and woe to the man who made a comment one way of the other about Monk's favorite species.

The boys were sunk into this milieu. They were growing up fast, they were both thirteen, going on twelve now, they were in a phase between childhood and adolescence, pulled this way and that, abandoning the toy soldiers of childishness for the real-life battles of the street-life. Harry hated boredom. He craved excitement. Tony was happy to just follow Harry's lead. After all, he was living in Harry's house, Harry wasn't living in his.

Then McKinley was shot. No one could believe it. The President, assassinated. And it happened in their state—although, thankfully, not in their city.

It didn't matter—they were all tarred with the same brush. It was an immigrant who did it, and an anarchist, to boot. So the Socialists, along with the anarchists, the nihilists, and all the "foreigners," indeed, the entire Lower East Side, especially, somehow, the Jews, were blamed wholesale. For hadn't they welcomed Gene Debs to Cooper Union, with open arms, in 1900? When Debs campaigned for President against McKinley, on the Socialist Party ticket, he gave a speech in the Cooper Union telling them, "If you are looking for a Moses to lead you out of this capitalist wilderness, you will stay right where you are. You must use your heads as well as your hands, and get yourselves out of your present condition!" And he was wildly cheered.

Now the Republicans were the outraged Party, the sinned-against. Including the very man who had been New York City Police Commissioner, as well as Governor of New York, and who now was sworn in as the President of the United States–Teddy Roosevelt.

Lately, young Harry, much as he idolized the Colonel of the Rough Riders, their all-of-a-sudden President, had given up checkers and chess for something serious, which the omnivorous Roosevelt, had they only known, also was devoted to: coin-collecting.

They would sometimes sit for hours on the sofa with Bubelah up in the apartment examining Harry's collection. He kept them in books and albums, holders, folders and capsules.

It had taken Harry a year or two to develop a level of trust deep enough to share with Tony his prized collection. Even so, Harry wouldn't let him so much as breathe on a coin.

Where did they get it, these Spritzkas? thought Tony, *this chutzpah? Now there was a word.*

At that moment, if Bubelah had not been sitting right there, between them, Tony might have spilled the whole treasury clattering onto the floor, happily, out of sheer spite.

One day the boys were in the back of the shop, almost at closing time, after Tony had arrived on the long trolley trip from Truant School, and Harry was finished with *cheder*. Old man Litvak, the bearded tailor, an Orthodox Jew, had noticed something about Tony that he brought to the attention of Louis Spritzka.

"This boy can handle a needle and thread, foter," he mentioned casually to Louis Spritzka, whom he never failed to annoy with his sly irony.

"What makes you say that?" said Louis, impatiently.

"I have seen him standing, watching me."

"So—he's watching you."

"To see if I'm doing it right."

Louis waved his hand at the old man, a gesture of dismissal, and walked off.

But one day he said to Tony, "Go out to the back. Take a bundle and do the same thing you see Litvak doing."

After a while Louis came to watch. Tony said nothing, he simply finished the job. Louis indicated he should pass it to Litvak for inspection. Litvak turned over the work and yanked and pulled a little bit. "Mm. It's good."

Louis said to him, "Find some work for him to do. I'm sick and tired of him and Harry hanging around doing nothing. Three dollars a week."

"Three-fifty," Tony piped up.

"Three bucks," said Mr Spritzka, "and don't be an ungrateful *yutz*, or I'll make it piecework." When Louis had gone, Litvak leaned over to Tony. "Where did you learn your trade?"

"My father."

"So. It runs in the family."

Chapter 10

The Tangled Cloth

"Whaddya doing? I been looking for you everywhere!"

Tony sat with his back to the city on a hump of refuse overlooking the stub-end of 62nd Street where it descended to melt into the lugubrious East River amid a tangle of tin shacks.

"I'm watching the water."

"What for?"

"It's flowing backwards. See?"

"So what?"

Harry's voice was changing. It growled like knuckles dragged across a scrub-board. "Come on! Let's go! I got big plans for us today."

"You got big plans every day."

"I thought we were pals."

"Yeah, we're pals—as long as you get your own way."

"Look, Tony—don't let me down, now!–come on!—I'll tell you on the way." With a groan, Tony got himself moving.

"Why you pulling such a long face? Don't you wanna know where we're going?"

They headed cross-town to 8th Avenue to take the trolley up to the Harlem River Speedway.

But before they could get past Fifth Avenue, they were diverted by a novel sight—an automobile accident. One of those contraptions that some people called a horseless carriage, others a self-propelled buggy, still others an infernal nuisance, was bent double from a collision with a horse-drawn coal-van. Two drivers covered in soot, one with goggles and riding chaps and the other in something like a street-cleaner's uniform, were arguing in the street.

"What happened?" Harry wanted to know from a bystander.

"Well, it was all the fault of the wheelman!"

"Did you see it?"

"I did, and he was coming down Fifth Avenue through the intersection at a tremendous rate of speed—with his head down, y'see, pedaling away, and he never looks up to see the watcha-callit pulling out behind the coal-van to pass it!"

Now they looked around and saw there was indeed a bicycle smashed and crumpled up against a railing on the far sidewalk—but where was the wheelman?

He was laid out on the sidewalk. "Is he dead?"

"By rights, he ought to be. But he was saved by the driver of the auto—when they hit, he went over the handlebars, straight into his chest—and then he sits up. Dazed as a sleeping baby, on the man's lap!—thank goodness! If he'd hit the pavement instead, they'd be scraping him off with a garden trowel!"

Harry laughed to see a pretty modern girl sympathizing with the prostrated wheelman as she stood over him, holding onto her bicycle.

"So he was chasing her! Serves him right! Tony, get a load of this steamboat." Harry was running his hand over the dented heap of the auto crosswise in the street. "I want one!"

"You know how much these things must cost?"

"I don't care. I'll get the money."

When they were finally on their street-car, Harry said, "Now, listen, this is what we're gonna do! Forget about Abba. All right, for now, you're working for him, that's all right—for now. But in future, you're gonna be working for me!"

"Harry, you need your head examined. You're a 14-year-old kid!"

"Not for long!" Harry insisted. "And I don't know why you're saying that, since, in fact, we're wasting our time right now, if we're not building our own business every minute of every day. Unless you're planning to be as old as Litvak!—for Crissakes, Tony, we could be dead by the time we're forty!"

"Hey—leave Him out of it, willya? Have some respect!"

"Will you just listen to me! I got plenty of respect for the Almighty that this whole town worships. And that's The Almighty Buck. And that's what's gonna get me one of them brand-new steamboats. And if you had any common sense, you'd want one, too. Why not? Everybody should have one— that's what I think! Look, Tony—if you got money, you can have anything you want! Money will make you happy! So, let's get our hands on some! I can't do what you do—sit all day with a needle and thread in my lap. You handle that end, and I'll handle the money. And I can't do what Abba wants me to do—you know, he wants me to go out to the shop in back and work like a *yutz*, like, like you! And someday, when he feels like it, he's gonna let me take over his little corner shop—maybe!—if he dies first!—which he ain't planning to do for a very long time—and only if I'm a good boy! And I can't do what Mabel wants me to do, either!—"

"Who the hell is Mabel?"

"Who do you think, asshole? Bubelah? My mother!—who else!"

"Her name is Miriam!"

"She's a Mabel to me—that's what she is—a Mabel. You know, she wants me to go to school— study and learn and grind my life away and end up after another fifteen years a doctor or a lawyer or something. I can't do that, Tony! Why should I?—when all you need in this life is a little common sense?"

Harry had every detail thought out. He was going to go into the very same business of hand-me-down vests-and-pants as the Salvation Army, only he was going to make a profit out if it. That neighborhood they had just passed through? He was going to go around Fifth Avenue and knock on doors and ask them if they had any old clothes they wanted to get rid of, and they would end up just giving them away to him. Of course, he'd offer a little money, but they would refuse. He might even let them believe that he was collecting for the poor. Then when he had the clothing collected, he would take these cast-offs down to Hester Street, to the re-sellers with their push-carts, and probably make a 100% profit, or close to it, or even open his own push-cart, and charge retail, and make even more. He couldn't miss. It was a goldmine. Money for nothing. They'd be rolling in it.

By this time, they were at 216th Street, their stop. When they entered the grounds through a massive marble arch, a panorama greeted them.

"Get a load of this," said Tony.

A more beautiful landscape, open to the wind, air, river and clouds, Tony had not seen in the city. Manicured lawns, piled-high sky, imposing cliffs, breathable air, well-dressed people, obviously, the better-off class of the town, decorously arranged, as if posing for postcards, out for the day's racing. Beautiful standard-bred horses, nothing at all like the workaday drudges of the ice and coal, beer-wagon and streetcar world. They were bred and trained as pacers and trotters, pulling low-slung two-wheeled sulkies, with drivers in colorful satins—on a perfectly straight stretch of level roadway, a dynamited shelf of land, an artificial plateau.

"Now ain't this where you'd love to spend your Saturday afternoons," said Harry, "throwing away your paycheck? Which I'm gonna put into your pocket?"

On the landward side of the raceway, the cliffs rose majestically and formed a hilly balcony where long lines of spectators stood on the edge of the grass looking down from their eagle-eye perch at the racing below. On the other side was an esplanade along the bank of the Hudson with a railing where more spectators took a ground-level view.

"Let's go over the embankment," said Harry, "so we can watch the girls up on the cliff."

"You going in the parasol business?"

"It's a thought, it's a thought. Obviously, they sell. You could do worse."

"How about girdles and garter belts?"

"Tony! I'm shocked."

The Harlem River Speedway was the creation of an immensely wealthy man named C.K. Billings. This was his estate, and his ornate manse, set back from the cliffs, fronted by a circular drive, which he then turned into the private, members-only headquarters of what he dubbed the Suburban Riding and Driving Club. Through his connections, he got the state of New York to pay for the dynamiting and construction of the graded and leveled gravel-and-dirt raceway, and the esplanade.

Harry was prepared for race day, having made certain beforehand that Tony and he were dressed in their very best in order to blend in. If they behaved like ruffians from the Lower East Side, they would not get to see the races, or the stables.

Billings had built accommodations on the grounds for not less than a couple of hundred horses, with paddocks, corrals and exercise lawns. A horse-lover's paradise. Tony was in heaven. He did not need to touch or stroke the animals—just to hang over the fence and look. He did not expect ever in his life to see such perfection, and he could only dream of actually approaching these fine, beautiful beasts.

It saddened him, too, to see their privileged existence, to compare this munificence to the dark, dingy stables of Baxter Street, to contrast their stately and elegant form to the poor, stoop-shouldered existence of his own beloved Fiorello, who deserved, every bit as much as these pedigreed animals did, to be coddled and pampered, but instead was worked to death.

"Horses?" said Harry. "You can have 'em. I'll take one of them steamboats. That's where we're going, Tony. The lap of luxury. Riding in style."

"You'll never see a motorcar as beautiful as a thoroughbred racehorse."

"Don't forget, Tony—I'm not in this alone. It's me and Robert—together. You know, my brother can be very helpful to us. And he wants to. The way I figure it is all we gotta do is watch Robert and copy everything he does. He's a smart kid, my brother—a very smart kid. He's got a lot of what it takes.

You mark my words. He's gonna be a millionaire by the time he's thirty. He told me so. He's already set that mark as his goal. And I believe he'll make it. Why not? He's got everything going for him—handsome, intelligent—handsome. People love him. People want *him* to love *them*, as soon as they lay eyes on him! He can't miss. And—any mistakes he might make—we learn from that, too."

Tony wanted to wave Harry away. He was like a mosquito in your ear. "Look at that chestnut with the black tail. And his mane—silky."

"So, you keep your nose to the grindstone in the shop, and watch how every little detail is conducted. I'll be the money man in the office, you run the factory for me, out on the floor. The new garment district in town is going on up around 34th street and midtown, up to Longacre Square."

"They changed the name, Harry."

"The name of what?"

"Times Square, Harry. It's not Longacre Square anymore."

"Yeah? How come?"

" 'Cause the New York Times opened up a new skyscraper on the corner down there. Don't you read the papers?"

"Me? That's what I got you for, Tony. All I know is that's where everybody's going for cheap space to open new shops, with electricity. Up there, around *Times Square,* okay? Power's the name of the game. With electric power, we make it easier, quicker, cheaper. My father's never gonna be anything more than an alteration business in his corner shop—he only wants to do custom-fitted for one guy at a time—measure 'em up and down with a tape and tailor to fit—whaddya expect?—that's what they did in the old country—that's all he knows. He hasn't got the imagination, Tony. Before they built this raceway, what was here? Nothing! It took imagination. My father's lucky he lets my mother bring in some of the ladies' trade—that's as far as he'll go. What he doesn't realize is not how much he's making—it's how much he's losing!"

Tony was stuck in thought. *He's selling me. That's what Harry does. A day at the races. Well– guess I'm sold. Now, if I'm smart, all I gotta do is go along for the ride . . .*

That day at the races was hardly the last time Tony and Harry had this little private talk. It quickly became the only thing they talked about every time they were together. When Harry fastened his mind on something, everything else became trivial.

Things like playing on the floor with toys, lounging on the sofa with Bubelah, listening to his parents remininisce at the dinner table, simply bored him now. Even his coin collection was set aside— although it did come in useful as a source of capital for his new business.

He had found that he could pawn a couple of album leaves down at Freundlich's on Hester Street for ready cash, not spend the cash, just keep it in reserve for times when he absolutely had to pay for merchandise to re-sell.

Harry's chosen territory worked very well for him. Most people were only too willing to have him take last year's closet off their hands—especially the lady of the house. It meant a new shopping spree was closer than she had thought—*tomorrow morning*. After all—look at this!—*I have nothing to wear.* If necessary, Harry would make friends with the servants at the delivery entrance in the back. They were always helpful— and a source of new leads.

Harry found new business when he moved north from Fifth Avenue up to 86th Street, the German neighborhood.

It was the German Jews who congregated here, in their own Little Prussia, and they considered people like Harry to be inadmissible to what they called "Our Crowd." To them, the "Eastern" Jews were little more than pack-animals, a disgusting lot with filthy habits and a miserable existence. Beneath their notice. Embarrassing. Almost shameful. But the cash from Freundlich's came in useful at these rear entrances as Harry found a little *schmeer* won him a lot of friends among the downstairs staff.

Harry was not surprised at how easy it became to make money, but Tony was amazed. Harry made a profit every single day down on Hester Street, his "overhead" was little or nothing, and he saved everything. He was soon accumulating a pile, a cash-reserve worthy of a bank account. He was never seen around the store on Division Street any more. He was either uptown or on Hester Street or in transit between. If he needed to know what was going on in his own house, he had Tony there, every day. But Harry was so busy that a week would go by before they saw each other.

For Tony, life seemed to be rapidly changing. The pace of everything was quickening. He was drowning in the onrush of Spritzkas. He needed to get away. He needed to start over, to get hold of himself. He started to commute back and forth on the Second Avenue line and stay every night at Uncle Eugene's. A day hardly began before it was erased from the calendar and turned into yesterday. A week went by and became the past before you knew there was a past.

Because Tony loved what he was doing now in Louis Spritzka's shop, the days did not seem long at all. He had the feeling that he had made his escape—that he would never have to haul ice or shine shoes again. He might be working seventy or eighty hours a week on the next bench beside his friend Litvak, but although they said little, when Litvak spoke, it was always about something new, that Tony had never heard of. There was a world out there. The theaters over on Second Avenue, the Yiddish Broadway, had dancing girls and song-and-dance men, comedy, slapstick, and even Shakespeare, in Yiddish, of course. The new movies they were showing in the nickelodeons, with the train robbers and the galloping horses—the phonograph cylinders which were beloved of Litvak—Chopin and Verdi and Schumann and Schubert—and even Enrico Caruso—the new buildings going up all over town, higher and higher—the new subway due to open soon on 2nd Avenue–and before you knew it, it was the weekend again.

And Tony would meet up with Harry, and they would go to the nickelodeon, or the Yiddish theater, or the Italian music-hall. At the Thalia Theatre on Second Avenue, they followed the career of the East Side's favorite celebrity, Jacob Adler, in plays ranging from *shtetl* comedies like "Tevye the Milkman" to historical pageants like "Bar Kokhba." Adler was a star, and he played not only the milkman, but also King Solomon and Shakespeare's Shylock. When he was out in the streets, crowds followed him just to get a glimpse.

At the Italian theater called the Neapolitan, on Mulberry Street, they stood around the balcony to listen to the crooners over from the old country singing the latest popular songs, or they watched the comedies, "*Pasquale, the Pig,*" and "*Il Pesce Pagliaccio,*" and followed the adventures of Harlequin and

Pulcinella and Dottore in the *Commedia dell'arte*, or out in the street they would find the puppeteers with their tiny stages enacting the *Siege of Troy* or the romance of *Dulcina in the Garden*.

In the summer, Tony resumed playing mandolin in Mulberry Park on Sundays, four to eight, at the Pergola with Maestro Siragusa's orchestra. This was his one day off from Litvak's back room, and he wanted to spend the time back in his own neighborhood, maybe even re-connect with his old pals.

When the absolutely sweltering months of July and August came, after the concert, they would troop over the Brooklyn Bridge with the rest of the city to try to cool off at Coney Island. From the nickelodeon, Tony added "okay, pardner" to his vocabulary, and Coney Island gave him "frankfurter," "hot dog," "relish and mustard."

Litvak, the Orthodox Jew, did not work on *Shabbat*. Threading a needle was one of the sub-categories of the 39 categories of work prohibited in the *Mishnah* by the Rabbis. But that did not mean Tony could not work on Saturday. Harry, however, being the new generation, and taking the modeling of his parents, Louis and Miriam, who hadn't been excessively religious even back home in Vilna, was not observant, and, never having threaded a needle himself, did not care if he tore Tony away from his work by noontime on Saturday. Being the growing young 15-year-olds they were fast becoming, they needed to blow off steam, they needed to run and jump and rid themselves of excess energy on a sunny afternoon. Saturday was their day to play. Tony was grinding every day away after school in Litvak's back-room, and Harry was doing the same Monday through Friday on his pushcart business. If they were not going to the races at the Harlem Speedway, they could always get up a game of stick-ball or stoop-ball to sweat out a Saturday afternoon, or even go over to the Henry Street

Settlement house to play the exciting new game of basket-ball that was spreading, flood-stage, throughout the streets of New York, with the encouragement of the physical-education fanatics of the Progressive Movement. In the winter, they could go skating in Central Park or stage snowball fights between the stick-ball teams. In these games, winter and summer, Harry and Tony both competed by drawing in their old friends from Little Italy and Rivington Street, so as to heighten the competitiveness, and add spice to the combat, making two sets of adversaries with a past history vie with one another anew and revive their rivalry. And as a consequence the street-fighting and brawling they loved to indulge in never stopped for a heartbeat.

Between the anarchists and the socialists, and the advocates of free love and the opponents of women's suffrage, and the Italians and the Jews, and the Irish and the Jews, and the Irish and the Italians and the Jews, between the police and the company goons, the ones Harry called *shtarkers*, on one side, and the soap-box preachers and union organizers and wildcat strikers, on the other side of the street; between the peacemakers and pacifists and anti-imperialists of the Henry Street Settlement House and the warmongers of the West Side docks, with their allies, the Spanish War vets, agitating for their long-forgotten benefits; between Dopey Benny's gang and the Yushke Nigger's gang, and Monk Eastman's gang, and the Tammany Hall auxiliaries, under Big Tim Sullivan, and Don Serafino and the Sicilian Black Hand over in Little Italy, and the Yiddish Gomorrah, and the Chinese Tong gangs, who were all jealously guarding their little territories and their private national-lotteries, their gambling and prostitution and protection rackets, trying to fend off the competition, the encroachers, the rival gangs; between all these contesting groups, the pitched street battles never ceased, providing the Lower East Siders with all the entertainment they wanted, as well as all the exercise they needed.

Then there were the automobile parades up Broadway to the newly-minted Times Square, which seemed to have become an annual event.

And they never went too long without repaying a visit to the Harlem River Speedway.

And if they got lucky on the Italian lottery or got a little graft or gratis benefit payment from the Yiddish Gomorrah, they could even get into the Metropolitan Opera, standing room only.

At one point, Tony had a serious problem with his increasingly downhearted and discouraged Uncle Eugenio. So he went to see Louis Spritzka to see if there was anything he could do to help out the family. Louis told Tony to let him see. Nobody ever wanted to leave Louis' shop, but Tony was hoping that Mr Spritzka might be able to squeeze his uncle in somewhere, somehow. Finally, Louis came up with a position for Tony's uncle as a presser, and a stitcher, and probably both, as needed, but it would have to be provisional—"as long as business picks up a little, and it don't fall off again—and the ladies department, Jesus, they'll drive you crazy—one season it's shirtwaists and skirts, the next season, who knows?—everything's gotta be new, everything's gotta be the latest!"

Another time, it was Harry who was stuck. His brother Robert had a can't-miss opportunity come along to buy a building up at 202 West 37th, a four-story brick, which had previously housed a cloth-dyeing operation that was going out of business due to the owner's demise from old age, sickness, illness and disease, but mostly, old age. The children were quarreling and one side wanted to sell out. If Robert Spritzka could get in quick enough, with cash, he could steal the place—and the first floor could be made suitable for a showroom, although it would be a lot of work to rid the building of its lingering odors and stains.

Robert was already a substantial property owner, having started out his career, as young as he was, buying residential foreclosures on the Jewish Lower East Side, and he saw himself as a real estate man, and his future in property acquisition. He had little or no interest in garment-making. He had little interest, for that matter, in developing. He would never commit capital to frills, decoration, renovation or building something new and stylish. He only wanted to buy cheap, sell high, and in the meantime, rent out space at the going rate or better, and have other people pay all his mortgage debt and operating expenses for him. He loved to lecture little brother Harry on how real estate was the perfect way to utilize other people's money to enrich yourself. But he did want to help out his younger brother Harry, too.

Because Harry was becoming quite a pest as he closed in on his sweet-16 birthday.

Harry was indignant about how much time, and money, he was losing. He had a pile of his own from his second-hand business already stashed away, but the competition was nosing him out in his chosen field—every day lost now, they were getting ahead of him, and Harry maintained that he had to start producing his own wholesale ready-made women's clothing, now, or maybe he'd be frozen out forever, on the chance, no, on the opportunity, of a lifetime.

Harry argued and remonstrated and protested over and over with Robert—and the brothers had to keep their father strictly out of it, for fear of his interference—their mother, too. It was becoming increasingly difficult to sit at the dinner table without all the tensions breaking loose.

So, Robert, in addition to Harry, was growing more impatient, even desperate.

Harry confided in Tony. All Robert needed was five hundred dollars, and he was into the deal— but he couldn't free it up liquid.

"I tell you—I'm at my wit's end."

Tony said, "Maybe there's something I can do."

"What the hell can you do?—with holes in the seat of your pants!"

But Tony had an idea, and he went back to the barbershop, to talk it over with Savastano.

Tony felt obligated in a way, to Harry, because of their friendship, their brotherhood, but also to Robert—because of Harry and Robert's father, Louis, and what Louis had done for Tony's uncle Eugene.

He explained this to Savastano, who marveled at the changes in Tony.

"You are becoming quite the young man, my friend. You remember the old days? I do! Especially that time with Don Serafino and the shoe! You know, people on the street, they still talk about that?"

"That's ancient history," said Tony. "Why don't they just let it go?"

"Ah, Tony, why you wanna be that way?"

"Everything's different now. Everything's changed."

"But some people will never forget, Tony."

"Yeah. So? Whaddya gonna do for me now, Pietro?"

"Listen to him! Now it's Pietro! Now he's all grown up!"

"Well?"

"I don't know, I don't know. Lemme see. Maybe there's something I can do. But I gotta talk to your friend, the Don."

"Well, you better talk fast. We're runnin' out of time here."

Savastano made a phone call, and when he finished saying, "Yeah . . . yeah . . . *si, si . . . certo!* . . ." he hung up the receiver and came back to Tony.

"*Va bene,* the Don says to set it up and have your friend come see him. He says to tell you he wouldn't do this for anybody else—but he likes you—he thinks you got a lotta balls. How about that, huh, Tony? A lotta balls!"

It suited Robert Spritzka just fine to do business with Don Serafino, in spite of the twenty-five percent interest, because he knew that this way his father would never find out about it—whereas, if Robert had tried the same thing on Hester Street, not only would Louis know all about everything before the paint dried on the contract—he might even have prevented it. And besides, Robert would never have to pay anything back out of his own pocket. He told Harry, "I don't care if you are only sixteen—you're gonna have to get the load outta your pants, brother!"

If Robert thought Harry was not up to the job, he underestimated his sibling—but Robert thought no such thing. He had a feeling this was going to turn out to be something they all remembered. After all, who resembled Robert more than Harry? Who modeled himself on Robert? Who idolized Robert? Who was the carbon copy of the original bill of sale?

Harry enlisted Tony in the new project immediately, and took him right out of Louis Spritzka's shop. Tony's uncle stepped into Tony's vacancy—and that solved that problem. Tony was happy.

Robert was happy—he owned a new four-story brick and had a brother who was going to turn it into a goldmine, and pay him rent. Louis was happy because he was ignorant—he knew nothing, and nobody told him anything, and he could just turn his back on all of them, wash his hands, and he considered himself well out of the whole mess—he was terribly disappointed in both his sons and the way they were turning out—both of them!—and even his wife could tell him nothing! Only Bubelah, upstairs on her sofa, knew anything, because in their terrible state of excitement, the boys, Harry and Tony, had to confide in someone, and who else could it be but Bubelah, who loved them both as she loved life itself, and even more, if that could be. But, of course, Bubelah could be trusted with all their secrets; she would never let on to her son-in-law Louis that she knew anything at all. It would all be just their own little romantic adventure to share. And what a story! "Imagine," said Bubelah, and her face was glowing, with her arms around them both on the sofa, "My boys! My boys are growing up!"

The boys plunged into the renovation of the new shop as if the place were on fire and they had to work fast to save it. They worked like low-wage day-laborers all over the four floors at one stretch for four days straight around the clock and only took short naps. They were afraid not to tackle everything at once, and the clock in Harry's head told them they were losing money every minute they were not already open for business. They became a two-man bucket brigade and attacked all the walls with stiff-bristle scrub-brushes on long poles and buckets of ammonia-water and solvents and turpentine and vinegar-water and even horse-linament, trying to get the stink of the dyeing operation out of the building, and then with hammers and nails they started to build the long benches they would need to travel the length of the long rooms upstairs, to hold row after row of sewing machines set up side-by-side, and the massive-sized cutting table they would need on the second floor. Fortunately, the building was designed for manufacture, originally, and came equipped with exactly the kind of freight elevator they would need to haul bolts of cloth upstairs on pallets and finished racks ready for wholesale back downstairs. Then they had to build the counter-tops and display cases they would need for the first-floor showroom; Harry thought he'd be able to sell finished product at retail from there, in the middle of the garment district.

Naturally, with lumber being delivered, and meals being sent in, and electricians hired to come in and re-wire everything, the boys attracted a lot of attention—especially because of their age—and in a couple of days they had loungers and loafers and slackers standing around on the sidewalk, just to watch, as if they were digging a subway tunnel. And many of these started asking about getting a job from the new neighbors.

But Harry had his plan in his head, and he was not going to go for a lot of men. He wanted women. They were easier, more docile, less trouble, you didn't have to pay them as much, they'd work cheaper. And he wanted young ones, too, especially since he and Tony were barely sixteen. He didn't want matronly mother-types as employees because he was afraid they wouldn't accept supervision from someone his age. Harry's plan was to get them young, and especially, untrained, and have Tony teach them what they'd need to know how to do, which, according to Harry, wasn't much.

Harry was not looking for tailors, he was looking for a small army of piece-workers who would keep their mouths shut and their heads down.

That's where the perfect man for the perfect plan fit in—his pal, Tony. Tony not only had the stitching expertise to pass along, he also had the other language, and that would allow them to tap into the pool of young Italian girls looking to help out at home by finding a steady job outside the house that would bring in cash. So their talent-pool, their target-workforce, they saw doubled by including the Italian girls in addition to the Yiddish-speaking girls. And maybe the Italians would even work for less. Depends on how desperate they are, Harry guessed. *We'll see.*

But they better hurry up—they owed brother Robert rent at the end of the month, and Harry was determined it was not coming out of his pool of cash reserves—it would have to come out of proceeds of sales—he was sinking everything he had into the renovations, and the expensive electrical fixtures and re-wiring, an enormous expense, that could not be avoided.

Tony, too, was in a hurry, as he had left a paying proposition at the shop on 68 Division Street to work for nothing—until they were up and running at 202 West 37th.

To both of them—this was the gamble of a lifetime.

A chance at success—on one throw of the dice.

But Harry had prepared for this. For a long time, he had been keeping his eyes and ears open, and watching. His used-coat and second-hand pants business on Hester Street provided an eye on everything. He was able to observe who was who and where the money was, what was successful and what sent you down the drain. In that little space of time he had been commuting, collecting, buying and selling, maybe two years at the most, things were developing and changing so rapidly it sometimes made your head spin.

All the talk was of something those in the needle trade began calling the new-model factory system. This was being promoted as the way to go, by mysterious forces that operated unseen, but which you felt every day.

One of these was the Edison Company. They stood to make a bundle by promoting electric power in the work-place, and their brand-new substations were going up all over Lower Manhattan.

They were digging the new subway on 2nd Avenue and that was due to open in 1904, and that, too, impinged on everyone because it meant that the labor force could get to work up in midtown from the Lower East Side cheaper and faster, with much less wasted time, and no lost work-days because of snow. For the people who had to scrape a living from needle and thread it meant that they could move out of the old neighborhood, and live further away, where rents were cheaper—and still get to work where the jobs were.

All the better-off old-lady do-gooders from the Settlement House Movement and the Consumers League were loving the new developments as heaven-sent. For years, they had been following the gospel of Jacob Riis and wringing their hands over the over-crowded living conditions and exploitative child labor of the sweating system, and now—that was disappearing—miraculously—overnight.

Even the big-shot operators of the garment trade who handed out the diminutive daily contracts of bundle-work that were the life-blood of the taskers saw the hand-writing on the wall. Their own futures, and worse, their own profits, were all at stake.

Before you knew it, the transition to the factory system had become mandatory—a matter of life and death.

The competition was ferocious, and those who got a leg up would survive—those who didn't, well—survival of the fittest, as they say. Manhattan was producing seventy percent of all the ready-made clothing on sale in the whole country, and if you wanted a piece of *that* pie—*well, get off your ass and get to work, dummkopf. Put your money where your mouth is.*

Of all the successful businessmen in the trade Harry observed, there was one pair at the top of the heap. Max Blanck and Isaac Harris were two immigrants from the *shtetl* who had arrived like so many others without a nickel to their names, but they were not the kind to go around the new world with their hair in ringlets wearing a long black beard. And like so many others, they also had started out in the tenement sweatshop, but now they were the owners and operators of the factory considered to be the model for all the others, situated in three floors at the top of a skyscraper building of ten stories, called the Asch Building, at the corner of Washington Street and Greene Street, a half-block east of Washington Square. Max Blanck and Isaac Harris were not their original names, but nowadays, what did that matter?—they had ridden to prominence on the wave of the latest in women's wear, the trend-setting fashion revolution that brought the lady's shirtwaist into absolute demand as the replacement for the old-fashioned wasp-waist single-piece shoe-top-length lady's dresses of the Nineties. Back then fashions demanded a waist-cinching girdle be worn underneath. Now, the very idea struck horror, and was hopelessly outdated. To the relief of masses of women. Especially the leaders of the Women's Suffrage, who considered the new fashion "liberating." The old confining strictures came to signify the old century, and women's second-class status, but this was the new century, and that was going to change, if they had anything to say about it.

For the manufacturing class, all men, it meant nothing more than money. *Money, money, money, baby.*

If you could get women to demand shirtwaists, which were long blouses with high necks and flouncy long sleeves, decorated with lace, then they would need a separate skirt to go with it—and now you could sell them two garments, instead of one, for their daily use, at home, at the market, in the work-place.

It was not hard to figure out. Sales figures might soar—and they did. At the crest of the new order, riding the tidal surge, were Max Blanck and Isaac Harris, whom people now nicknamed "The Shirtwaist Kings."

Harry Spritzka selected the Shirtwaist Kings as his models, and in order to observe their operation at close hand, he decided to apply for a job at the Triangle Shirtwaist Company, which was what they called their business at the top of the Asch Building.

Harry had no intention of taking a job there, but, as it was a big city, and they were prominent men, they did not know who he was, and he did not say anything about his real intentions to the underling who provided him with the nickel tour.

What Harry saw that day was what he replicated in exact detail, from memory, when he set up his own shop at 202.

That meant that by his own calculation, he was probably around the thirtieth or thirty-fifth in line of a mob of operators who copied Blanck and Harris. He was just jumping into a pool of sharks, and it was already 1904.

Meanwhile, for his sixteenth birthday, his brother Robert had a surprise for Harry. After they had cake and candles with their parents and Bubelah, at the first chance he had, Robert drew his brother aside behind a door in another room upstairs.

"Harry, I'm sorry I didn't have something all wrapped up for a gift for you—but I don't want you to think I forgot all about your birthday."

Harry was intrigued. *Why the secrecy?*

"Not a word now," said Robert. "This is just between us."

Robert arranged for Harry to meet him at a café on Hester Street on Saturday night—and all Robert's friends were there—but not their girlfriends–something Robert never did.

He and his friends formed their own social circle and never went anywhere unless they could show off the sweet young ladies they were practicing on. Whether it was the beach or the skating pond, the theater or the nickelodeon, they always did everything as a crowd, which seemed to make it so much easier to mix with the feminine gender and the idle set. On this Saturday evening, however, they all focused their attention on Harry—and it seemed their intention was to get him relaxed and comfortable—very relaxed and comfortable. In a strictly male conclave. And the more Harry drank, the more comfortable the idea became.

Finally, Robert came to the point. "Harry—there comes a time—in every young man's upbringing—when the social graces have to be mastered—and certain rites of initiation have to be passed through, so to speak—"

His friends could not stifle their wicked grins, and thought Robert's elaborate, exaggerated choice of verbiage hilarious. Harry was not the only one getting drunk that evening.

"Now I don't expect you've failed to notice, Harry, a certain strata of society around the— Bowery, for instance—which, I am sure, a young fellow of your upright disposition, has never visited after dark, unaccompanied."

Harry said, "Robert!—is this the night we pay a visit to Tillie the Toenail?"

"Harry!—I'm surprised at you!"

"Holy Moses, what are we waitin' for! Let's go!"

"Not so fast, my fine-feathered friend. First of all—not even Jake or Hymie here would take his own life in his hands down on the Bowery—and I advise you, as any good brother has to, to steer clear of that particular stretch. The good Jewish girls of Allen Street are plenty good enough for you to try out your spurs on!"

"Jumping Jesus!–Fancy Ladies—here we come!" cried Harry in sheer inebriated overflowing joy. It was all things considered, in Harry's estimation, the best gift anyone had ever given him. And it brought him closer to his older brother, a being so superior that Harry had always stood in awe of him.

This completely unexpected night on the town sealed a compact between them as brothers—a kind of a deal. It laid out a contract between them: henceforward, they were equals in life, no longer the older versus the younger, but different versions of the same heart, the same mind, the same soul. It gave them a shared secret that set them apart from the rest of their family, especially their mother and father. And it was not a secret that Harry could share with Bubelah, either. And that, more than anything else, turned Harry into a man—a fully grown adult man, at the age of sixteen—a man, no longer a child.

Nor did Harry breathe a word of all this to Tony. It seemed to him that Robert had had his own reasons for making sure that Harry's friend was excluded from any awareness that this little debuntante's ball had ever taken place.

And that gave Harry pause. He hated to forego the greatest opportunity to boast and to gloat that he had ever had, but, dammit, he would have to. Yes, there would have to be some other way, if he could only think of it, eventually, to reveal his secret to Tony. There had to be. Otherwise, what good was it to finally get laid if you couldn't brag about it to your best friend!

On the other hand—there was something to be gained from going about the usual, knowing he had his own little secret that Tony could not even suspect. And when they were finally engaged upon the greatest endeavor of their young lives, attacking the new building at 202, in a hectic fever of demolishing, rebuilding, tearing up and putting down—Harry gloried in hoarding his treasure and biding his time.

They had the building ready by a nose at the finish line, for there was a queue winding down the street waiting for them to unlock the doors on hiring day, a Friday. And Harry was adamant they had to start full operations the very next day, Saturday or not. And most of the girls in the queue were Jewish—there was a smattering of Italian girls, and Harry walked up and down the line out on the sidewalk, checking.

The one or two young girls he found who were obviously *shvartzes* he told to go home—they would not be admitted to the building. He simply stated to them, "No colored allowed." After all, it was just what they had expected. A hum of satisfaction went through the other girls, and they eyed him up and down, wondering just what they were getting themselves in for with this young *mashugenah*. But Harry was dressed in a three-piece suit and keeping himself very aloof and professional. He spent most of the day with his arms folded in the office next to the showroom, where he had set up his desk—and placed his brother Robert in the owner's chair. It made a better impression. At 23, Robert, handsome and tailored, looked to be obviously the man in charge. Nobody needed to know anyone's real role in anything—it was none of their business. Harry had Tony in the office as well, since he could converse with the Italians—and Tony ran his own little test, if he was doubtful. He had the girl thread a needle, and instantly he would know if they had ever done it before, or weren't very practiced at it. Harry only wanted the youngest, most untrained, and if possible, the most desperate girls—if they were good-looking, so much the better, but he really did not think that was such a good thing. Actually, he thought, the fatter and uglier, the better. But in one or two cases he could not help himself. The three of them had discussed everything amongst themselves, with Harry doing the talking, Tony the listening, and Robert the approving. Robert was their cover. With him in the office, the younger pair felt almost older and wiser themselves—and the nervousness with which they had opened their eyes in their bedrooms that morning, on a day of days, disappeared.

Chapter 11

Maestro Of The Plaza

It was not long before Harry Spritzka was making money (and by that, he meant *profits*) at a rapid rate. He had hit the track with a running start, and in a matter of weeks, he was feeling nothing could stop them, nothing at all.

Not only did he find he had a talent for organizing and delegating, he surprised himself with discovering unknown instincts to draw upon. He never saw a deal he did not like because deep down he was a *schnorrer*, and he delighted in it whenever some *goyisher yutz* told him he was trying to "Jew him down!" Harry would walk away counting his money and say to himself, *American gonif!* . . . His years of knocking on doors on the Upper East Side, he thought, made him a hell of a salesman. He was convinced he could sell ice to the Laplanders. And his knowledge of who's who and what's what down on Hester Street was impeccable. Before he ever began this business, he already had outlined in his mind his suppliers, his wholesale customers, and his brand. Women's daily wear, for the mass market, cheap, but high volume, that was his road to making a fortune.

On hiring day, he had stalked out of the office, placed his hands on his hips, and yelled at the giggling girls, "No talking!" Might as well start them off the right way. In his place of business he was damned if he wasn't going to run a tight ship. He expected the same attitude out of Tony. He had placed Tony on an equal footing with the two or three older, experienced women he had hired as floor-ladies, and he expected Tony was going to act as his enforcer, and free Harry from the onus.

But Tony had an entirely different manner with the girls. They were all girls to him, even the floor-ladies. As such, he treated them with more respect than they themselves were expecting, and they noted this. He was polite and courteous—a gentleman—he never yelled at them, like that other one. He might take one of them aside, by the elbow, if he had something critical to say, but only at the end of the day, so as not to embarrass them in front of others. The Italians girls called him *simpatico*.

But it was the only way Tony knew how to be. When Harry stuck his head out of the office, which was seldom, Tony might make a show of saying loudly, "All right, over there—no talking! You know the rules!"

But the girls only giggled at him. Sometimes they would wait for him after work, near the exit, until he came to let them out—the doors were always locked. They wanted to know, *Tony, who's your mother saving you for? Have you got a girl?* Tony would blush, and the girls would go home happy. Sometimes the Jewish girls would say something like, *I don't suppose you'd take home a Yiddisher girl to your family, huh? But you know, I could keep your toes warm at night!* All the girls delighted in teasing Tony LaStoria. One day Harry said to him, as if in passing, "Have you picked your flower yet?"

"Harry—these girls are all 14 years old!"

"I know. I picked 'em that way. Budding young virgins for you to train. You got a whole garden here, dying for you to pluck 'em!"

Tony knew very well that Harry had already made his own flower arrangement. In fact he had a whole bouquet. Harry was very definitely in it for that—but, Tony supposed, that was the difference between them—*to each his own*. Besides, he liked Harry, *he made money offa Harry*, but why would he ever want to be Harry?

One day Spritzka pulled up at the door of 202 at six-thirty in the morning in a brand-new Hispano-Suiza. It was like Dewey landing in Manila.

"How do you like my new rowboat, Tony?"

Tony was at a loss for words, but Harry was bubbling over, and pulled Tony inside with both arms wrapping his shoulders, hugging and shaking him.

"If you're a good boy, I'll take you for a ride! But only after work! She's built like a Spanish galleon, huh? Solid steel! Whaddya think?"

That was the day Harry called Selma Goldstein into the office to take her measurements. He joked with her that he wanted to find out if she would fit into his new automobile. He didn't want her to break the dashboard with her chest. "No. Really. Just joking. But honestly–I need to make sure that some of our blouses are gonna be the right proportions for the buxom girls out there—you know, Selma, the ones like you—built like a brick shithouse–so, be a good girl, and help me out here. Just stand still, and stick out your chest."

After that, in addition to his French cravat, or his Mardi Gras pocket handkerchief, Harry was never seen around the office at 202 without a measuring tape dangling around his neck. The Jewish girls all whispered amongst themselves about who would be pulled into the office next. If any one of them was invited for a ride in the Hispano-Suiza after work, it sparked a round of unbridled speculation. But Harry was not about to fall for any of their tricks—and he never pulled any girl into the office who already had a diamond on her finger. This only increased the anticipation. The girls were all sure he was measuring for a bride. But to Harry, they were just something to toy with. He studiously avoided bothering the Italian girls—he was afraid of going too far, and he figured they could be trouble—you know, *temperamental*—they all thought they were opera singers. Besides, there was the language barrier. That's what he had Tony for—to deal with them. And it wasn't a bad idea to play off the two groups of girls one against the other—keep 'em on their toes.

The Italian girls were all scandalized by the splashy stones on the ring-fingers of the Jewish girls. They said they didn't know how they could do it—these girls could keep a young Jewish fella engaged for six or seven years and never let him get past a peck on the cheek. As for themselves, they figured they were only here for two or three weeks, or six months at the most, and then they'd be married. Italian guys couldn't wait. *They'd die if you made 'em. You gotta give in, and sooner rather than later's probably smarter anyway. Who wants to work for a living? Have babies and stay home, and send him out to dig the subway tunnels. This is only a temporary thing here. Let the Jewish girls scrimp and save for seven years to set up house—that's not our way—and anyhow, they don't know what they're missing, huh? You only live once.*

One Saturday Tony and Harry went up to the Harlem River Speedway; they had begun to use that Saturday ritual as their escape-hatch from the factory building, their steam-valve; the floor-ladies could handle things for the few hours remaining in the work-week. They took the new motorcar, and riding along, Harry said to Tony, "I think I know what your problem is—you're just shy, that's all."

"What are you talking about?" Tony was offended.

"You! You're around the girls constantly—and you treat 'em like tea-cups—like you're gonna break 'em—they're so fragile."

Tony felt needled, but he had to be careful not to rock the rowboat. After all, it was Harry's Hispano-Suiza he was riding in.

"I see how you handle them. Please this, and if you don't mind that. Tony—you gotta take charge—let 'em know who's boss."

They looked at each other. Then Tony said, "Watch where you're going, will ya?"

"Nevermind. You leave it all to me. I know just what you need."

The following weekend, when they climbed into the car on Saturday, instead of turning up Broadway to head for Harlem, they started the other way. Tony didn't want to ask what Harry was up to, so he just sat there, glumly—then they found themselves in Chinatown.

Harry parked on a tiny street where he figured they had never even seen an automobile before, but he let 'em look. He and Tony stepped out to greet a small number of the curious, who were quickly adding up to a show-window crowd, and he slipped a couple of quarters to a young guy, and said,

"Watch the wheels for me, willya?"

He beckoned to Tony from a dimly-lit doorway. The young Chinese guy started barking at his countrymen in their own lingo to back off of the big man's automobile. Tony put his hands in his pockets and, trying to look as casual as he could, but feeling eyes on his back, he followed Harry.

They stepped into a cavernous room so dark that it smelled like a cave.

It took a while till Tony could finally make out a rectangular-shaped bar and little paper lanterns.

They pulled out two stools and an obsequious little man came over to offer service, but he had no English. Harry held up two fingers and motioned with his hand tipping to his lips, as if cupping a glass, and then pointed at Tony and himself. The bartender brought back two glasses of a foul-smelling liquid, which Harry gulped down, and Tony sipped, though the odor went up his nose and he felt nauseated.

For a long time they sat there without saying a word and nothing happened. Then a little man appeared at Harry's elbow.

"You likey little lovin'?"

The next thing Tony knew Harry was gone, and a tiny woman was tugging at his own elbow. She reached into his lap and pulled his hands into hers. She gently turned him on the swivel-stool and got him to his feet. She was backing away, pulling him by both hands.

Tony hardly knew what was happening, but his heart was beating and he didn't dare say or do anything. The young woman was very short, but she was in a sheath-like dress that widened her hips, and her lips were painted red, and her eyes purple, and they pleaded with him, and narrowed into slits as if she were eyeing a snake or a rabbit.

A small smile came over her, and she turned and pulled Tony by one hand up a back stair, with her hips bobbing back and forth under his nose.

Tony, thinking he could back out, or say no, any time he wanted to, would go as far as to permit himself to follow her up the staircase, until he found himself in a room with a bed, like a boarding house, or hotel room. But he had never been in a boarding house or hotel—or a brothel. So until he found himself in this room, he didn't know what to expect, or what to do, except to sit down on the bed with the dragon bedspread when she guided him there.

Then the girl, for that's what she was, now that he saw her under the single light-bulb dangling from the ceiling, looked even younger than he was. And she was kneeling in front of him, and then she was trying to undo his celluloid collar, and all Tony could think of was that he was soiling his clean white shirt, the clean white shirt that he wore every day, that he had adopted as his uniform in life.

For it was said that clothes made the man.

"No, no, no!" he cried, and he stood up, suddenly filled with revulsion that she had touched him, and he ran out of the room and down the stair, groping his way along the bar in the darkness until he virtually stumbled back out into the street.

He sat in the Hispano-Suiza surrounded by curious onlookers who were groping him with their eyes for what seemed like forever until Harry re-emerged, passing a finger under the collar around his own neck as if it were choking him. Then he stooped in front of the auto and turned the crank handle with vehemence. When it wouldn't start, he kicked the fender. Tony was becoming alarmed. The crowd of Chinese stood back as if this machine were a breathing dragon. Furiously, Harry cranked it again.

The car rumbled and groaned into sputtering life and Harry climbed in and roared off down the narrow street, irrespective of bystanders, pedestrians or onlookers, who jumped for their lives.

All the way back neither one of them said a word. When they parked at the door of 202 and got out, they met on the sidewalk, as Harry came around the car. Tony was waiting for him. He stubbed a finger into Harry's chest.

"Don't you ever do that to me again!"

"Hey! Tony!" Tony was walking away, Harry had to speak to his back. "Who puts money in your pocket, huh? Who? Who?"

They didn't speak for a week. Tony resolved not to ride in that Hispano-Suiza again. Nowadays he was back to where he belonged, living with Uncle Eugene and the family in the Italian neighborhood on the Upper East Side, and he took the streetcar back and forth to work every day. That gave him plenty of time to stew and steam. He hadn't seen Bubelah in ages, and he wished he could talk to her, and feel her put her little arms around him—but he would never go back there again. The way he felt now, he wished he had never met Harry Spritzka in his life.

But of course the following day was Sunday and it was time to sit in with the Professore's orchestra. Sinking into the music, he felt at home again, and he wondered at himself. When it came time to pack up the instruments and leave, when the interlude of music, which took you away from, apart from, life and all its daily dilemmas, it occurred to him that he didn't understand himself at all. What made him act the way he did? Feel the way he did? Why was he a mystery to himself? And why was his own life a problem to him?

Monday morning he was back at work. When Saturday rolled around again, Harry was back at it. "Let's go. It's time to get out of here."

"Harry–!" Tony had been pulled aside, but he felt everyone watching them nevertheless. The girls in the shop were like the cousins at home—you couldn't get anything past them. They knew more about what was going on than you did, and the week's worth of the silent treatment between the two bosses certainly did not go unnoticed. "Whaddya want now?" Tony lowered his voice.

"I need you, Tony." Harry had lowered his voice, as well. "For a special job."

Tony folded his arms and looked like he wanted in the worst way to tell Harry to go to hell. Harry nudged his elbow. "Come on, Tony—you're not gonna let me down now, are you?"

Tony's lips were pressed together, but his eyes were dark and smoking.

"After all I done for you?"

So Harry was going to play that card.

"I didn't think you were that way."

Tony was furious. "I trusted you." He wanted to turn on his heel, but he felt fastened there; the sewing-machine needle had just pierced, not his forefinger, but his stubborn male pride.

"Ya gotta understand, Tony—you're the only real friend I got."

Harry would have his way. Harry would always have his way. He just wouldn't let a thing go until he had his way. He wore you down. Tony found himself riding in the Hispano-Suiza seated next to Harry, and he didn't even want to look around to see where they were going. Harry was talking.

"I never meant to piss you off, Tony. I was trying to help you—that's all. I was trying to help you get over the hump. With all my heart, Tony—I would never do anything to hurt you. I was only thinking of you. Why else would I have gone through all that *magillah?* For myself? I don't need it. I was trying to do something good for you. Why can't you understand that?"

Finally, they were stopping. Parking in front of a hotel. The Hotel Essex on 17th Street. They went inside. In the elevator, Harry said, "Didja bring your brass knuckles? You might have to back me up."

Tony felt like he was riding in a vertical coffin, going down, not up. It numbed his whole frame. They knocked on a door—Number 324. A voice bid them to enter—it was unlocked.

A man with his back to them at the windows of the hotel room, dressed in a good suit, picked up two shot-glasses from a small table in front of the filmy white curtains that admitted dreary daylight with the green window-shade up. Tony saw that there was a bottle of whisky standing on the small table. When the well-dressed man turned with the two glasses of whisky in hand, he said, in a distinct English accent, "Well, hello, lads. Like a drink?"

The man stepped forward, smiling, crinkly, offering the drinks. Harry was shutting the door behind them.

Then Harry turned and slapped the drinks out of the man's hands.

The shot-glasses went flying; one bounced off a full-length mirror on the door of a wardrobe and spilled the smell of splattered whisky.

Grabbing the man by the lapels, Harry threw him to the floor. Then, collapsing to his knees, he straddled the horrified, startled Englishman, sitting on his chest. His defenceless victim threw his hands up to ward off the blows that Harry was firing, but Harry kept pummeling him, left, right, left, right; then he jumped up, to start kicking him, and Tony grabbed his friend by the elbow to pull him off his feet. "Stop, Harry!—that's enough—come on, now—do you wanna kill him?"

Harry had spittle on his chin, his hair was wild, his hat had fallen off, he was breathing hard, his eye glared like firelight. He was still straddling the stricken Englishman at his feet.

Then, vehemently, Harry yanked his elbow away from Tony's iron grip. "Now give me your wallet!" he yelled at the supine man, who was using his heel on the carpet to inch his body backwards, trying to get away from Harry at the same time that, propped on one elbow, with his other hand, he was pulling his billfold from the inside pocket of his suitcoat. "Please—please—take it!"

Harry snatched the billfold, ripped the folding cash out of it, and tossed it, flapping empty, at the Englishman on the floor, who turned his head and buried his face in his hands in shame.

On the way back to work in the auto, Tony said nothing and just stared straight ahead. Harry said, "Don't you wanna know what that was all about?"

Tony did not reply.

Harry began to laugh, a strange laugh—not a laughing at something funny, but a defensive laughter, guffawing hoarsely at the wildness, the horridness, the disgust, the pity of–of everything.

They never spoke of it again.

A year went by before Harry dared to try his initiation rites on Tony again, and in the meantime, the two friends had developed separate territories at 202.

Tony found that he truly preferred to carve out his own little empire within the factory walls, and drew the boundary line around Harry's office, down on the first floor.

Outside of Tony, the only male employees who worked for *Spritzka Ladies' Wear,* were on the second floor, in the cutter's room. That was the make-or-break part of the operation. Your profit margin could be won or lost by the scraps thrown under the big table on the cutting-room floor. Cloth-cutters were the most highly trained, experienced skilled-labor. Throughout the garment district, the cloth-cutters were considered the aristocrats of the industry.

But you could hire untrained young teenage girls, unskilled labor, with no previous experience, pay them accordingly, and turn them into stitchers, because all they had to do was to sit at the machine, push the material through, and perform the same identical piece-work operation over and over again all day long. They got so they could have done it with their eyes closed, or while holding a conversation with the girl at the next machine on either side, or both at once—which was strictly forbidden, because it slowed everyone down. That was one of the main jobs that Tony and the floor-ladies had—patrolling the stitchers on the top two floors to enforce the *No Talking* rule.

It was a firing offense, and as much as Tony hated to do it, he had to—if you let one get away with it, next thing you know, all the girls were complaining about your favoritism. Tony tried to get the floor-ladies to do this kind of dirty work for him, as much as he could.

But sometimes, he was stuck, and on the spot, so he employed the three strikes and you're out rule—"just like baseball." Usually that worked, because it gave a girl a chance to mend her habits, or try to curb her talkativeness, and it seemed fair, and spared a lot of heartache for everyone, on both sides.

But then again, sometimes a girl just didn't work out. Maybe she couldn't be quiet. Maybe she wasn't expecting that they would be so strict. Perhaps she found the whole thing unnatural. For this one, Tony would suggest that maybe a parting of the ways was best for both.

There were a million reasons why people got into this work, and some stayed, some didn't. Some just couldn't cut it. The roar of all those electric-powered sewing machines going at once on the factory floor was deafening. It was cold in the winter, sitting in one place all day long, never moving. In summer, you quickly found out why they called it a sweatshop. All those human beings trapped in a box with never a breeze and windows that, half the time, didn't work. The doors were always locked, and the girls knew it. It was the same all over the industry, everybody knew that, and it was never going to change. Sometimes claustrophobia set in on a girl, and panic was always only a stitch away.

There was a lot of turnover, and it all fell on Tony to teach the new ones, and keep everything running without interruption. It was the largest part of his job, and took a lot of his time, standing over someone's shoulder, encouraging, guiding, directing, coaching them—he would pull out the chair and demonstrate himself how it should be done. His value to Harry Spritzka Tony proved a hundred times over in this way.

Often, Tony would stand back near the windows on the third or fourth floor, and just drink in the sights. It gave him a sense of accomplishment and satisfaction. Unconsciously, the order and layout of things appealed to him. You were standing in a seemingly vast room, with rows of straight benches spaced across the width, running lengthwise from your feet all the way to a distant point. It was like looking down rows of straight railroad tracks at Penn Station. Everything was symmetrical. You could walk back and forth or up and down or circle the wagons, your viewpoint constantly altering, but the same symmetry was evident at each point. The windows encased in between tall piers of red brick were tall themselves, and admitted acres of daylight into the room—on sunny days you could see bars of sunlight, adjusting their angles as the day progressed, with clouds of circling dust-motes dancing in them, which gave the light-bars a texture almost palpable. Fabrics were always shedding lint that would stick to your hands and clothing, and somehow they evaporated cloth-dust, too, which rose into the room like steam from a pond on a cool morning. On a grey day, there was still more light coming in from outside the building through the tall windows than the amount of light provided by the electric bulbs. These ran off the same wiring running along the rafters as the cables which descended from the overheads to each work station from the overheads to run the sewing machines—so electric light was spaced at intervals that guaranteed every stitcher had enough light to work by at her station. Often, standing back by the windows, overseeing, Tony would feel a deep-seated sensation, transcending all thought, that this was how his life was meant to be, this was where he belonged: in charge of his own little fiefdom where he was the undisputed, indispensable man-in-charge.

It was a far cry from the old days of working in the cramped unheated cold-water-flat of Uncle Eugenio's, with one bare bulb, and a sink full of dishes at your elbow, and a hot coal-stove pumping out warmth that never reached the corners, while the humid overheating of all those people elbow to elbow with not enough space to stand up, suffocated you. And dark, dark all the time, never any light.

He was doing what he was trained by his father to do from the time he was seven years old, the traditional age of reason back in the hidebound, priest-ridden Old Country, with its feudal class-divisions; a society where customs centuries old dictated your every move, yet—gave values to your daily existence founded in, built on, a thousand years of thought and experience—*maybe that was it.*

Being in charge, and yet keeping the respect of those under him—*maybe that was it.*

He felt no need to be mean or flaunt an authoritarian manner in people's faces; instead, he fed off the respect that he gained when he was helpful to them. He could see it in their eyes. They were grateful. They passed beyond the labels they might have put on him, such as boss, supervisor, overseer, and perceived him warmly as some kind of mentor, coach or even friend; they saw him for what he was—*Tony's good people*—"listen to Tony, he will help you"–*he's one of us.*

That was as far as they could get, and all he needed. A moment that passes between two human beings. A hand on a shoulder. A smile, a shrug, a kind word. It made people like you. And if they liked you, they would do anything for you.

To Tony, it was like music. Like him and his mandolin.

Elusive moments of solo glory would come and go, when it was just him and his notes, echoing from a plucked string.

But now he had assumed the position of the maestro. He was the conductor of the orchestra, and his stitchers on the manufacturing floor were his players, and what he made out of their back and forth was—harmony. Now Tony was the one with the baton in his hand, whose children adored him, without knowing how or why: a man of respect.

There was a glory in the garment industry, too, a different kind of glory though it may be. You could make a living, support a family, and put clothes on the backs of thousands, maybe more, who would not otherwise have them. Imagine the good you were doing, for everyone—if you want to look at it that way. It was a universe unto itself. It was more than an occupation, it was a way of life.

For it was said that clothes made the man.

As long as you could keep Harry Spritzka in his place. "No interference. You stay in your office and out here, on the manufacturing floor—I run things. That's the only way this is going to work."

Then there were the cutters on the second floor. The nobility. The artists. The craftsmen, so jealous of their prerogatives. A strictly male domain. Women were barred from the profession. It was a male preserve. An enclave of privilege.

Tony never ever tried to tell them what to do. Most of them were a lot older than he was—and anyway there were only two or three on staff for an operation the size of Harry's. Would it kill you to keep them happy? Of course not. But was it essential? A good cloth-cutter who knew his business was worth his weight in gold. Their performance was the whole difference between profit and loss–and if you pissed them off, they could even sabotage your business. Because it was a matter of fractions of inches.

The bulk cloth you needed to make your orders came in the back of the building to the loading dock in bolts. You had to take these bolts and unroll them out on the huge tables on the second floor, and layer them, 10 or 15 layers thick. Everything smooth and even. Then the cloth-cutter had to take the paper patterns of the parts of the garments you were making, lay them out on the topmost layer, and figure out the puzzle.

He had to cut all 15 layers identical—but in such a way as to minimize the waste.

Sure, you could throw out the patterns, a sleeve over here, a tail over there, a collar over here—but how close together could you fit them? That was the magic in what the cutters did. Could you fit the patterns in all their shapes on the surface of a flattened roll? The bolt unrolled on the table could be anywhere from 40 to 100 yards long, and possibly as little as 36 inches wide, or up to 54 inches wide, depending on the type of material.

That was a vast area, and you would see the cutters crawling on their hands and knees on top of the cutting table fitting their patterns, or leaning over from the waist and reaching in as far as they could over the sides.

Every inch of waste they had to throw away was completely useless—and yet the owner had paid for that amount of wastage, and now it was gone and he could not get his money back.

And that was the difference between profit and loss in this industry.

Although Tony did not make himself seen on the second floor, Harry had to.

When Harry was putting together his operation, he had thought of the parallels between the factory floor and a ballteam. He was the owner, and he would pay for the bats, balls, uniforms and salaries. Tony was his manager on the field. So Harry could afford to let his manager have his own scope in daily operations—but he could not let him pick the team.

For that, and the most essential pieces, he went to Litvak, in his father's shop. Litvak told him who to hire for cutters—if he could get them—if he could pay—or if not, if they were unavailable, Litvak would get the second-stringers for him.

So Harry had guidance in his hiring, from a priceless old-timer, the kind who gave it away for nothing, out of a sense of duty, out of humanity. Also, you could trust Litvak to keep his lips sealed. And therefore Harry did not have to go through his father.

Between Litvak and his brother Robert, Harry managed.

But once he opened, he could not bring himself to place his whole trust in these same highly-recommended people, the cloth-cutters. One thing he made sure of—his three hirings for cloth-cutters were all Jews. He could not place any trust at all in anyone else. He had to feel that he could draw on their religious convictions, their identity as fellow commiserators, to bolster his own youth and brashness, as against their age and experience. This was not an unskilled position. You had to bring to the cutting table solid training and, preferably, years of experience and success. So they would be a lot older than he, and automatically inclined to dismiss Harry. He had to counterweight that with some sense of, "after all—we're in this together—we're all Jews here."

But then he still worried—will they get along together—is three too many—will I end up with two who do all the work, and a *schlepper*? So, he could not leave them alone. He would wander in and out—try to talk to them—try to make friends. He would stand and watch—he would ask their advice. In the end, he hovered over them. At least they would know he had his eye out.

In this way Tony and Harry each carved out a piece of the pie for themselves. And they were able to get along. They did not fight, because they did not talk about what bothered them.

Underneath it all, somehow, after all they had been through, each one thought he could not do it, that is, live his life, without the other. And neither one of them could figure out why. It just turned out that way. They had to accept it. They had no choice.

In this way, another year went by, and finally Harry knew he had to resurrect his mercy mission for his friend Tony. But this time he would have to finish the job once and for all. He knew he wasn't going to get any chance at a third strike. So he hit on a plan to make sure he got Tony good and drunk first, before they got to the real business of the evening.

Harry set the plot afoot on a Saturday night after their usual afternoon off at the races, when he proposed they should go for a drive.

"To where?" said Tony, suspiciously.

In the car, Harry was trying to keep everything offhand, make it look casual. He knew that Tony had been acting standoffish for a long time now, that he was wounded by a breach of trust coming between them—but it happened that another circumstance came to his aid, strictly by chance.

Tony had won big at the track that afternoon, so maybe the wheels were greased, and he could get Tony to skid.

"Don't worry," he said. "I'm not gonna take you down to Chinatown." Tony shot a look at him.

"You know, Harry, really—I'm tired—it's been a long week—I just wanna go home."

Tony looked away, but he didn't really see the passing scene—he was picturing coming home to the cousins and his aunt and uncle loaded down with cold cuts and Italian pastries, and walking in with his arms bulging, saying, *oh, you know, I kinda hit it lucky today* . . .

"Hey—Tony—don't give me that look—I know better than that—I'm your friend, remember?"

"I just don't feel like it tonight."

"Well, then do it for me! Humor me, for once."

Harry got no response. Tony wouldn't let him see his face—he kept his head turned.

"Okay. Be like that. You know, you're like a girl—she's trying to say no, 'cause she don't want you to know she really wants to."

He nudged Tony's elbow. Making funny wasn't working.

"Oh. I get it. I see the picture now. You got lucky today, so now you're holding onto it like a goddam Scotchman. Yeah. I get it."

Tony noticed they had missed the turn for the East Side. Harry was heading for midtown. He was up to something, but Tony couldn't figure out what.

He realized first of all that he was in no position to insist. Tony liked it only too well when they went out riding. He always felt privileged—he felt that everyone noticed them—it made him feel good. He knew that without Harry he wouldn't be surveying things from any lofty perch—and whatever else Harry was or wasn't, Tony worked damn hard for him, and he had earned these perquisites. Sometimes it was awfully hard to imagine giving them up.

And then—one way or another, usually Harry got what he wanted.

Now he was telling Tony, "Look. You're tired. So we'll stop for a cup of espresso, and you'll wake up. Tony! We'll make it a special night. We'll go to the Plaza—whaddya say to that? We'll go take a gander at the quality. We'll have something nice to eat—I heard they got a new shipment of Italian wines in. Come on, Tony. Whaddya say?"

The Plaza was the height of sophistication, the destination of the moment. It had just opened, and everyone wanted to be seen there. Twenty stories, with a façade in the elaborate style of a French chateau, with soaring mansard roofs, its main entrance faced on Fifth Avenue at the Grand Army Plaza in Central Park South. When they walked through, Harry said to Tony, "You know they're charging $2.50 a night to stay in a room here?—and they're booked!"

They strolled through, marveling. Tony was glad they had dressed for a day at the races. All of a sudden he felt on top of the world—without coffee.

Harry said, "I hear they got butler service 24 hours a day!"

There were literally waves of people passing back and forth, like traffic on Second Avenue. The whole town had turned out. It seemed for once that all the sightseers were not greenhorns, but native New Yorkers. They had flocked here on a Saturday night as if it were one of those new automobile showrooms, only fancier, more sophisticated and suave.

Harry and Tony meandered through the Grand Ballroom, the Champagne Bar, the Rose Club, and the Persian Room. When they had finally arrived at the Terrace Room, Tony was amazed—there was Maestro Siragusa and his little orchestra of accordion, violins, cello, trumpets, clarinets and cornets— complete with trombones! Tony could not get over it. He was scheduled as usual to be there tomorrow afternoon in Mulberry Park. So—this was the Maestro's real orchestra! Tony could see they were the well-seasoned, professional musicians, older men with families, members of the musician's union, that formed the best that Italy had brought to New York Harbor. He felt a surge of native, Neapolitan pride—to think that this band had been selected to play the opening of the Plaza. Of course, there were other bands, other ensembles and orchestras, one in every lounge of the Plaza—but to be considered one of that company—and for the Terrace Room!

In the Champagne Bar, Harry had the prime rib, with trimmings, and Tony a 12-ounce tenderloin. Harry had onions, Tony had mushrooms. The steak was juicy and tender, the sauce delicate and lasting on the tongue. When they pushed back from the table, they lit cigars; Tony had recently felt he could afford store-bought cigarettes, and his smoking was becoming a habit; they finished their wine and ordered coffee, when into the door of the Champagne Bar behind them walked old friends from Little Italy—Mousey, Knickers, Il Gatto and Long-Johns—whose real names were Federico, Giovanni, Piero and Francesco—or Freddy, John, Peter, and Frankie, which, in fact, they preferred—they were dressed to the nines, no second-hand hand-me-downs, no nicknames tonight, because, after all, this was *The Plaza*.

Tony was not really that surprised to see them, as he had been able for some time now to get Freddy and Frankie hired on at 202 on the loading dock operation, where they handled supplies coming in and finished racks going out—but to see them out for the night, with the other two—here? What was up?

Into the other door at the far end of the Champagne Bar walked Harry's old pals from Rivington Street.

Harry had a wicked grin on. "Surprised?" Tony did not know what to say.

"It's a reunion, Tony! All the guys that were with us from the very beginning—you remember? You remember how we met? Everybody else does! My gang, and your gang!"

And so the party began. They did not spend the entire evening at the Plaza. Far from it. For one thing, the drinks were too expensive, for another the company too polite—they were young guys out to have a good time, out for wine, women and song, and for once, Tony, with money from the track in his pocket, wasn't telling himself, *I don't feel like it.* They passed over Times Square—that was the Broadway theater crowd. They avoided Chinatown, at Harry's specific behest. His plan was working as long as, with each bar they hit, Tony was getting a little more inebriated, but still on his feet.

They ended up on Allen Street on the Lower East Side where the vaudeville was a little spicier than it was in the Yiddish theater row on Second Avenue. Harry steered them to the flamboyant, *déshabillé* district. "I'm thinking of getting into ladies' undergarments," Harry joked. "I need to do a little research."

The Italian boys didn't mind, they figured the Jewish girls were easy—not pure, saintly and untouchable like the good girls of their neighborhood. Of course, they had their own bad girls, too. *Face it, a woman, she's either a Madonna or a whore, right?* They knew that there were Italian girls walking the streets—or that you could visit one of the Don's parlor houses any time of the day or night, in Little Italy. It was just that you didn't wanna be like a tenement-building cat and piss in your own back hall.

The Jewish boys called the Little Italy guys spaghetti-benders and other fragrant names. The Italians called them names back—potato-mashers, and other more monosyllabic epithets. Kike, guinea, sheeny, wop—it was all the same to them—it was Saturday night in New York, they were out to have a good time, they had all already imbibed more than a little of what was good for them.

They were passing open doors in the dark on Allen Street. Lights in windows invited them inside.

Music, dancing, drinking, having a fling, letting loose all inhibitions.

The Jews don't mind if you're potting their sister, the Italian boys were thinking. *Now with us it's different.* And the Jewish boys were thinking, *why would I wanna dip my wick into something I can't be sure they're unclean or not, you know?* And both groups were thinking, *anyhow, it's nothing to be ashamed of, but on the other hand, you wouldn't go home and tell your mother, now, would you?*

The last thing Tony heard before he passed out with his head on the bar was Harry saying, "Tony! Did I ever tell you about Tillie the Toenail? Jesus Christ—what that woman can do with a toenail!— Tony, you would not believe it!"

When Tony woke up he had his head leaning back on the seat-cushion of Harry's Hispano-Suiza, and Harry was passing his finger back and forth under Tony's nose.

"Tony. Tony. What's that smell like? Huh? Do you know where that finger's been, Tony?"

Tony opened the car-door and fell out on the pavement. He staggered to his feet.

Harry was pulling him up.

"Tony! Tony, it's time you bit off a piece for yourself. Now get yourself turned around—that's it— get headed up the steps–."

"Where swee goin' now, Sarry?"

"What's the matter with you, you drunken *putz!* Don't you realize I'm doin' you a favor?"

Tony had broken away and lurched back to the car where he had to grab on to hold himself up.

"Tony! It's all paid for! My treat! All you gotta do—!"

Harry stopped himself. He realized that trying to reason with this drunken mess was getting him nowhere. He had to say something that was gonna get under his skin—he had to come up with something that was like—like—*a firecracker up his ass!*

He grabbed Tony by the collar and put his nose right in Tony's muzzle.

"Tony—you're startin' to get me worried. That's right. Worried. That there's something wrong with you, you know? That, maybe, you just don't like girls, you know?"

"What's youz sssstalkin' about, Harry?"

"Tony—I wouldn't wanna find out you're leanin' the other way on me, Tony."

"Allsright! Allsright! Leave me alone, you sonna ma bitch."

Tony broke off and wobbled toward the stairs. Harry heaved a prayer to the skies and the air came out of him like a deflated balloon. Tony was actually pulling himself up the steps. Harry could not believe it—then Tony turned and looked woefully at him.

Harry had lost all patience. "Go on, go on!" He waved both arms at Tony. "She'll show you what to do, ya *schmuck!*"

For a while Harry stood there breathing in and out as if he'd just run a sprint. Finally, he fumbled around in the darkness trying to find which pocket he had left his cigar stub in. He lit up and leaned back against his car to wait. He smiled to himself and said out loud, "Holy Moses!" He didn't have to wait long. It seemed he had barely closed his eyes and started to take a nap on his feet and started thinking about how nice it would be to climb in the back of the car and just lay back and close his eyes—when Tony came stumbling down the steps—not the same way he had gone in, but practically sobered-up and rearranging his necktie.

"Well—did you do it?"

"I did it. And now she wants to marry me!"

"Aw, hell—she tells all the boys that! She's hoping some fool might fall for it sometime."

"No, sheriously, she means it! I had a bitch of a time getting away from her. She wants me to take her away from a shife of lame and make a honest woman outta her!"

"Aw, hell–she tells all the guys that!"

"You know shummthing, Harry Ssshplitzka? I think I hate you. In fuct—I mean—shit–I can't even shay it–Mother of God, you spucking sonna ma bitch, God help me, but I hate your spucking guts!"

"I love you, too, you stupid guinea."

Chapter 12

The Uprising Of The Women

Every time Tony turned around, he heard Harry asking "How many pieces?"

It was the same with the floor-ladies. Harry wanted a strict accounting in the morning, and again in the afternoon, before six, and if they worked late, again at the end of 14 or 15 hours, at eight or nine or ten at night. How to increase, that was the problem. It would not leave him alone. Harry always wanted more.

Of course, he had great ideas, of that he was convinced. His concepts were superior. His ideas always worked. He knew before he ever began this enterprise that it would work. He had some kind of gift, the way a salesman has an instinct that he can get you to buy. In his own territory, he was without peer. All he could do to explain this to himself was compare his way of doing things to his father's, or his brother's.

"My brother Robert has absolutely no interest in clothing, although," he told Tony, "we grew up in the same house— where it was the family business! That amazes me. My brother Robert is strictly real estate. Louis, my father, he has the passion for garment-making, like me, but his ideas are hopelessly outdated. He's so much the European Jew, worrying what the well-to-do Fifth Avenue mob, and, yes, the *goy chintzers,* are gonna think of him."

Tony had heard it all before. Sometimes he was glad to just get away to 62nd Street after work, because any leisure time spent with Harry, which was most of his time, was taken up with nothing but shop-talk—it was Harry's obsession.

"You know, what the problem is, is with my name. It's not commercial—"Spritzka." They can't spell it, they can't say it. Sure, it's fine to file papers here at 202 calling this place *Spritzka Ladies' Wear.* After all, I'm proud of what we done here. But it's not gonna do to hang that name over the door on the factory outlet on the first floor. And this location on West 37th is horrible. The whole city's my marketplace. I need to reach my customers. I'm producing 20,000 pieces a week, and I gotta transport them to retail all over town, owned by others, some of them my own competitors, and for what?—to make *them* rich? I need a name, Tony. Come up with something for me, Tony."

"You're the genius, Harry."

Harry shook his head and made a gesture with his hands like choking Tony. "You know, sometimes."

The problem was consuming him. Harry was a numbers man. He knew the machines were putting out a capacity of 3,000 stitches a minute—per machine. Why wasn't he getting more finished pieces?

He did not worry about making a quality product. He figured that the middle of the road was the widest boulevard you could find, with the most people in it. He wanted quality sufficient for the average buyer, paying what they could afford—that was the way to the biggest numbers. He was paying other people good money to worry about quality, that was not his job. His top two cutters were making a fortune. They were on salary at $20 a week! The third he paid $18, and the man was falling over faint at the thought! Even Tony LaStoria, at a salary of $12.50 a week, was raking in a princely sum.

Because of Tony's payscale, Harry had been forced to pay the floor-ladies $13 week—they were older, more experienced, and frankly, tougher. They were Harry's enforcers—Tony was his persuader. The floor-ladies were strict and unyielding and merciless on the girls—"You there—never mind fixin' your collar on my time! It ain't six o'clock yet!" Or, "You know where you're headed? Out the door! So, get movin', and watch your step. I got my eye on you." Or, "Your production is lousy. You can't cut it. You're fired!" They were a cross between a bath-house attendant and a truant officer, and their vocabulary was as raw as a stevedore's. Tony was a coaxer, and far too tender-hearted.

Harry himself managed the design department, and he saved himself a bundle by copying everything out of the newspaper advertising of his competitors, who were so fond of artistic line-drawings of buxom women in shirtwaists. But the problem of selling what he produced would not leave Harry alone. He had to think of some better way. He was charging the girls for everything he could— the thread they used, the needles, the electricity that drove their Singer sewing machines, even the chairs they sat on! It all came out of their pay packets at the end of the week. But those numbers were just petty change–he was only skimming the surface! And he had to listen to complaints from them to boot!

One day one of the girls stopped him in the street. He was outraged. She started in on her ailing mother at home, and how tough it was to make ends meet—just like all of them—whining, sniveling, weak-kneed creatures that expected the world to provide them with a living, instead of the other way around— "Didn't you hear, Mister Spritzka—Lincoln freed the slaves!"

"Listen," said Harry, "count yourself lucky I don't make you buy your own sewing machine and carry it on your back to work!"

"Well, mister, that's just ridiculous!"

"Is it, now? Tell me—didn't you have your own machine at home? Back when you were working out of your flat, with your poor sick mother, and your dying father, with the consumption, from workin' in the sewers? You bet your rump-feathers you did! And bought and paid for with your own money. Else you were out of business. But, now—when I *give* you a job— you expect *me* to assume that expense!"

Harry had to walk away before he choked on his own spleen.

When he was in his office feeling bedeviled, he would throw his legs on the desk, peer at the young lady he had at a typewriter punching out invoices and bills of lading, and twirl a pencil in his fingers. Or he would take some scrap cloth and cut out circles with the pinking shears. Somehow the crown-shaped cut-outs with the many-pointed teeth helped him to think. One day, it just came to him— just like a bolt out of the setting suns that streamed in the plate-glass windows of his showroom in blinding, golden shafts and sun-bursts.

For a long time he had been thinking about Buster Brown shoes. It frustrated and yet fascinated him that someone else had thought of a way to create a buying frenzy before he did. He had not yet solved the problem—and someone else had beat him to it. And it all began with a cartoon in the Sunday papers! Buster Brown was a cheerful, fun-loving young idiot with a streak of mischief, in the comic strips, a girlfriend named Mary Jane, and a talking dog called Tige. The whole thing was patent nonsense, because none of the adults could hear the dog talk, only Buster Brown. But it caught the public's fancy and became a sensation overnight.

Then came the World's Fair of St Louis in 1904. The papers were syndicating the comic strip, and St Louis was a big shoe manufacturing center. All of a sudden they were selling shoes for children named after Buster Brown, and the company making them hired a child actor to impersonate the cartoon character in the flesh. Then they put him on a train and sent him right around the whole country, from Chicago east, complete with his talking dog and his girl, Mary Jane—and if you bought a pair of Buster Browns for your kid, the kid got a free booklet of comic strip reprints.

It was a sensation. They built it up big like the circus coming to town well ahead of Buster's appearance in your little village—direct from the World's Fair in St Louis!–and they attracted crowds at the train station—and sold a lot of shoes. What an angle they had! Harry believed that whoever thought that one up was not only a genius, they ought to let him run the country!

Harry might have missed this entire phenomenon had it not been for accidentally noticing a shop in Hester Street called Jakob's Workingmen's Clothing.

Not only was 1904 the year of the World's Fair, it also brought a disaster that rocked the entire Lower East Side, when the General Slocum caught fire and sank in the East River, and over a thousand people, Germans, from St Mark's Lutheran Church, died from drowning, trapped in the sinking paddle-wheeler.

Harry was not really affected by or even aware of the loss of life, he didn't like Germans anyway—but it resulted in a mass exodus of those people moving away from the neighborhood to relocate to the Upper East Side, far away from their awful memories of lost loved ones, who had set out on a holiday excursion organized by their church, and instead, drowned.

When the people moved away, so did the shops that catered to them. The next year, 1905, another disaster, this one far, far away, across oceans, seas and continents, had an equal impact on the Lower East Side—the Russians managed to lose their war with the Japanese out on the far Pacific rim of Asia. But when their defeated army came trudging home, all hell broke loose. There was evidently a major uprising of some kind in St Petersburg and Moscow, and the Tsar called out his Cossacks. But worse than that, the defeated soldiers decided the way to take out their grievances and anger and problems was on the backs of the bowed-down Russian Jews, and a wave of pogroms swept over the country, which then resulted in a wave of fleeing Russian Jews landing homeless and destitute in the Lower East Side.

It was one of these refugees who set up shop in one of the abandoned storefronts left empty by the General Slocum Germans.

One day Harry stood in front of this shop, having gone there as a new source of outlet for his pieces, and he was amazed. The red-colored Yiddish writing on the storefront glass spelled out

Jakob's Workingmen's Clothing

But on the fascia above the windows there was Buster Brown, from the comic strip, instantly recognizable, with his golden pageboy locks curling down round his shoulders, his wide-brimmed red sailor's cap, his royal blue bunched-up neckerchief, and his arm around his grinning dog, Tige—all executed in a hand-painted wooden logo, that told you everything you needed to know in a single glance, without any writing except the words, "Buster Brown."

What a crazy world, thought Harry. Here's one of these Russian *potzes*, infected with all that radical socialist bullshit—joining forces with the latest in American capitalism—to sell a pair of kid's shoes!

Harry was sitting at his desk with his pinking shears and the late afternoon sun, picturing himself standing in front of this storefront, when the solution came to him. "Hey, Sybil," he yelled at the typewriter girl, "what I need is a brand of my own! That's just what I need! I want you to work on that right away."

"What are you talking about, Harry?"

"I'm talkin' about Buster Brown shoes, that's what I'm talkin' about. Ah! I don't know why I waste my breath." He jumped up. "Tell Tony, and the floor-ladies, I went out. I'll be back when I'm back."

He left the Hispano-Suiza parked in front of the shop, and started down the street, towards midtown, striding purposefully, head down, hands in his pockets.

He kept repeating—Buster Brown, Buster Brown, Buster—Richard Paul! First part's got that little sing-song—then—bang!—with a thud!

His hands came out of his pockets, and he punched his right fist into his left palm.

He decided he needed a big juicy steak and a nice bottle of imported wine, and he veered his steps toward the Plaza.

Yes! He would sit down and treat himself to a big juicy steak with all the trimmings and gloat and glory in his triumph of vision—for by this time he had pictured not just a brand name plastered on a storefront, but an entire methodology of how to market his pieces, including convenient locations on streetcar lines, newspaper advertising headlined by his brand name, lines of clothing with labels carrying his brand name—and why not men's wear, as well as women's?

Instantly, his stores became twice as big, his inventory doubled, just by adding the other gender—why hadn't he thought of this before! His eye swept over the magisterial sight of women's on one side of the floor, men's on the other—and don't forget children's sizes! But—not like a department store—only one product! Clothes! *Clothes make the man!* Clothes make the woman and the child, too. What do people need to live? Only three things! Three basic things! Food—shelter—and clothing! And I got the market on one of 'em!

I'm gonna make wheelbarrows full o' cash

Along with the name came a plan. A series of stores—not located on West 37th—location, location, location. Why—why couldn't you have two stores in Manhattan–one—here, at the shop, and one say, on Second Avenue, in the department store row, alongside the big boys. And maybe—one across the river in Brooklyn! Yeah! Why not? What about Jersey, too? They got a shoreline over there! There's Hoboken, there's—

Harry by now had become so excited that he was opening entire new factories, to produce his men's lines, and children's. And Robert Spritzka, his beloved partner, his own brother, was buying up the buildings to house them in!

Harry said to himself, *I'm going to the Plaza, I'm gonna sit myself down, and I'm gonna have the biggest, juiciest steak you ever saw!*

People in the street seeing him charging toward them with his arms raised up to the heavens heard him shouting, "I am a genius! I am!"

Harry Spritzka enjoyed his steak, in the Oak Room Bar, and topped it off with a snifter of Pernod, recommended by the bartender, Alphonse, and when he put down the snifter at the end, he felt glowing.

He hardly touched the surface of the sidewalk as he walked back to his office, twenty-five blocks and more. He felt leisurely and with his hands in his pockets, strolled, gazing at the tall buildings, taking in the world—he felt he could have balanced the globe like a teacup in the palm of his hand.

While Harry Spritzka went into his office next to the showroom through one door from the street, Tony LaStoria came in the other door which entered from the factory floor.

Tony spoke first. "Harry—we got trouble."

Harry did not hear him. He started in saying, "Tony, I want you to sit down for this. I gotta tell you something, and we gotta get started right now—there's no time to lose—Tony, we gotta expand. Now, here's what I want you to do—"

"Harry—sit down—I gotta talk to you—I think—we got trouble."

Harry looked at him, dumbfounded. "Whaddya talking about, ya dumb wop!"

"The girls, Harry."

"What about the goddam girls?"

"They been talkin'."

"So, what else is new? What else they got to do with their little pea-brains—yak, yak, yak!"

"I been hearin' things, Harry."

"What things?"

"They're talkin' about walkin' out!"

"Walkin' out! What are they, crazy? How can they do this to me! Just when—you tell me who, and we'll fire 'em! And that'll be the end of that!"

"Not this time, Harry."

"Look, Tony—when hasn't this happened before? It never works! They don't know what they're doin'! Let 'em walk! In five minutes, I'll have the whole crew replaced—why, girls like them, they're a dime a dozen! Their own sisters'll come flockin' down here to take their jobs off 'em!"

"This time it's different, Harry."

"Are they talkin' union?"

"It ain't just that."

"Tony, I swear to God—I pay you good money to keep the union outta here! Why didn't you let me know about this before!"

"There wasn't nothin' to tell you, Harry! This just came up! It's not like it's been goin' on. Why do ya think I'm tellin' you now? 'Cause I'm doin' my job, that's why!"

"A wildcat, huh? Ah!—they don't know what they're doin'. They got nothin'! Whaddya so worried about!"

"Harry—the talk is about takin' the whole district out!"

"Whaddya mean—the whole district! Are you insane!"

"There's a meeting on, for Thursday night. At Cooper Union, Harry."

"That's a big hall. Why so big?"

"I dunno, Harry."

"Well—we gotta find out! Who else is gonna be there?"

"Looks like Gompers, and the A.F. of L."

"Those shit-heads!"

"Yeah—those ones."

"Fuckin' Christ! Tony—I want you there. I can't go. They'd hoot me outa there. They hate my guts. Tony—you gotta be my eyes and ears."

"What makes you think they'll let me in?"

"You're their pal, Tony!"

"I'm not so sure about that, Harry."

"Look—just play big-brother-Tony—just watchin' out for his little guinea sisters—know what I mean? But, Tony—ya gotta do this for me. Just now, at this moment, we can't afford to be takin' chances. Are you with me? And—Tony—ya gotta think on one thing—*whose side are you on?*"

Tony was there, on the night of November 22, 1909, in Cooper Union—and for something so eventful, that marked both an ending and a beginning in the lives of so many, the meeting began in a remarkably uneventful manner and proceeded at a humdrum, droning-on-and-on, meandering pace that took all the wind out of the sails of the three thousand young seamstresses, most of them still in their teens, whose palpable anticipation drained away over the course of two hours of endless speeches from the men on the platform.

Fifty years earlier Abraham Lincoln had denounced slavery in this very same damp and drafty, vast basement auditorium, and the three thousand girls came that night expecting something as stirring as that, thinking of themselves, calling themselves, "wage-slaves," a terminology they had picked up from the many soap-box orators who had brought with them the slogans and battle-cries of the 1905 Russian Revolution.

The people on the stage were all men. They were not garment workers, but union leaders, nearly all well-dressed and well-groomed, indistinguishable from the factory owners themselves, people such as A.F. of L. President Samuel Gompers, who had been invited as the guest of honor for the evening, a man in a suit and tie and high-top patent leather shoes and a funny cap he wore that resembled a Turkish fez. With his portly demeanor and his longish hair bulging out over the back collar of his suit, Gompers could have been the ragman driving his horse-wagon down your street, except that this ragman did not holler and gesticulate, he presided.

The others on the podium were equally celebrities in the eyes of the union-organizers and socialist press that crammed the front and sides of the room. The Chairman of the meeting was Benjamin Feigenbaum, the editor of the Jewish daily *Forvitz,* who droned on in Yiddish in speech after speech while the girls in the hall grew restless.

Others on the stage, like Big Bill Haywood, were invited guests, but he was from Montana, did not understand Yiddish, and represented the IWW, at that time mostly a miners' union of the western copper mines, remote from the concerns of the streets of the Lower East Side.

Then a girl suddenly stood up. She was well-known to her sisters as the most outspoken girl in Local 25 of the I.L.G.W.U.— the International Ladies Garment Workers' Union.

That did not mean a great deal to the men on the stage, as they knew that Local 25 had only 100 members, and $4 in its treasury.

But when this girl stood up and said, in Yiddish, "I want to say a few words," people began shouting, "Get up on the platform!"

"Let her up on the stage!"

She did get up on the platform, and she did continue in Yiddish. "I am a working girl, one of those who came tonight to speak out against intolerable conditions. I am tired of listening to speakers who talk in generalities—I offer a resolution that a general strike be declared. Now!"

The hall erupted. Every girl there stood up, cheering. A wave of excitement swept over them. Tony was skulking down in the back of the hall with a slouchy tweed cap, like those worn by Tammany poll-workers, pulled down over his eyes, trying to remain out of the way, unnoticed and unobtrusive. Most of the cheering girls were Jewish and used Yiddish every day, but the minority in the hall were Italian girls, some of them from 202 West 37th, and they turned to translate to Tony, with their eyes bright, and their lips moving. Tony could not hear them, the uproar in the hall was so loudly immense, but, like them, he knew just enough Yiddish to understand—and anyway, the meaning was unmistakable.

Tony was looking at an uprising. He was witnessing a rebellion, and who knew where that would lead.

He suddenly understood a great many things that had nothing to do with his former life, which he knew instantly, was gone.

It was like standing there when the ocean broke in on the streets of the Lower East Side and overwhelmed them in a flood that drowned everything in sight.

It was power—raw power. And in its own way, electric.

Feigenbaum on the stage was equally carried away. He stood up and cried, "Do you mean it in good faith? Will you take the old Jewish oath?"

Thousands of hands shot up.

Feigenbaum recited. "If I turn traitor to the cause I now pledge, may this hand wither from the arm I raise!"

A thousand voices repeated the oath.

Tony left. He had heard enough. He met Harry waiting in a tavern down the street. He told him, "I don't know what's gonna happen tomorrow, but I know something happened tonight."

In the morning, Harry told Tony to get the bat out of the car. "What bat?"

"In the back seat."

Harry no longer had the Hispano-Suiza. His new car was a personal monolith, an Edison Touring Car, enormous because the electric batteries in the back gave it the stern of a battleship.

Harry didn't like it, he was thinking seriously of going back to internal combustion, but the Touring Car seated five, with an ample back seat. Tony found a baseball bat was in fact wedged on the floor between the front and back.

"Harry, what's this for?"

"I'm gonna paddle some asses, what do *you* think?" Harry said, laughing.

He wasn't laughing when he went upstairs to the second floor machine room. Seven o'clock in the morning arrived, and so did all the girls. But they assumed their chairs—and sat there with their hands folded in their laps, and did nothing. Harry made a circuit of the entire room—up the window side, 60 yards, across the rows 30 yards, down the back side, and across to where he started, the whole time eyeing them while they sat there, nervously fidgeting, and he kept beating his palm with the bat.

When he got back to the middle window, he roared at them, "Whaddya think you're doing! Start your machines! I ain't paying you people to sit here!"

He stalked back and forth beating the bat. But nobody moved, and there was frightened silence. "Go ahead! Go ahead! I'm watchin' yez! I'm dockin' the pay of every one of youz that sits here like this! It's comin' out of your pay packets! It ain't comin' outta my pocket! That's for damn sure!" Harry went up to Tony. "Whadda they think they're doin'?"

"I dunno, Harry."

"Well, *do* somethin'!"

Tony looked at the two floor-ladies, who, for once, looked pale and panic-stricken.

They, more than anyone, knew they were hated—even despised—and if they could have crawled under the floorboards, they would have gone there on hands and knees.

Tony appealed to his girls—that's how he thought of them—his girls.

"Look, ladies—we can't just sit here like this—it's five minutes since starting time already!"

Somebody giggled, and someone else said quietly, "Tony—you're so cute when you try to get mad!"

Harry shouted. "All right! I've had enough of this! Either you get to work immediately, or I'll get the police in here, and you'll all be arrested!"

Someone in the back, far away, yelled, "We don't take orders from you anymore!"

"Who was that!"

Harry was running back and forth with his bat. "You tell me who it was!" Fifteen hands shot into the air, followed by twenty more. Girls were looking around at each other, and some broke into grins; they were feeling defiant now, there was strength in their numbers, they were all in this together. "It was me! It was me! I did it, you bastard!"

"Don't you people realize that what you're doing is against the law!" Harry roared. "I could have you all arrested and carted off! Keep this up, and that's exactly what you're gonna get! I'll ruin you people! You'll never get another job in this town again! And when I fire the whole lot of yez—I'll have a whole new staff in here in the morning to take your jobs! Is that what you want!"

Somebody yelled, "Hey, Harry, what are you gonna do with that bat? You want me to tell you what to do with it?"

Everybody laughed—even Tony, and the floor-ladies.

Harry raced over to Tony. "Get up to the third floor and see what's goin' on up there!"

"All right, Harry—but it's gonna be the same thing. I don't hear no machines runnin.'"

"Just do it, Tony!"

When he came back, he just went up to Harry and said quietly with his lips next to Harry's ear, "Same thing."

Harry was standing there with his futile baseball bat. Nothing had happened for what seemed another eternity. Finally, he said, to Tony, in a low voice, "I'm not accomplishing anything here. I'm wasting my time trying to talk to these people. I'll be downstairs in the office. Try to find out at least, if you can, what their intentions are. Maybe if they see me leave the room, they'll talk to you."

Harry's tactic worked exactly this way, and when Tony went downstairs he told Harry, "They're waiting for instructions."

"From who?"

"From their leaders."

"The union? But, Tony, don't you see—they can't just sit here and refuse to work. What do you expect me to do? They're on *my* property. They are preventing *me* from running *my* machines! No court in the land will uphold their side! Look—go down street and see what's goin' on other places. If they're just wild-cattin' me, Tony, then we got 'em licked. I gotta know—this crazy talk about a general strike—where do they get the nerve!"

Tony went and came back to report, "It's the same elsewhere. Nobody's liftin' a finger. Nothin's runnin.'"

When he came back, Tony found Harry on the telephone, talking to the police captain. The captain was telling Harry that he already had as much trouble as he could handle. Harry put down the receiver, looked at Tony, and said, "This is bad. This is bad."

Then there was shouting in the street. Voices were calling, "Come out! Come out!"

"Join us! The strike is on! Everybody's coming out!"

Tony and Harry heard the voice above their heads calling out through the open windows, "We can't! The doors are all locked!"

Voices in the street started chanting, "Let them out! Let them out! Let them out!" Harry told Tony. "Go up and unlock the doors. I don't want them here anyway!"

The first day ended right there, but Harry was far from stymied. He took a breath, gave Tony instructions.

"Lemme see. Okay. Go down to your neighborhood—see if you know anybody there that knows the *shvartzes* over in Washington Square, you know, the niggers. I want the colored girls over here in the morning. They'll be only too glad to take the jobs off of our girls. I don't want any sympathizers comin' in here, you know, half-asses, not sure if they're doing the right thing. The colored girls— they're always desperate. We'll be doin' them a favor—getting 'em off the streets! We should get a medal from the mayor! For goddam public service!"

Tony went on his mission, but in a foul mood. He had stepped into the horse manure this time, and there was no getting out of it, over it, or around it. He felt things slipping out of his control. And he was angry, because this was not the ferryboat he had signed up for. But what could he do? He owed everything to Harry. His Uncle Eugenio was working in his trade and supporting his family, including Tony's cousins, and Tony's own domicile, through Tony's connection to the

Spritzkas. Everything was so complicated, so tangled up. Tony could not think just of himself. He had to put his aunt and uncle and his cousins, and yes, Harry, ahead of himself. And now he had a goddam war on his hands— Harry's war. And Harry expected Tony to fight his battles for him. And now this—this foul-intentioned, dirty, thankless task of signing up the colored girls to do Harry's bidding. Tony cursed himself for having sold himself body and soul to Harry. Was Harry not going to be satisfied till he had Tony's mind enthralled in debt, too?

The next morning, Harry was back with hired goons from the old neighborhood down on Allen Street, but the union was back, too, this time with pickets. Harry and Tony were supposed to be managing the job of signing on all the colored girls who showed up between six and seven in the morning, but the next thing you know, they had a riot on their hands instead.

The pickets wanted to walk the sidewalk outside Harry's door, but his *shtarkers,* which is the ugly name the Yiddish girls called down on the heads of Harry's hired sluggers, pushed them away across the street.

They wouldn't go away further than that, so they were well within earshot of the poor colored girls, who were as frightened as rabbits. They had shown up hoping they were getting their chance at a decent job for once, only to have verbal abuse heaped on them at the hands of angry girls with sticks and umbrellas and signs in their hands, and the most polite thing they heard was, "You dirty rotten lousy stinkin' scab, you!"

Harry had the police called in for fear of getting the plate glass windows broken on his showroom, but by the time they showed up, there was blood all over both sidewalks, from the *shtarkers'* clubs and bats, and the wooden-handled signs and lead-filled umbrellas of the picketing strikers.

Cries and screams and threats of all stripes filled the air when the police started dragging the picketers into their vans.

"Spritzka, you dirty skunk! We're gonna get you for this! You ain't seen the end of us, you rotten bastard—not by a long-shot!"

"Hey, Officer!—what's your badge made outta? Dirty copper, that's what! Get your hands off me!"

Within a week, Harry was completely out of business. Shut down. He might as well lock the place up and walk away. The only reason his pockets weren't empty was that he had his hands in them.

Inventory was moldering in a locked building. "I'm losing my shirt!" Somebody far away in Cleveland or Pittsburgh or Philly was filling his orders. New York was at a standstill. Twenty thousand garment workers were out. The newspapers were filled with sympathetic accounts of their grievances, their down-trodden conditions, at work, and at home, as if that was central to the matter!

And the heinous practices of the bosses, such as charging you for the seat you sat on to stitch his bundles for him—the public found they were outraged at some of the things they were hearing.

With the law, the judges, the courts, the police, Tammany Hall, the state militia, and the governor on the side of the rightful owners of garment factories—they still could not get a fair shake out of the press on this damned illegal strike from hell!

Harry was dumbfounded. How could it be? The cartoonists in the papers were having a field day caricaturing the garment bosses as cigar-chewing Simon Legrees, as evil toadies in top hats. How had it happened that all of a sudden everybody was on the side of the law-breakers?

By the end of the first week, an additional ten thousand had walked off the job. And you couldn't even call them women! They were girls, that only came up to your elbow!

Never in the entire history of the United States had a bunch of women held up a whole city like this. And this was New York. Seventy percent of all garments made in the country were made here, in these factories, by these girls. Even the colored girls—the absolute bottom of the barrel—had had second thoughts about strike-breaking—and their ministers and congregations held meetings in their chapels and churches to discuss whether or not it was fair that colored girls take work away from others.

That was the last straw for Harry. What in the world was the world coming to?

All Harry knew was that it sure sold papers. Harry was losing his shirt and Randolph Hearst's profits were going through the roof.

And the publishers were not even the worst of the worst.

What about Mary Dreier? Now here was a woman, wealthy in her own right, upper-middle-class, and college-educated—certainly not a street-scrapper out of the Lower East Side, like Harry Spritzka— never had to spend a day in her life wanting for anything—and she goes and appoints herself not only the guardian of the morals of today's young women, but she gets herself elected the President of the Women's Trade Union League—an outfit Harry had never heard of, but which he soon found out that he was sorry he ever did.

This woman, Mary Dreier, organized her well-off college-educated suffragette girlfriends to help the striking women with their every-day problems behind the scenes while they were out on the picket line. They rented meeting halls for the striking women and set up telephone networks so that strikers in different locations on separate blocks and streets could keep in touch and coordinate tactics and strategy. And most of the immigrant-class strikers did not even know how to work a telephone, they had to be taught.

The WTUL, as they called them in the papers, then went out and got reform-minded lawyers to defend strikers in court—gratis, no less.

The strikers were being arrested on a regular, wholesale basis. Some of them who were repeat offenders, and unlucky enough to appear before a puritanical or conservative-minded judge, were sent to the Women's Workhouse on Blackwell's Island in the East River. Most of the time the arrested were hauled away in the horse-drawn police vans and brought in to Night Court, where Tammany judges would fine them either three dollars or five and lock them up in the Tombs overnight, where they were let to go home in the morning. But Judge Olmstead, when he found repeaters before him, declared to them, "You are on strike against God and Nature—whose firm law is that man shall earn his bread in the sweat of his brow! You are on strike against God!"

And he thereupon sentenced them to five days in the Women's Workhouse.

One repeat offender, a girl named Rose Perr, who was sixteen, but small and undernourished, and a girl who had a child's voice, and a braid down her back, so that she looked like she was ten, not sixteen, was sentenced by Judge Olmstead to five days on Blackwell Island, where she did hard labor alongside prostitutes, petty thieves and shoplifters, pickpockets and drug addicts. Not surprisingly, when the papers picked this up, it backfired on the factory-owners.

In jail, wearing a scratchy woolen dress and heavy Dutch-wooden shoes that gave her blisters, Rose Perr scrubbed floors on her knees with a pig-bristle brush, and had to wash mounds of dirty clothes, which she lifted with a heavy paddle, on a washboard, by hand, with lye soap, which burned her hands—and then had to stir them in a vat of boiling water with a wooden pole, after which she had to lift them out with a stick, rinse them twice, in cold water, and then hang them up to dry.

If Rose Perr failed to finish on time, she had to spend a sleepless night in what the prisoners of Blackwell's Island called "the dark room," a pitch-black dungeon infested with rats and cockroaches.

If she broke the silence rule, same punishment—the dark room.

By the time Rose Perr was released, she had become a *cause célèbre*. She and Lena Lapido and five others were brought by boat to Manhattan, where Mary Dreier and other members of the WTUL greeted them—and handed each one of them a bouquet of American Beauty roses.

The press were there, taking photos. The Lower East Side, Jews and Italians both, turned out to welcome them home as heroines. Rose and Lena were interviewed and dubbed in the daily *Forvitz* "Our wonderful, fiery little girls!"—"*Unzere wunderbar farbrente meyd lekh!*"

And that was not the last of it. To Harry's bewilderment, and eventual dismay, Alva Belmont entered the fray. She was the widow of a millionaire banker, and represented one of the most influential, old-money families in the city. Her family owned the 2nd Avenue Subway line, the very first to open in New York, back in 1904—and every other line opened since then.

According to Harry, Alva Belmont was an out-and-out madwoman. "A so-called feminist, one of them damned suffragettes, or whatever you call 'em, and a traitor to her class," he told Tony. "She actually advised one of her diehard female followers, 'Pray to God. *She* will help you.'"

"She called God a she?" said Tony.

"Listen, she's a nut. Do you know she actually wants women to be allowed to be priests in the Catholic Church? Your church, Tony! Not only that, she wants women judges, women athletes— women everything! She probably thinks a woman oughta be President! She's down in the Jefferson Market Court at three a.m., getting strikers out by using her mink coat to post bail with! I swear! She did that one night when she ran out of money—and the judge accepted the coat!"

Harry reserved his special scorn for another member of the "Mink Coat Brigade"—Anne Morgan—none other than *the* Anne Morgan—youngest daughter of J.P. Morgan himself!

This "deluded female," as Harry called her, could not have had a life further removed from the "squalor and degradation" of the Lower East Side, as, Harry added, "the pathetic scribes of the almighty American newspaper combine call it."

In December, after four weeks of a general strike in bitter cold and snow, this woman, Anne Morgan, organized the women members of her exclusive Colony Club and held a "motor parade," in which a line of fifteen chauffeur-driven automobiles moved down Fifth Avenue all the way into the Lower East Side. Anne Morgan and Alva Belmont rode in the two lead autos. Each car was decked with posters spelling out strike slogans such as,

THE WORKHOUSE IS NO ANSWER TO DEMANDS FOR JUSTICE

and

VOTES FOR WOMEN

In the cars, strikers sat next to socialites, while crowds, cheering, thronged the sidewalks, and the inevitable press photographers snapped their immortal masterpieces, which were made indelible, instantly, in that same evening's edition.

Then came January.

An all-out rally was held in Carnegie Hall. The same Carnegie Hall built by one of the richest tycoons in the country, the "steel magnate" himself. The wealthiest scions of the city's most prominent families turned out to listen to the dunning refrain of the abuse of power by the police, the courts, the militia, the judges, the governor and the captains of the garment industry. The factory owners, from Blanck and Harris to Harry Spritzka, were portrayed, mocked and denounced, in purple prose, by a lineup of phrase-makers that included a prominent lawyer from the Lower East Side, Morris Hillquist, who was also a leader of the Socialist Party, giving the main speech.

On the front of the stage, alongside the array of speakers, sat twenty ex-Workhouse inmates, each one wearing a sash that read either

Eugene Christy

PEACEFUL PICKETING IS THE RIGHT OF EVERY WORKER

or the other slogan used in the Auto Parade,

THE WORKHOUSE IS NO ANSWER TO DEMANDS FOR JUSTICE

Everything was choreographed for maximum impact. Behind the girls with the sashes sat a further 350 women who had been arrested, hauled into court in police vans, fined and jailed.

The rally organizers outdid themselves, and the audience was moved to tears by little Rose Perr, who came to the front of the stage to say she had been sentenced to Blackwell's Island because she had asked non-union workers "not to take the bread out of their sisters' mouths."

She had been coached not to use the word "scabs," and she did not.

However good the rich and thrifty felt about their attendance at this rally, the poor and spendthrift strikers felt equally bad about their chances as the strike dragged on.

It was all well and good for the well-fed and warm to go on about injustice, but the workers in the street felt the cold, and faced evictions for non-payment of rent, and had to eat hand-outs of soup and bread because there was nothing else.

On the picket line, they faced bad winds driving merciless rain in their faces and were chilled to the bone till they felt like walking icicles.

When snow fell, it soon melted into slush from so many tramping feet, and their cheap shoes with their thin soles were full of holes from plodding the line.

When they got home at night to the cold-water flat they peeled off light-weight overcoats, hung them up, and could only hope they dried by morning—when they would be back out there on the picket line facing the same, or worse weather, with the same prospect of no money coming in, and the thought of actual starvation staring them in the face.

Sometimes they had to question whether or not a raise in wages and shortened work-hours were worth all this suffering, or whether they could win at all, or whether they were being sacrificed by their leaders just so that the unions could win the closed shop.

As the strike dragged on, the other side, the employers, known in the press as *the garment-industry operators,* was also chastened. Unable to fill orders, the smaller shops actually had to go down, because they could not pay their bills. Many had to close their doors, and they feared that such a step, once taken—with a business which had taken years to build up—meant the business could be permanently lost, in the wink of an eye.

Once these shops were out, the organized league of owners was seriously endangered. After all, it was only circumstances that had forced them to band together. Normally, they were competitors, and in that arena, the law of the jungle prevailed—the high and the mighty, the large and the strong, devoured the small and the weak.

The dozen largest firms were led by Max Blanck and Isaac Harris and the Triangle Shirtwaist Company, which everyone had long looked up to as the model for the industry. They stood fast—but they were not about to spend any of their own capital to rescue their inferiors. After all, they were competitors—*let 'em go down! So much the better for us.*

Eugene Christy

One day during the strike, after 53 days of staring at lifeless machines, Harry Spritzka showed up at six in the morning to find his beautiful plate-glass showroom windows lying in shattered pieces on the showroom floor.

He thought he had never seen anything so sad.

He had been through all the ups and downs of the strike. Attended all the meetings of the owners. Pleaded with the police for protection. Humbled himself to accept that he had to allow the pickets their "rights." Now this.

He had paid good money to *shtarkers* to frighten off the pickets. It was money down the drain. He himself had charged them, fought them hand to hand, when things got out of control, as they sometimes did.

Nerves were frayed, and hatred boiled just below the surface, on both sides. Walking into his own shop, Harry could feel their eyes on him.

In spite of everything, the other side was not backing down.

Was he going to be forced in the end to hire back all these same people, who called him names in Yiddish?

It was inconceivable to him.

Tony came into the showroom. All he said was, "Well, boss, we had a good four-year run." Harry could not believe it. Now even Tony was calling him "boss."

Harry said, "Would you get a broom, Tony? If you don't mind? Help me clean up this mess."

For Harry Spritzka, the last straw came when he read in the *Herald-Tribune* that a striker's mother, who was dependent on her daughter for the support of five little ones, was quoted by a reporter. The man with the notepad asked whether imminent starvation would force this family to yield. And the striker's mother replied, *"We will eat grass, if there's any to be found, before we give up this strike."*

Chapter 13

The Fire Above

After twelve weeks in the dead of winter, the strike of the 20,000 women of the Manhattan garment industry ended when the owners conceded, on February 15, 1910.

Harry felt betrayed—by Max Blanck, the very man, co-owner of the Triangle Shirtwaist Company, whom he had thought to emulate.

Blanck had met, secretly, with Mary Dreier and the Strike leaders. Harry heard that he had humiliated himself, and all the operaters, including Harry. It was going around that Blanck had caved in, going so far as to say that he didn't want it to seem that the strikers had beaten him into making changes; and that if they would only help him to "save face" and let the girls go back to work, that he would meet the strikers' "demands." Mary Dreier herself was boasting of this.

Harry thought he had never heard of anything so cowardly from a man of such prominence and influence. To make a deal was one thing, but this was an outright, abject surrender. Local 25 of the I.L.G.W.U. got a 12 percent pay raise—12 percent! How Harry would like to be able to jack his wholesale prices 12 percent! And that wasn't all—they got a 52-hour work-week, and an end to what they called "petty abuses," like charging for needles and chairs. And every owner whose shop had struck was going to be forced to take back all the same girls, this time, as union members.

Nothing was ever going to be the same again. Harry had lost control of his own business.

And yet Max Blanck wanted him to believe that he had won the fight on the closed shop, because the I.L.G.W.U. had agreed to concede that point in return for all they won.

What that meant, Harry thought, was a win on paper—and a loss on the factory floor. Sure, they couldn't force a new employee to become a dues-paying union member—but did anyone really believe that any new girl was not going to join? In this atmosphere? To hold out against all the other girls, flush with victory?

Harry was disgusted, and he said so, when he and Tony got together with brother Robert over egg creams at Auster's on Second Avenue.

Robert said, "I told you, but you don't wanna listen."

Harry turned on him. "And I'll tell you, Bobby, I'm gonna make this work! You feel free to make your money any way your little heart desires."

"When you own residential, they gotta pay up—they need you! They got nowhere else to live!"

"You build your little empire, I'll build mine."

"But you have no control over your people anymore."

"Oh—like you don't have people movin' out the furniture in the middle of the night, skippin' out on the rent!"

"And the next morning I fill the space. But at least when I chase 'em, I got the laws and the courts on my side! You got nothing."

Tony was standing there sipping on his egg cream thinking that he was right back in the middle between these two again, where he had always been, and always would be: *a slab of pastrami in the Spritzka Brothers' sangwich.*

"Don't you worry, Bobby, I'm gonna show you. I'm gonna make this work—in spite of everything. I got my plans, let me assure you. I got more ways of making money than you ever dreamed of—"

"Yeah—you and Abba both. Cut from the same cloth!"

"Does Tatti have 135 employees—all making money for him? No, he doesn't. I do. Do you? And I ain't stopping there, either—not by a long shot."

Harry was delighted with himself for this idea—if he doubled or tripled his employees, why, it was plain arithmetic—production and sales would double or triple and up goes his gross! And he was going to be very tight-fisted with his gross, and make sure his profit margins stayed in solid, indelible black-ink. He felt good about himself for the first time in weeks. That was all he had needed, apparently—a good argument with his brother.

On the way back to West 37th, Harry was pumping Tony. "Expansion, Tony—expansion, expansion, expansion—we gotta do it. It's gonna be a big job, and I'm gonna need you—I'm gonna need somebody I can trust to help me keep the union out—somebody who knows what we been through with these people—that's why I need you, Tony. I got nobody else—there is nobody else! Now listen. This is what we're gonna do!"

By the time they got back to the showroom office, Harry was back to form, ready to spit in the customer's eye. But one little lady with a pink parasol stopped him in his tracks.

She stuck her head in the office door.

"How do you like things, now, Mr Big Shot?"

It was the same little wizened, whiney creature who, before the strike, had told him "Lincoln freed the slaves!"

Harry was out of his chair. He was angry. The effrontery of this—girl!

"Oh, don't get up for me, Harry," said the young woman. "I was just leaving!" Harry stuck his hand inside his suitcoat, he was reaching for his waistband.

The girl was turning her back, insolently, so sure of herself, in the doorway, and did not see what Harry had in his hand.

It was a gun.

Tony lunged for Harry's hand.

He knew about the gun—Harry had told him the story.

In the latter days of the strike, Harry had been going home to 68 Division Street, very late one dark night, when, after parking his Edison, Dopey Benny jumped out of the shadows at him. He confronted Harry. When Harry told Tony, he acted it out, playing the part of Dopey Benny.

"You know what your trouble is, Harry Spritzka? You got no loyalty. I got loyalty. Lucky for you, I got loyalty to your old man. That's right—a gentleman named Louis Spritzka. Somebody wanted me to take a contract out on breaking your knee-caps, Harry—but I said no—'cause your father's a decent man and always treated me like a gentleman."

After that, Harry wore the gun in his waistband through the rest of the strike.

That's why it was in his hand now, when Tony lunged for his wrist. "Harry! Stop! Don't! Whaddya think you're doin'?" said Tony, through clenched teeth. And he twisted his hand on Harry to get the gun-barrel turned down to point at the floor.

Briefly, Harry made as if to tear the hand with the gun in it away, so that Tony felt he had to hang on. Then just as suddenly he could feel the heat in Harry's wrist go slack. Harry's anger melted away, as quickly as it had come on.

Harry said, "Ah—whaddya worried about?"

Tony released his grip and Harry stuck the gun back where it came from as he straightened up.

Tony stood back, and Harry looked him in the eye. "What?" he said. "I was just gonna show her the gun and tell her to get the hell out of my office!"

Tony said, "All right, Harry, all right."

"It's still my office, ain't it?"

"Harry, sit down, will ya? You're makin' me nervous."

"Well, is it my office, or not?"

Sometimes there was just no talking to Harry.

In many ways, they were right back where they started from—before the strike. It was business as usual. In other ways, subtle ways, everything was changed.

When they were at work together, they avoided one another. If Harry wanted to go out someplace, Tony felt free to say no. If it was a case of going to the Harlem River Speedway on a Saturday afternoon—because of the shorter work week, they, too, had more leisure time—Tony might refuse a lift, and say, "I'll meet you there—I'll take the streetcar."

Sometimes these days it seemed to Tony that he spent his life on a trolley. Gone were the old horse-drawn, lumbering and creaking wooden streetcars. Nowadays overhead electric wires crisscrossed what open sky was left and the streetcars were rumbling, loaded and screeching. Still, Tony LaStoria much preferred them to the new subways, as you could take a look around, see people, and things, buildings, street scenes, and breathe actual air instead of tunnel-vapors.

It was a long time ago now since he had lived in Harry's house. Nowadays Tony was in transit, constantly back and forth from the Upper East Side to the garment district. Most of the time, his mind was on idle, like a sewing-machine between bursts of rapid-fire stitching. Sometimes his eyes closed; and sometimes eyes-wide-open streetcar daydreams overcame him, and he had to remind himself not to miss his stop.

One day, she stepped on at 2nd Avenue and East 59th.

Three blocks from where Tony lived with his Uncle Eugene and Auntie Marietta and the cousins. He had never seen her before.

He thought that if he had seen her before, he would certainly have remembered– this girl. Where had she come from? Who was she? What was her name?

When he tried to go to sleep that night, he could not, he found, unless he first spent his thoughts, his powers, on trying to retrieve her image, so that it would reappear before him, magically, as if glowing on the nickelodeon screen, bathed in a halo of light.

The next morning the terrifying thought occurred to him that—*what if he never saw her again?* He hurried to the trolley stop. For three blocks he rode gripped in fear and doubt—even his hands were clenched.

Then she stepped on board again, at the same stop.

Oh, Mother of Angels, Tony thought—*bless you. You sent her back to me.*

He soon found that he should not expect to see her on the streetcar when he was going home in the evenings. Often he worked late—and if he did not, then, their schedules must still vary, such that the timing made it impossible.

Nevertheless, he had her with him every morning—and Tony thought that to be remarkable, fortunate, and momentous.

That second morning when she boarded the streetcar, she sat with her back to him. Tony was immensely relieved because that meant he could gaze upon her all he wanted. He could study her. The slope of her shoulders. The carriage of the way she carried her head on her neck, the tilt of her chin, slightly uplifted, seen from over her right shoulder.

He tried to memorize the details, so as to recall them when he wanted to go to sleep at night, but she was elusive—she would not come to him, he could not call her up at will.

He thought that he must not stare at her—or let her catch him looking. Certainly she would be offended—if he stared. A girl like her was not a statue in a church. Tony thought, in fact, that if she knew that she was adored, she would be offended by that, out of modesty.

But she was certainly aware of him on the streetcar. How, Tony could not divine. It was a mystery, but the feeling that she was aware of his eyes on her back—that she knew he was watching her—grew on him.

It made him uneasy to think that he might be causing her any discomfort, but there was more. It was not just that she knew she was being watched, it was—that she knew who was watching. That she knew him.

They had never spoken a word to each other—they had not even made contact with their eyes— yet she knew him.

One day he was studiously avoiding looking at her on the morning streetcar, because it was mobbed that day—she could not find a seat, she was coming down the aisle, trying to wedge herself past strap-hangers; like a bird, she was peeking, trying to see through the branches to an opening to the sky, craning her neck to try to see the back rows of seats.

Tony did not dare rise and make any show of offering her his seat. That would have been so forward. Better if she found another seat, even some other man who was polite enough to give his up to her. Tony would have preferred even that to risking her shaking her head, no, I'll stand, thank you.

What if he had to speak to her? What would he say? Tony tried not to be watching her, but when he finally did look up—she was standing right in front of him where he sat.

Their eyes met. It was a shock to Tony, like fresh water thrown in his face.

Her eyes were brown. He had never known that before. He would like to know why he had never realized that, or guessed it, or assumed it. Her face was oval, her cheeks were blushing, like the red skin of a peach. This sweet young girl had no need of rouge. She was too young to wear makeup. She was perfectly beautiful the way she was. *God made a rose and Man did imagine he could improve Perfection by adding his love.* To Tony, this girl was put upon the earth, and into his path, to prove to him that there was beauty, that it was not lost from the world. The incessant roar of the trolley wheels grinding and the sewing machines stitching did not drown out the music of life. The drudgery of day after day, of sameness and repetition and helpless, hopeless routine, was not all there was.

And when their eyes met, in this happenstance way, she did not look away. Instead, she looked into his eyes, for the briefest moment, though it felt like a flicker of eternity before she lowered her eyes, demurely, and he was left to gaze on her lowered eyelids, which floated like rose petals on a still pool. And as he lowered his own glance, so as not to stare, he found a crucifix, the kind you could find at Woolworth's, plain, unadorned, silvery-white, resting on a delicate chain at the base of her throat, her throat, which was as white as amaryllis.

He shook himself like a dog, and jumped up to offer his seat to her. He was mortified.

Calmly, she sat. She placed her pocketbook on her lap, her umbrella at her knee. She quietly looked straight ahead, past Tony's midsection.

Neither of them had said a word.

Tony felt the crimson flood into his cheeks, he felt he was burning, his neck was on fire.

He was not at all conscious that he was staring at her, but she was. And when she looked up into his eyes again, he was stunned to see there, in her subtle brown eyes, a question. *Are you following me? What do you want? Do you not care how I feel?*

Tony did the only thing he could do. He lowered his own eyes, so as not to see her, to avoid her gaze by looking at the floor. He wanted to cry out, *No, No, that's not it at all, I would never—what you see is adoration—please!*

But his lips would not move, his voice died strangled in his throat, his forehead felt about to burst into flame, he was paralyzed. And as he fastened his gaze abashedly to the floor, he saw her shoes.

The toe of her shoe, as she sat there, calm and composed, was virtually kissing his own on the crowded, jostling streetcar.

Her shoes were the usual style of all the other young girls who worked in the garment trade. The style was high-button, but hers were laced, not buttoned, and the uppers were of cheap Moroccan leather, they were blocky, stout, made for walking, made for pressing on the sewing-machine pedal over and over, not stylish shoes, but every-day, useful shoes, for a working girl to wear—not meant to be noticed by young men, but meant to be tucked modestly away. She could not have been more than fourteen or fifteen. And so her modesty was of the virginal kind of a girl not yet, but about to be, on the verge of womanhood.

He thought these shoes must hurt her feet. He wanted to kneel down and kiss away the hurt, but the thought shamed him, and he did not dare in reality do such a melodramatic thing, it would be ridiculous, it would call all the wrong kind of attention to her, who should be enshrined in a holy, high-walled sanctuary in his soul.

And at that very moment when he was feeling a surge of tenderness toward her, he remembered that shameful episode with the Jewish whore down on Allen Street—it flew into his mind, the entire shameful scene, unbidden—and he could not command it to stay away. Of all times to be thinking of that!

She must never know. Never. He must shield her from that, protect her from all that was shameful. And without knowing it then, he had found the most powerful reason for not speaking to her at all. Fear. Fear that if he once opened his mouth all confession of his deepest secrets and innermost soul would come pouring out, and that he would not be able to contain the pain, the hurt of his entire life, from the moment he left his mother, clutching in his hand her hard-won coins, to the instant he turned his back on the lady in blue.

In the coming weeks and days and months Tony descended into the most painful, personal agony he could ever have imagined, while at the same time he was lifted up to the highest plateaus of mountainous joy. At times he thought he would be simply overwhelmed.

And this did not go unnoticed by others.

For one, his Uncle Eugenio was sitting or standing beside him on almost every day of this singular streetcar journey through the "vales of his tortured soul." Those were Uncle Eugenio's very words, in a moment of inspiration. In fact, he delighted in teasing Tony. "Who is she, son?" He would nudge Tony with his elbow. Over the years, Uncle Eugenio had slipped himself into the role of Tony's real father, nominating himself as the replacement, the stand-in for his brother— another thing that annoyed Tony, to no end. "Want me to find out for you?"

Tony shot him a murderous look.

"Perhaps I could arrange a meeting between the families?"

"You will do no such thing!"

"You know, you really should be thinking of getting married. Madonn'! How the hell old are you, anyway? I think you must be at least 22, no? Let's see—let me calculate. What, are you planning to be an aging spinster? You know, Tony, you can only milk the cow so much before your hand gets tired!"

Then there was Angie, at work. The girl on the streetcar was not the only blossom on the tree, or so Angie thought. Angie had a whole handbag of her usual tricks—"Tony! Tony! I need you! Come over here—come on—one minute!"

Then she would lean over and hide the piece of sewing so as to make Tony have to bend over her other shoulder to see, which brought his face down close to hers, and she would say, "When you gonna ask me out for an egg cream?"

"A month of Sundays."

"Are you really that stingy? Tony, how come you never give any of the girls a tumble? Don't you know they're dyin' for you?"

And Angie, from Brooklyn, who walked over the Williamsburg Bridge every day, to save on the transfer fare, before taking the trolley in Manhattan up to West 37th, would give him her little cackle of a laugh.

It mystified Tony that somehow Angie knew all about the girl on the streetcar. How in the hell would she? But of course Angie arranged to "bump into" Tony, literally, on the freight elevator, where she told all the other assembled girls riding up to start the shift, "Tony's got a secret!"

"Come on, Tony—tell us! Who's the lucky girl?"

Tony was furious with Angie and wouldn't speak to her at all for a week.

"She can stick her whole hand under the needle and bleed all over the bundle and I don't care!" he told Harry, in a moment of pique. "I'm not gonna play her stupid games anymore!"

But Harry had other ideas. He thought Angie was just the girl for Tony. And he tried to use her as bait. Unlike Angie, Harry did not plunge after a person's depths, where the still waters run; yet he too was worried about Tony.

Ever since the strike, it seemed that he could no longer entice Tony into renewing their little amusements, which, formerly, they used to enjoy immensely—together.

Harry missed that. He was at a loss what to do about it, when it came to his attention that Angie was throbbing at the starting gate for Tony.

So one Saturday night Harry arranged for Tony to meet him at Auster's for an egg cream in the booth along the side wall nearest the sidewalk of 2nd Avenue.

When Tony got there, he found Angie curled up like a cat in the corner of the bench seat against the wall.

There was no room on the other side because Harry, as usual, had his flavor of the week, which these days, was Roxanne, with him.

So Tony had stepped into the muck and mire yet again.

Actually, Tony liked Roxanne, quite a lot, and she certainly didn't deserve Harry, who treated her like he picked her up in the street.

Roxanne was not like that at all. It wasn't her fault that she was a buxom white blonde with full Jewish lips that seemed made for long, langorous kissing. Or that she handsomely filled out the currently stylish pigeon-breasted shirtwaist, or the knock-offs of Paul Poirot that all the girls were ravenous for. Harry treated her as if she were a professional chorus girl from Minsky's burlesque, but she was a doctor's daughter. To her misfortune, she was hopelessly in love with Harry, and deceived herself that they were soon to become engaged, and Tony would have hated to wise her up.

"Tony, meet Angie," said Harry.

"I've already had that pleasure," Tony said, as he slid into the booth gloomily.

"Say—are you gonna be a *sour-putz* all night? 'Cause the girls wanna have a little fun."

Angie said, "Tony's in love."

Harry said, "We know that. All the world knows that. We wanna get him marooned off his island, that's all."

Angie slipped her arm into Tony's, and he let her. He was pausing, and pressing his palms together, thoughtfully.

"What's her name, Tony?" Angie asked. "You can tell me, sweetheart."

Tony looked down at his hands and twined his fingers. He resented Angie for so casually calling him sweetheart when she knew there was nothing between them. People should not joke about such things. Some people called everybody *honey* and *darling* and all that did was drain these endearments of all meaning. Then he raised his head and looked back and forth into the eyes of people who cared about him. That he could not gainsay. "I honestly don't know her name."

That's as much as he would confess. That's all they would get out of him on that evening. They all went out for a little dinner, went to the Jewish theater to hear Shakespeare in Yiddish, and the Jews in the audience laughed and wept, at the Merchant of Venice, and so did Tony and Angie, a couple of Italians, who understood everything whether they spoke the language or not, because it was one of those evenings when life becomes knowable to the most ignorant, and visible to the most blind.

After that, he became determined to speak to the one he loved. He would have to steel his resolve, but each day that was passing his determination grew. It was already a year since he had fallen desperately in love with an ideal of womanhood, a heavenly beauty, an angel on earth, and he still did not know how to approach her, how to take her hand, how to put his arm around his beloved, how to whisper her name on his own lips. Long ago he had given up trying to conjure her face, when he was lying down on his weary bed to go to sleep after another long day, although it was a face he had memorized, a face he would never forget, never be able to forget—it was easy enough at work all day long doing a million busy little rituals and performances, thoughtlessly, automatically, his mind off somewhere, a million miles away—it was then, in daylight, easy to recall her face, having seen her again that very morning on the streetcar—in actual fact, the image came to his minds, his many, distracted minds, at all-and-every tricky moment, unbidden, when he was supposedly doing something else altogether, so that sometimes he felt he couldn't concentrate at all.

But late at night, weary, sleepless, he could only see her shoes. And so he looked down at his own feet, and then when he saw her shoes, then he could drift off, then he could sleep, then he could dream.

But to speak to her, he had to meet her.

This he planned out meticulously. He had to make sure his uncle was not to be found in that imagined scene, as he planned it. Not Harry, either, or Angie. He and his beloved would have to be alone together. He pictured coming face to face with her. Where? Somewhere where she would feel natural about it, and not threatened, or startled, at all. He would not jump out at her from the shadows, the way Dopey Benny had with Harry. Somewhere where she might almost be expected to see him. Where might she be hoping to see him? Perhaps coming out of work, one night?—with the long day over, her thoughts turning homeward? Perhaps she had dreamed of that moment—that he would be waiting there for her. Yes, she must have. He would walk up to her—slowly—he would hold out his hand to her—the way the Americans did, to shake hands—he would say simply, "Hello," or "Buona sera." She understood Italian. He knew that much. He had seen it from the first, but it was also in her face, and her manner. She was a shy young Italian girl, sheltered, and sheltering, in her family. She loved to go home to them at the end of a long day. She dreamed of one day not having to go to the factory, to drudge her life away, but to have a family of her own, children, a man who loved her, and respected her, the kind of man whom she could, with all her heart, adore.

And also, there was the small matter of apologizing to her for that day on the trolley when he had made her uncomfortable, when her eyes had spoken to him out of protest, out of injured feelings—no, no, no, he must correct that impression, he must at least give himself a chance to explain himself, to say that he was so in love with her that he could not help himself, but that he would never, never do anything to hurt her feelings, that he only wished to cherish and adore her and give her everything and make her happy.

Therefore, Tony thought, he would have to find out where she worked. He would have to follow her. Again.

He hated to do it, but there was no choice. He could have simply talked to her on the streetcar, some morning, say hello, introduce himself, but, no, that would have been wrong, wrong, wrong— overcrowded, noisy, even thunderous, those wooden contraptions, with rattling glass—*how romantic!*

Besides, she would never find out that he was following her. He would never divulge that to her.

And he could not let her discover it.

He knew that she continued on the streetcar, every day, when Tony got off at his stop. Where did she go? She was a stitcher, Tony could tell from her hands—also from her posture when sitting on the trolley. She kept her back straight, knowing that all day she would be bending over a machine, pushing cloth through the resistance with her arms and shoulders, pedaling her feet. Tony's conjecture was that she worked somewhere in the lower 30s, south of 37th Street.

He was wrong about that. He had formulated his plan to one day follow her so that she would not know it by using the new motor-taxis that were all the time becoming more and more industrious and plentiful on the streets of Manhattan. He had never in his life taken one, but he would have to now.

He carried out his plan on a Saturday, when things were likely to be slightly more relaxed and not as pushy at work, with five days behind, and the day-off coming. Then they would not miss him if he came in a half-hour late. That was all he needed, he thought, if he used the cab. If he did not use a cab, there was a chance he would lose her streetcar on foot. A chance he could not take.

The day came, in March, of 1911, and to his surprise, she did not exit the streetcar until it was all the way down Second Avenue to Houston Street. Then she took a transfer on West Houston, and got out at the corner of Macdougal Street, where she walked northerly, towards Washington Square.

Tony smiled to himself, as he thought, how perfect!—she's working at Blanck and Jacobs' Triangle Shirtwaist, Harry's loathed and despised competition—perfect!

Everybody in the needle trade would have known that was the only place she could have been going, as it was not only the biggest, but the only garment outpost in that district.

Tony paid off the cabbie and walked all the way back to work at 37th Street that Saturday morning, not only to save money, but also to savor his plans, and their coming fruition—which now was within a fingertip's grasp.

He could not wait any longer. It would have to be the following Saturday. It was the only feasible day. It would have to be now. It was already 1911, for God-sakes. He knew in his bones that everything was going to work out perfectly. As Monday, Tuesday, Wednesday ticked off, he could no longer contain himself. On Thursday morning, on the streetcar, when she boarded, he leaned over to his uncle and whispered, "I found out where she works."

Uncle Eugenio gave a shrug. "I could have told you that. *The Triangle Shirtwaist Company.* Do you want to know her name?"

"No, no, no!" Tony was furious. He immediately got up and walked as far in the trolley as he could, away from his uncle. He even forgot that she was aboard, he was so angry. Again, he wanted to kill the man. He would have placed both hands over his ears to block out the sound of her name on his lips, if he had not thought he would look ridiculous. So he had to get away, as far away as he could.

Uncle Eugenio was enjoying himself immensely, and invited a young lady coming on board at the next stop to occupy the empty seat Tony had left, pointing to his nephew down the aisle as he explained.

As they were leaving home the next morning, Tony, thinking about how he had followed his beloved in a taxi to the Blanck and Jacobs building, said to his uncle on the sidewalk before they got to their stop, "How could you not tell me you knew where she worked?"

"You didn't want to know!"

Tony stalked off, furious all over again.

"I did not want to spoil your daydreams for you!" Uncle Eugenio pleaded, only half-jibing.

Tony continued to walk away. "Don't you dare interfere with my life!"

"Argh!—you are *un giovane pazzo!* A crazy young *pazzo!*"

"I don't need your help! I don't need anybody's help! I can take care of myself!"

"A young *pazzo* in love—the worst kind!"

Saturday arrived at last, and Tony launched his plan. He made sure to suggest to Harry that they should knock off early, as they often did on Saturday—leave the floor-ladies in charge, they were more severe than a pair of Prussian drill instructors—and head up to the races in Harlem.

Although the strike was a victory for the I.L.G.W.U., it was already a year in the past, and Harry, like most of the other operators, had reinstated fining for petty offenses, locked bathrooms, charges for needles, thread and chairs—he had even devised a way to get rid of all the union girls by having Tony supervise them in teams of six, as they were instructed to teach all they knew to six new hires— whereupon, Harry dismissed the union girls, as soon as they and Tony had finished training their replacements.

The result was that Tony was busier than he had ever been, when he fell in love with the girl on the streetcar. A whole year had literally flown by the factory windows. "I have a couple of machines to take care of—so, I'll meet you there—you go ahead—I'll grab the streetcar."

With Harry sent out of the way, Tony grabbed the streetcar, true, but he headed in the other direction. He would find some excuse or other when the time came.

Meanwhile, he could think of only one thing. To be there on time. Since it was Saturday, he knew they would be letting out early, about five o'clock. However, Harry had left the office just after noontime, to have lunch before the races, so Tony had time on his hands, and by two o'clock, he was so restless, he had to leave.

He had almost three hours to waste, or spend. He could not bear to think of standing outside the ten-story Asch Building, a modern skyscraper, for three hours. What if she should look out the window of the 8th or 9th floor, where the Triangle machine rooms were located, and see him, malingering on the sidewalk?

So he decided to visit Savastano's, maybe see old friends, from the old neighborhood, catch up, to while away the afternoon.

"Tony!" said the barber. "We never see you no more! How come?" Heads turned in the barber chairs. Every waiting-seat was filled.

Savastano announced to the whole shop, "Look who's here! You know who this kid is? This is the kid who talked back to the Don—to his face! Tony LaStoria!"

They all knew that old tale, but they never tired of telling it, or hearing it again. "Only now, I guess he's too big and important for us Mulberry Street types."

As word went around the neighborhood, one by one, Mousey, Knickers and Long-johns arrived— followed by, as usual, dead last in the mud, Il Gatto. It was like a school reunion. They went out on the sidewalk to catch up on old times, and from there, Tony could see Savastano beaming at them from the window. Finally, Tony had to go back inside to use the bathroom at the back, and to use the mirrors in the front—make sure he was ready.

Savastono joked, "Whaddya got a hot date, Tony?"

Tony left in plenty of time to leisurely stroll over to Washington Square, and he got there by 4.30—a decent interval, he thought—he would not be hanging around long enough for it to be called loitering by some nosy cop.

As he paced back and forth, however, he could not resist looking skyward—he wanted to see her in a window. He had his hands in his pockets, but he kept turning his head to look up, as he paced.

The time could not go by fast enough. He had his eye also on the door where the girls would be exiting to the sidewalk, on Washington Place, at the bottom of the building, the ten-story skyscraper, the modern, fireproof, thank God, skyscraper, where his beloved worked, where, any moment now, she would be coming through that ground-floor doorway, perhaps laughing with her girlfriends, perhaps happy to see him, waiting for her on the sidewalk, and she would, no doubt, smile.

As he began to step into the roadway and cross over Washington Place, he looked up one last time. He knew it was silly but when he was on the sidewalk next to the building, he would not be able to see up there, straight up over his head. The angle of view would be decreased.

So he looked up one last time, and saw smoke billowing like bubbles from around the edges of windows up there.

Alarmed, his heart began to beat fast, and he took his hands out of his pockets. At almost the same moment, he heard fire-bells.

He stepped back, to the far sidewalk he had just stepped off of, to see better. Already smoke was pouring from the air-tight windows.

He heard smashing glass, up high.

Fire-engines with horses breathing hard appeared on the corner, skidding wheels. Tony began to run back and forth, beside himself.

People were running toward Washington Place from every direction.

Ladder engines were arriving, screeching, skidding. Tony looked up. Dense black smoke in awful ribbons dissipating into grey feathers were pouring out of the upper windows of the Asch Building.

It was all happening too fast. The firemen were already jumping all over that side of the street, more arriving, with more engines, every second. People were shouting, "Do something! Oh, those poor people! Oh, my God, my God!" The firemen on the ladder wagons were extending them upward as fast as they could.

Looking up, Tony saw faces appear at the windows up there. Now he could see the red and yellow glow of flames as they reflected on the black, billowing undersides of clouds of smoke. The smoke was no longer seeping out in streamers. It was pouring out in angry black cauldrons. He ran across the street towards the building. Firemen were screaming, for some reason, "Don't jump! Don't jump! The ladders are coming!" Horrified, Tony looked up to see the first girl fall. Firemen had large circular basket-like nets already spread out, and they tried to catch her—but falling from nine stories, her body went right through the net, to hit the sidewalk with a sickening sound.

Tony did not have time to think. Voices were screaming, "Oh, my God, my God!" from the sidewalk, when more girls started to come down, heavily through the air, some of them holding hands, some of them in pairs, chest to chest, holding onto one another—some of them trailing smoke or actually on fire, it seemed, how could one tell, it was all happening so fast, what to do, what could you do, they were coming down faster and faster, horrendous shrieks filled the air, there were too many falling bodies, not enough nets, Tony had to watch it all without being able to do a single thing to stop it or to help anyone, nor could the firemen, who were also beside themselves.

Then, suddenly, no more bodies were falling through the air.

Nobody knew just then, or thought of it just then, but incredibly, it did jump into their minds to ask, God, how long did that take? Five minutes?

"We were here in five minutes from the first alarm, and still, there was nothing we could do!"

Tony heard the firemen exclaiming, as they pushed back onlookers, who had flooded into Washington Square in alarming numbers, the usual obsessive fire-chasers amplified by dozens more, maybe even hundreds more, scarred and scared but nonetheless captivated by the horror of the awful sights they had just witnessed.

The fire was still raging, even more intensely, and the laddermen, who knew only too well that their extensions could only get them up as far the sixth floor, were having all they could do to haul their heavy hoses up that high only to shoot futile squirts at the raging inferno.

Fire captains with megaphones were ordering the crowd back, policemen in stronger numbers were now on the scene, and pushing people back, firemen were covering lumps of skirts and bundles of blouses on the sidewalk with their own coats, as they ripped them from their shoulders and struggled out of their sleeves—there was nothing else to cover them with, they were like the undraped dead of the slaughterhouses.

Tony was pushed back by a hand in his chest, and he was thinking, absurdly, only an hour ago, I was looking at the calendar at Savastano's, by the mirrors, thinking March 25th, 1911—*the first day of my life. Oh, please, God, please, God, Madre di Dio, don't let it be her . . .*

How would he know? How would he ever know?

He did not even know her name.

He could not ask someone, did Maria?—Teresa?—Adelina?—Giulia?—did she make it out? The fire raged on for hours more and Tony stood there, unable to move or speak or even feel anything.

But finally he heard someone say, "Where are they taking them?"

"To the Charities Morgue."

There was no question he would follow. He followed in the footsteps of all the others as they drifted to the Charities Morgue, and he was not even aware of where he was going.

The Morgue was like a warehouse. The bodies were laid out on pallets or trestles of wood, with their feet placed together, in a long row, 146 bodies.

The pallets were slender, the bodies were small.

They were like schoolgirls waiting in line for the bell to ring.

People were walking slowly in single file, as directed by the police who were present, looking down to their left, as they filed past the long row.

Screams and crying. When a family member recognized their daughter or sister, it was senseless how the howling grief poured out. It was like wolves in the dark. The warehouse, with its many pillars and pylons supporting the beams of a ten-foot ceiling overlaid with rafters, seemed like a forest in the wilderness. There was concrete, exposed steel, brick, cold to the touch, remote wooden rafters high overhead, the darkened smudge of the floorboards of the warehouse floor above filled with shadow, the bare bulbs swinging on light-fixtures pooling dim puddles of sulfurous yellow light amid the howling, bent-double echoes of grief, echoing from the throats not of human mothers, but of lions, weasels and starlings.

Police and morgue doctors and city officials were present with clipboards asking fathers, mothers, families, to identify their loved ones.

Checking names off on a list.

Writing names onto another list. Comparing one with the other.

Tony filed by, shuffling along with all the others, before and behind, looking down to his left.

Then he saw her shoes.

He backed away. Tears flooded from his eyes and flooded down over his chin onto his chest.

A woman behind him or alongside him somewhere began to scream, a wounded, half-strangled cry of utter misery.

"Ah, mia figlia, mia bambina, la mia povera bambina—guarda, è la mia Laura!"

Officials with clipboards stepped forward. Seeing that a body was recognized, they approached.

Laura's mother sank to her knees beside the pallet that held her dead daughter, and she raised both arms to heaven, wailing against God, against life.

A man in a suit was asking the father, with four more children in hand, the family name. Tony heard him say, "Antonelli."

Laura Antonelli.

Tears streaming down him, Tony walked slowly backwards, a disembodied ghost, feeling with his hands behind him for some support, anything. He came to a pillar as he slowly backed up, and he placed his back up against this pillar, because he was afraid that if he did not, like Laura's mother, he would fall to the ground.

As he felt the pillar behind him, and as he felt his back against the pillar, he looked up and saw the lady in blue, on the pier in Napoli, with her husband and her children, beckoning to him to come on board the ship.

Chapter 14

Arrivederci, New York

Harry Spritzka was worried about Tony LaStoria. His friend was like a man who had lost his mind. You would think he had lost perhaps the very will to live. He walked around like a living person, but he was dead to the world.

Harry thought the Strike in '09 had been destructive, to himself, his business, to the city, even to his relations with Tony, who was like a brother to him, and had been for–how many years now? The Strike was nothing compared to the devastation of this fire.

It was like a fog, a permanent fog, had settled over New York City. Nobody talked about anything else and it went on and on—you couldn't walk past a newspaper without another headline, another reminder, another re-hash.

Now all the do-gooders, commiserators, hand-wringers, and holier-than-thou's in town had charred bodies and coffins to throw at the operators.

In the end, the Strike had changed very little of what went on. This was different. This was going to change everything.

But you couldn't tell from Tony. He wasn't interested.

The first time Tony initiated a scrap of conversation, in weeks—not just mumbling a reply to a question with his eyes pasted to the floor—he came to the office and said to Harry at the end of the day, "Send me to Boston."

"Boston!"

"I have to get out of New York."

"But I was planning to send you the other way–!"

"Where?"

"New Jersey."

"I don't want to go to New Jersey. It's too close. I can't stay in this city. I have to get away."

Harry had noticed that Tony had come into the office with his mandolin in his hand, and it had made him wonder what was up. Now he watched as Tony turned his back to look out the window while he placed the mandolin standing on the floor next to him with the neck balanced up against the wall, unconcerned that it might fall down. "But why Boston?" said Harry. "We don't know anybody in Boston. Do you know anybody in Boston, I should ship you there?"

"I don't need to know anybody. I know they got cheap floor space up there."

"How do you know that?"

"They got cheap floor space everywhere."

"Yeah. Like New Jersey."

After all these years, Harry knew well enough that sometimes there was no talking to Tony. And he reflected with some chagrin that all this should have been done by now, had Tony listened to him. Before the Triangle fire, Harry had spoken to Tony about sending him down to Camden, outside Philly. He had located space there for manufacturing, but the real attraction was the start-up of his chain of *Richard Paul* stores. This was because the real estate on offer included the corner location zoned for commercial, situated downtown on the streetcar line, which was going to be the first grand opening of *Richard Paul Men's and Women's Apparel.*

As the weeks went by, Harry started saying to himself, *All this lost time, I'm losing my shirt here.*

But at the time, Tony wouldn't hear of leaving New York—because of that girl.

Then, came the Triangle fire. But Harry couldn't bring himself to bring it up again to his friend Tony. He knew his friend was suffering.

Now, he said to Tony, "I'm worried about you, pal. If I send you to Boston—are you gonna let me down, Tony?"

"Have I ever let you down?"

"No, but I never seen you like this, either—and I'm not the only one."

"Have I ever?"

"No, but—"

"It's all right, Harry. It don't matter."

"Tony–ya gotta make me say it."

"I don't have to work for you."

"I need people I can trust. I need you."

"You ain't the only guy in the world to work for."

"I can't accomplish what I'm trying to accomplish without trust."

"Why don't you send my uncle to New Jersey. Him you can trust. He's the same as me. He can do the same things I can for you."

"That ain't a bad idea."

"And he's tired of your father's place—no advancement, always the same old–."

"Enough already. We ain't gonna talk about this anymore."

"Good. I was leaving in the morning anyway."

"When were you gonna tell me?"

"I just did."

"Well—it's not like we'll never see each other again."

Tony was standing at the window, looking out on the street with his back to Harry. This had been his normal posture for weeks now. *When there was ice on the East River—you could skate to Brooklyn– but when it started to thaw, that was the treacherous time.*

"But, why Boston, I'll never know," said Harry, to Tony's back.

"They got a river up there where they cut ice in the winter."

After a time, as he reached up his right hand to rub the scar on his left cheek, which sometimes bothered him, Harry said, "Well . . . I hope you freeze your balls off up there in Boston."

Without turning around, Tony left the office. Without saying goodbye to his friend, Harry Spritzka, Tony LaStoria left through the street door and walked away down West 37th Street, towards midtown, alone. And then he felt the first idle drops fall on his face, and he wondered if it was going to rain, and then a few more fell, and, of course, it might rain, that is, *it ought to rain,* he was thinking, and as he was walking towards midtown, he realized that *rain could fall,* because, *you know, everything happens in New York.*

Harry Spritzka sat there in his office, and for the first time in years, in his busy life, spent constantly anticipating, furiously, the next big deal, he felt completely alone.

And then, he noticed the mandolin. Tony had forgotten it. Or maybe he left it behind on purpose. *Maybe I should run down the street after him. Nah. He'll send for it, if he wants it. I'll just keep it here for him.*

When she was alive, when he lay in his bed dreaming of her, then, he had been able to conjure up only her shoes. Now, Laura Antonelli's face appeared to Tony LaStoria every time he sought rest. And it was the appearance of her eyes looking into his, for that fleeting moment when their eyes had met, that day, that one time, on the streetcar, which stabbed him directly underneath his heart.

Over and over again he excused himself, stood up, felt embarrassed, and awkward—and yet their eyes met again, for that instant of time.

With those eyes she had transmitted her whole, entire soul, mind and being to him, and now she lived in him, though, to the world, she was dead.

Perhaps she had divined that this one look would change him forever.

Acknowledgements

There are so many people without whom I could not have made it through the six years of creative solitude to fashion the five volumes of The Twentieth Century Quintet, beginning with this novel, *Arrivederci New York*.

First of all I should like to give a heartfelt *mille grazie* to my dear sister Janet and her husband, Patrick Gable, who nursed and cared for me, put me up at their home during months of cardiac recovery, and donated to the writing a wonderful Florida wintering on Gulf Coast Boulevard in Naples. Most of all, Janet and Pat led me through the wilderness when Janet and I lost our mother, our beloved brother Jan, and our father, in three consecutive years; events which turned out to be seminal in the motivation for my venturing upon this journey of composing a family saga that would at least attempt to pay tribute to the family which gave us life and so much more.

To my beautiful daughter, Aisling O'Leary, and her husband Kevin, as well as their children, Eoghan, Grace and Oscar, my wonderfully handsome and brilliant grandchildren, I owe undying gratitude for coming to my relief in 2016 by paying me a memorable visit, all the way from County Kildare, shortly after my first heart attack. Everyone should be as blessed as I have been, both in childhood and as a parent, in the family of which I'm proud to be would-be historian.

Next I would like to thank profusely my best friend of fifty years, Rodney MacDow, of Portland, OR, by way of North Carolina, whose freely-given consultation on a weekly basis through the medium of the modern internet made this a journey I did not have to take alone. I am forever in Rod's debt. No one on this earth could have understood and supported me more, from the inside out, in my endeavors to create indelible prose, than Rod.

Richard Wise, best friend of both Rod and myself, made up the third member of our triumvirate, the self-styled Three Amigos, and to this man, goldsmith, certified gemologist, and novelist, and America's leading expert on precious metals, author of the best-selling *Secrets of the Gem Trade,* as well as the novels, *The French Blue*, and *Redlined* (Rick is a colorful character . . .) I owe a debt of gratitude, to him and to his lovely wife Rebekah, not only for several expensive dinners which enhanced my waistline, but also for material support of my bank account, for services rendered as an editor, and for services rendered as musical entertainment at a gala evening at *Chez Wise*, as well as for visiting me while I was in cardiac recovery and graciously losing a game of chess.

To Christopher Nye, Editor and Board Member of Orion Magazine, the noted environmental journal from Great Barrington, Massachusetts, and moderator of the writer's workshop he ran at the Orion offices, I owe deeply felt thanks for his early and ongoing support of my overly ambitious and ridiculously unrealistic idea of concocting a six-year project, on spec, by a previously unpublished novelist, which never had any honest hope of ever seeing the light of day, and yet Chris never stopped for one moment in believing in me when I was most direly hard-put to believe in myself.

My thanks go also to the other members of that workshop, who steadfastly put up with me through two years of composing the first two novels in this series, and they are the late Steve Applin, dearly-departed friend and poet and fellow graduate of the University of Rhode Island, Jan Hutchinson, of Simon's Rock in Great Barrington, a division of Bard College, Emily Pulfer-Terino, teacher at Miss Hall's School, and poet Frances Roth.

I need not mention here, since in this book they are elsewhere cited, but my thanks go to Dr Carla Simonini, Ph.D., of Loyola University in Chicago, and the Editor of *Italian-Americana Magazine* and to the inimitable Christine Palamidessi Moore, writer, artist and benefactor of 20 years of international students to whom she has graciously opened her home and family in the Boston area for their extended sojourns in America: Christine is the woman who contributed "the lady in blue" to my story when she served as my fiction editor in 2017.

At this point I must mention the ladies who are co-founders and organizers of the writer's group here in the Berkshires, called *Writing is Better Together,* of which I am currently a devoted member, and they are Dr Julia Kirst, Ph.D., formerly of Bard College at Simon's Rock, and now an independent linguistic expert and translation consultant, and Dr Jenna McIntire, Ph.D., Professor of Biology at Williams College; as well as Cheryl Hulseapple, Editor at Laurin Publishing, poet and visual artist Rosemary Starace, and poet and writer M. Betsy Smith. These are the ladies responsible for enticing me to emerge from my long, solitary sojourn in my creative cave, back into the light-of-day of friendship and companionship and above all, community in the writer's journey.

And now I come to the present time, 2020, and acknowledge my thanks to Joy Baglio, Founder-Director of the

Pioneer Valley Writer's Workshop, and to her sidekick, Kate Senecal, Assistant Director of PVWW, who have granted me a full scholarship to the year-long Fiction Writers' Workshop, the only scholarship they have given out this year. I am so pleased to have been awarded this grant worth $1200 and to have won their trust and recognition and the chance to work under Kate's instruction as part of their esteemed program; thank you.

As a long-time resident of Pittsfield, Massachusetts, heart of the beautiful Berkshires, the town where Melville wrote the greatest novel in American literature, *Moby Dick;* and yet, as a transplant to the area, from further east in Boston, I must extend my gratitude to so many of the local residents who made me welcome here from the very beginning, including, not limited to, the men, women and children of both the Irish-American Club of Berkshire County, and the Irish Sister-City and Italian Sister-City Committees, starting with Pat and Marie Gormalley, of Pittsfield Community Television and the Pittsfield schools, going on with Dr. Kevin Cahill, Ph.D., head of *Soldiers On* and President of the Irish-American Club, and Jen Glockner, of the Pittsfield Office of Cultural Development, continuing with Fran and Linda Curley, Stephanie and Mark Abrams, Rob Dwyer and Whitney, Clark Nicholls, Eileen Kane, Cam and Rachel Collins, Patrick and Connie Gray, and Patrick Gray, Jr, Bobby Sweet and Lara Tupper, Andy Kelly, Tessa Kelly, Chris Parkinson, Mary Tart, Perry Daniels, Eileen Markland, Rick Leab, Greg Steele, Paul Rice, Bridget Howe, and so many others, who were fellow musicians or followers of my Irish band, *The Dossers,* for ten years here in the Berkshires; and of course, to Pittsfield's greatest living writer, Kevin O'Hara, author of *The Last of the Donkey Pilgrims* and *A Lucky Irish Lad,* and his lovely and long-understanding wife Belita.

To my fellow Dossers, Bill Morrison, on six-string and vocals, and multi-instrumentalist Rick Marquis, vocals, guitar, banjo and mandolin, thanks, from the bottom of my pacemaker-heart for ten years of irreplaceable memories as members of *The Dossers;* to Bill, who has always been my best friend in Pittsfield, thanks for standing by my side at so many gigs in so many places, from Portsmitt's to Jiminy Peak; to Rick, thanks for keeping us laughing, and for giving us Teresa, Sophie, Scottie, Sammy and Elaine to be part of our circle of harmonies; Ricky and Bill, you are the lads who made Tuesday Nights what they were; and can we ever fail to recall, at the end of our final year's engagement at the Crowne Plaza in downtown Pittsfield, that unforgettable Farewell Concert in June of 2016, four hours of non-stop dancing, singing, music and hilarity?

On the Italian side of my life's arc, my thanks go to Professore Alessandro Nardacci, Anna Zaffanella, Kathie Penna, Dante D'Aniello, Enrico and Cookie Lamet and all the members of *Club Cappucino;* and of course, I must not forget Judge Rudy Sacco, my fellow Boston College alumnus, a figurehead of Berkshire County, who preceded me at BC by 20 years, and who has been someone I have looked up to as a model and inspiration ever since I came to the Berkshires. Nor can I fail to highlight Enrico Lamet, an author in his own right, and a very fine one too, who wrote a memoir entitled *A Gift From The Enemy,* available from Syracuse University Press, a memoir of life under Mussolini's regime of internal exile during World War II and who therefore spent his own unforgettable childhood in a village only a few miles from my grandparents' home town of Alta Villa Irpina.

Lastly, I must say thank you so ever much to members of my now far-flung family who grew up with me in a tight circle of cousins, aunts and uncles, an extended Boston-Italian family scattered through the close-in suburbs of Revere and Watertown; to Linda Mihelis, formerly Linda Scioscia, and her husband Nick; to their son-in-law, David Holscher, transplanted here from faraway Ohio, who freely gave of his immense talents as a graphics designer to provide me with five specially-beautiful book-covers for my novels; to Tom DiPace, of Miami, FL, my exact-counterpart first cousin, companion of my childhood, in Revere and Watertown, without whom I would have never played hardball or shagged flies at the Hosmer School; to my cousin Lenore and her husband Ron Meehan; to Marie Scioscia of New York and her brother Leon, of Alexandria, VA, and their sister Joanna; to Geri Zani and Tony Taverna of Watertown, MA; and to the *grande dame* of our family, my aunt, Mrs Anna Silva, who, this summer will attain the great and prestigious age of one hundred.

Mrs Anna Silva is the last remaining sibling of the family founded by Antonio Scioscia and Giuseppina Fabrizio of Alta Villa Irpina, in the South of Italy, and of Boston, Massachusetts; this is the family who were the models of the fictional LaStoria family portrayed in my books.

Finally, as the son of a coal miner, I would be remiss if I did not give my thanks to my parents, my father Mel and my mother Gerry, who gave me love when I didn't deserve it, and discipline when I did, and finally, a college education, to reform me altogether, and give me the chance they never had.

If not for them, I would never have lived to know my grandchildren, to write books, and to spar with the stars in the heavens.

Chapter 1 Acknowledgement

Chapter 1 of this novel was previously published in the Summer 2017 issue of Italian Americana Magazine, Editor, Dr Carla Simonini, Ph.D., Paul and Anna Rubino Endowed Associate Professor and Founding Director of the Italian American Studies Program at Loyola University Chicago. This chapter, "A Game of Chance," appears here as edited by Christine Palamidessi Moore, Fiction Editor of Italian Americana. I wish to acknowledge her fine, professional work on my story. Ms. Palamidessi Moore was at the time 2017 Artist-in-Residence at MassMoCA in North Adams, MA, and also, simultaneously, 2017 Visiting Artist at The American Academy in Rome, Italy.

About the Author

Eugene Christy is a novelist, poet and musician currently enjoying retirement in his home in the Berkshires. His maternal grandparents Antonio Scioscia and Giuseppina Fabrizio came from Alta Villa Irpina, near Avellino, in the South of Italy. He has studied under Sean O'Faolain, James Dickey, and Larry McMurtry. Appearing as Gene Christy, he was previously known around the Berkshires as the singer-songwriter and accordian-player who led The Dossers, the Irish-themed pub-band trio featuring Bill Morrison and Rick Marquis. His current project, six years in the making, is called The Twentieth Century Quintet, five novels telling the saga of Antonio LaStoria and his descendants through three generations in America from 1899 to 1972, to be published by Adelaide Books, New York, in 2020 and 2021.

www.ingramcontent.com/pod-product-compliance
Lightning Source LLC
Chambersburg PA
CBHW030318100526
44592CB00010B/476